# THE SOCIOLOGY OF REVOLUTION

## READINGS ON POLITICAL UPHEAVAL AND POPULAR UNREST

EDITED BY RONALD YE-LIN CHENG

HENRY REGNERY COMPANY·CHICAGO

*Library of Congress Cataloging in Publication Data*

Cheng, Ronald Ye-lin, 1933—                                        comp.
   Sociology of revolution.

   Includes bibliographical references.
   1. Revolutions—Addresses, essays, lectures. I. Title.
HM281.C453            301.6'333'08            72-11194

I wish to thank Mihaly Csikszentmihalyi for his assistance
and patience; C.K. Cheng for his help in improving my
style of writing; and the publishers and authors for
permitting me to use their publications.

Manufactured in the United States of America.
Library of Congress Catalog Card Number: 72-11194

# CONTENTS

# INTRODUCTION

In a world of rapid change and recurrent disruption, a growing number of people have become fearful and uncertain of the future. Their increasing concern over social unrest has prompted many researchers to direct their attentions to the "etiological study" of revolution. But the subject matter of revolution is often emotionally charged. Some defend revolution as the instrument of inevitable progress; others condemn revolution as the outburst of primitive emotions.

In the aftermath of any great revolution, such as the French Revolution of 1789, there are always myths, legends, and legacies that complicate one's thinking. For instance Michelet thought that the French Revolution destroyed the evil of the old regime, relieved the misery of the masses, and led French society to inevitable progress, liberty, and justice.[1] On the other hand Burke thought that the French Revolution was the embodiment of evil, that it led to an outbreak of popular violence and wanton cruelty; if not checked, it would end by subjecting all people either to anarchy or to a ruthless master.[2]

As distinguished from philosophical and historical studies, sociological studies are not concerned with the moral aspects of revolution; neither are they concerned with the historical uniqueness of a particular revolution. The main purpose of sociological research is to understand the phenomena of revolution in different societies so that generalizations may be made on their causations, processes, and consequences. In line with this purpose the present volume brings together a collection of outstanding studies in the fast-developing field of the sociology of revolution.

**Definitions and Classifications**
There are basically three ways of defining revolution: (1) revolution is any political change that brings about a shift in the locale of sovereignty (e.g., from an absolute monarch to the people); (2) revolution is an abrupt, violent social change in any of several aspects of social phoenomena (religious, economic, or political); (3) revolution is a fundamental change in all aspects of social phenomena. (See Part I.1 of this volume, Yoder) The present volume is mainly concerned with the type of revolution that leads to an abrupt, violent political change.

In the study of political revolution two forms of classification have been suggested. The first divides revolutions into five types: (1) private palace revolution, (2) public palace revolution, (3) colonial revolution, (4) great national revolution, and (5) systemic revolution. This method of classification is based on two criteria: the degree of social change involved, and the size of population and geographical areas covered. (Part I.2, Pettee) For instance, private palace revolution and public palace revolution aim chiefly at changes in the government's structure and personnel within a very limited geographical area; colonial revolution and great national revolution aim at changing the whole complex of governmental institutions (e.g., from monarchy to democracy) throughout a nation. In the case of the systemic revolution the replacement of one system of government by another aims at governmental changes on a world-wide scale (e.g., democracy replaced monarchy as the dominant system of government in the world). This method of classification has proved useful in studying the causations, processes, and consequences of each type of revolution. However, many in the social sciences and the humanities prefer to call changes within a system of government a rebellion. Therefore the distinction between "rebellion" (change within system) and "revolution" (change of system) may be retained here. According to this classification private palace revolutions, public palace revolutions, and some colonial revolutions are "rebellions"; and some colonial revolutions, great national revolutions, and systemic revolutions are "revolutions." The latter group provides the subject matter of this volume.

Another method of classification uses six categories: (1) Jacquerie, (2) millenarian rebellion, (3) anarchistic rebellion, (4) Jacobin communist revolution, (5) conspiratorial *coup d'etat*, and (6) militarized mass insurrection. This classification is based on four criteria: targets of revolutionary activity (government, regime, and community), identity of the revolutionaries (masses, elites-leading-masses, and elites), revolutionary goals or ideology, and whether the revolution is spontaneous or calculated.[3]

The term Jacquerie is used to characterize a mass rebellion of peasants with strictly limited aims such as restoration of lost rights or removal of specific grievances. Millenarian rebellion arises from the hope that a complete and radical change in the world will be achieved in the millennium. Anarchistic rebellion occurs as a reaction to changes that have already been brought about in the social system. Jacobin communist revolution is a movement for fundamental and sweeping change in the political system. Conspiratorial *coup d'état* is an attempt on the part of a small group of people to replace existing leadership. Militarized mass insurrection involves mobilization of the masses under the guidance of a conspiratorial general staff in an attempt to overthrow the government.

With reference to Pettee's "extent of social change," this method of classification specifies that if the target of revolutionary activity is the community, social change is likely to be most extensive; if the target is the regime, social change is likely to be less extensive; and if the target is the government, social change is likely to be the least extensive of all. The distinction made here between spontaneous and calculated revolutions is also used by Huntington to classify Eastern and Western revolutions.[4]

## Preconditions to Revolution

Some people are more susceptible than others to certain types of disease. In the same way it seems reasonable to hypothesize that certain kinds of pre-existing circumstances are more conducive than others to revolution. If these pre-existing circumstances can be identified, revolutionary potentials may be assessed long before the occurrence of a revolution. Therefore those pre-existing circumstances likely to increase revolutionary potential are an important area for research.

According to the "law of evolutionary potential," the more specialized a society is, the more conservative and rigid it becomes and the greater will be its difficulty for change from one stage to another.[5] If a society is not able to move from one stage to another through peaceful change, then revolution becomes more probable. This is especially true if the ruling group resists change. It seems therefore reasonable to conclude that the more specialized a society is, the greater will be the probability of revolution.

Lyford P. Edwards, who proposes a similar thesis, states that the nature of evolution is replacement: a dominant species of plant or animal does not evolve from another but replaces another, and this principle can be extended to social evolution.[6] As Edwards points out, the coal barons and the steel kings occupied positions of dominance in America similar to those of the feudal barons and kings in the Middle Ages. But the coal barons and steel kings did not evolve from the feudal barons and kings; they evolved from lower class ancestors in the Middle Ages. Thus the transformation of social institutions or social systems is often accomplished through the destruction of the old by the new rather than evolution of the new from the old.

Edwards thinks that an organism creates the conditions for its own destruction by increasing its size and complexity. For example, just before they perished the dinosaurs grew to an almost incredible size. They were too large and clumsy for their environment, and so they became extinct. The same principle applies to the transformation of social institutions or social systems.

> The medieval church flowered out into the most luxurious riches of cathedrals, abbeys, statues, pictures, painted glass, and every form of expensive beauty and ornament just before the Reformation. The extravagant luxury and profuseness of the old regime in France culminated very shortly before the Revolution.

At present this hypothesis is too general and therefore very difficult to prove without further specification and the development of sub-propositions. Nevertheless, the idea is worth pursuing because it provides a different perspective from the prevalent notion that the widening gap between the highly industrialized nations and the less developed countries makes those countries in the early stages of industrialization prone to revolution. On the contrary, the evolutionary hypothesis suggests that the highly industrialized countries also have some disadvantages in their development. Due to their specialization, rigidity, and overcom-

plexity, they have more difficulty in moving to a new stage
of development, and therefore they are not immune to
revolution.

Other circumstances held to be conducive to revolution
include the confusion of values with other components of
action (e.g., norms), the lack of means to express grievances,
the lack of methods for the isolation of value-oriented
movements, and the availability of communication for the
dissemination of revolutionary beliefs. (Part II.1, Smelser)
When values are not differentiated from norms, violation
of a norm will be interpreted as a defiance of general values.
An increasing dissatisfaction with social arrangements may
lead eventually to a protest against values. Revolutionary
ideologies arise when alternative means of reconstituting
the social situation are unavailable. If revolutionary movements can be insulated, or isolated geographically, the probability of their success will be reduced. The spread of such
movements depends on the dissemination of revolutionary
ideologies, and therefore the greater the effectiveness of
communicating these ideologies, the greater the probability
of revolution.

There is evidence that a centralized political system cannot
adapt itself as well to a broadening of political participation
as can a decentralized one; therefore the former is more
conducive to revolution. (Part II.2, Huntington) According
to the above hypothesis, the communist countries, as well
as a number of highly centralized monarchical and dictatorial countries, would be very susceptible to revolution.

Certain types of ecological conditions also might be conducive to revolution. For instance, the establishment of a
communist revolutionary base in China and Vietnam might
have been predicted in terms of the political ecologies of
those areas.[7] The probability for the establishment of a
revolutionary base increases in areas that have the following
conditions: (1) previous political or revolutionary activity,
(2) access to major political targets and sources of power,

(3) weak or confused political control, (4) terrain favorable for military operations, and (5) economic self-sufficiency. The identification of such base areas could be useful for both revolutionary and counter-revolutionary forces.

## Increasing Contradictions and Conflicts in Society

Although certain pre-existing circumstances might be conducive to revolution, they are not sufficient causes for a revolution. By themselves the predictive value of these circumstances is not very high. For instance, the traditional Chinese society had developed to a high level of specialization and the government was highly centralized during the Ming and the Ch'ing Dynasties. But revolution did not occur until the end of the Ch'ing Dynasty in spite of the presence of a variety of favorable conditions over a period of five hundred years. The simple reason is that in their initial appearance, various social contradictions in the traditional system could be contained by existing mechanisms of control. But as basic changes led to greater contradictions and conflicts, the traditional system became less stable and less effective, and as a result the revolutionary potential increased. Therefore it is important to understand the nature and development of contradictions and conflicts in society.

For instance, there are basic contradictions of functions between domestic government and foreign governments. From the theoretical standpoint the primary function of the domestic government is to protect the country against foreign aggression. In its relations with other countries the foreign government is oriented in the direction of political and economic expansion in the world. Western European colonial expansion during the eighteenth and nineteenth centuries and the native governments' attempts to defend their countries against Western aggression are good examples.

The main function of an economy is the maintenance and development of production, exchange, and distribution of commodities in a society.[8] Between the government and its economy there are two contradicting functions. On the one hand the government needs economic resources for the maintenance and expansion of governmental activities, and there is a tendency for the government to over-tax the resources of the economy through its system of allocation and to deny the economy needed resources for development. On the other hand rapid economic development and expansion may lead to substantial and abrupt social change and create considerable dislocation and disorder, which will increase the problem of maintaining law and order by the government.

The main function of religion is explanation of the problems relating to the meaning of life.[9] As religion can both legitimize and challenge dominant values in a society, there is a contradiction between government and religion. In times of widespread distress and hardship religion might encourage disorder and rebellion. For instance, there were repeated rebellions of secret religious societies in Chinese history during times of widespread distress and hardship.

The main functions of education are the pursuit of knowledge, the development of personality, and the acquisition of skills.[10] There are contradictions of functions between government and education. Development of new knowledge combined with a new type of personality might promote revolutionary or subversive thinking. Newly learned skills might be used for corruption and subversion, thereby undermining governmental efficiency.

During a period of rapid social change, various parts of a social system are not changing at the same rate.[11] Since different parts of the social system are interdependent, a rapid change in one requires adjustment and readjustment in the others. But frequently there is an adjustment lag. The result is an increase in contradictions in the overall adjustment mechanism. For example, increased political contradictions and conflicts may arise from internal or external sources. A declining consensus in a society is an important internal source of conflict because it will increase the gap between governmental output and public expectation. (Part III.1, Tsurutani) Foreign intervention is another important source of conflict. World War I definitely was a contributing factor to the Bolshevik Revolution of 1917. Western encroachment on the sovereignties of Japan and China during the nineteenth century led to the Meiji Restoration of 1868 and the Chinese Revolution of 1911. French attempts to suppress political opposition in Vietnam before World War II led to an increase in underground political activity. (Part III.2, McAlister) When the French colonials wavered in the 1940s, the pent-up political energies erupted in a revolution that no amount of French force could subdue.

It would be difficult for a revolution to succeed without economic incentive for a substantial number of people to revolt. (Part III.3, Edwards) Rapid industrialization and urbanization, underemployment in the cities, dislocation of traditional industries, growth of modern industries, and an increase in economic aspiration may all contribute to economic discontent. It has been pointed out that economic discontent reaches its highest level when an upward development in real income is interrupted by a sharp decline. (Part III.4, Davies) When this happens the groups that experience relative deprivation might be inclined to take part in revolutionary activities.

Confrontations of different religious groups may lead to an intensification of conflicts. For instance, after the French Revolution of 1789 attempts on the part of the new government to curtail the fiscal privileges and political power of the Church led to increased resistance from the clergy and the general populace and resulted in the counter-revolution in the Vendée. (Part III.5, Tilly) During the second half of the nineteenth century the intrusion of Christian missionaries into the Chinese world order led to an increase in resistance among the Chinese that was partly responsible for the Chinese Revolution of 1911. (Part III.6, Cohen)

Education is an increasingly important agent of socialization in modern societies. The education of Chinese abroad (especially in Japan) introduced new ideas and knowledge to many who became increasingly nationalistic and revolutionary. (Part III.7, Hackett) They expressed strong dissatisfaction with the Ch'ing government and promoted revolutionary ideas and activities in a variety of ways. In the modern world student movements have become increasingly radical. Eisenstadt (Part III.8) attributes the growing student radicalism to an increase in "intellectual antinomianism" and "generational discontinuity and conflict" in the modern world. Even though students' ideas are still unclear and their powers limited, their demands for a free, just, humane, and ecologically balanced world must be taken seriously.

Rapid political, economic, religious, and educational changes in a society often heighten and intensify conflicts among the various groups in the stratification system. Because members of these groups belong to different political, religious, economic, and educational organizations, changes in these organizations often lead to changes in the relative sizes and social positions of the groups and a possible emergence of new groups.[12] As a result, demands will be made by relatively deprived groups for a reallocation and redistribution of wealth, power, and esteem. If the government's outputs and social controls are not capable of meeting these demands, more and more people will be alienated and frustrated, and conflicts and violence will become more and more general. This situation will further undermine the government's ability to meet demands from the people, and so the gap progressively widens. This process, if continued, will lead to an increase in revolutionary potential. The greater the duration and extent of the gap between these outputs and inputs, the greater will be the potential for revolution in a society. This may be illustrated by three examples.

De Tocqueville showed that at one time the duties and privileges of the French nobles were fairly well balanced.[13] But during the eighteenth century the aristocrats' traditional administrative duties largely disappeared while many of their privileges were retained. Meanwhile an increasingly larger proportion of the peasantry had become free land-holders. Under these changed circumstances the continued existence of aristocratic privileges without corresponding duties brought an unjust and unwarranted situation into focus and intensified peasants' hatred of the nobles and of the feudal system. Therefore the greatly increased contradictions and conflicts in the stratification system were contributing factors to the participation of the peasantry in the French Revolution.

Marx and Engels (Part III.9) showed that technological development in capitalist societies, especially during the early stage of industrialization, may lead to a widening gap between the rich and the poor. If a government's outputs and social controls are not capable of meeting demands for a more equalized allocation and distribution of wealth, power, and esteem, the conflict between the bourgeoisie and the workers will intensify and a revolutionary movement will develop.

Finally, Wolf (Part III.10) has pointed out that peasants suffer from the impact of three great crises: (1) demographic crisis due to rapid increase in population; (2) ecological crisis due to commercialization of agriculture and a concomitant increase in rentals and taxation that deprive the peasantry of the fruits of their labor; (3) a crisis of authority due to the development of a modern market economy, which results in the rise of the bourgeoisie and a widening gap between the ruler and the ruled. However, peasants have to depend on the leadership of the intellectuals to carry out a successful revolution, as is shown in the Chinese

Revolution of 1949, the Cuban Revolution of 1959, and the on-going Vietnamese Revolution.

## Mobilization of Resources in Revolutionary Struggle

Certain pre-existing circumstances highly conducive to revolution may be present in a society along with considerable contradictions and conflicts, and still a revolution will not necessarily occur. Whether revolution will occur remains to be determined by the outcome of a struggle between various political groups.[14]

When various groups mobilize their resources in a revolutionary struggle, four outcomes are possible:

1. The traditional system of government is overthrown and destroyed by the revolutionaries.
2. The traditional system of government is reformed in conformity with revolutionary demands.
3. The traditional system of government is restored by a reactionary movement that suppresses all revolutionary and reform activities.
4. The government collapses and the country is divided into independent political units.

Which of the four alternatives is realized depends on the interplay of five groups of forces. First, pre-existing circumstances will obviously have an influence on the outcome; for instance, if the traditional government still has considerable influence in a society, the possibility for reaction will be greater. If on the other hand geographical conditions favor guerrilla warfare, the possibility for revolution will also be greater.

Second, the nature, scope, and duration of various contradictions will have considerable influence on the revolution's outcome. For instance, persistent contradictions of functions and interests will likely sustain the process of mobilization at a high level. If contradictions are reduced to a very low level and most people are satisfied with extensive reforms, conditions in society will return to normal. But reform takes time. If time is limited (e.g., due to the threat of colonization) and extensive reform cannot be brought about, increasing impatience and frustration may explode into a revolution.

Third, competition between reactionary, reform, and revolutionary ideologies will have to be taken into account. A well-developed revolutionary ideology will give unity, direction, and purpose to diverse groups and will increase the chances of revolutionary success. The absence of such an ideology will greatly reduce such chances. For instance, in traditional China there were many rebellions but no revolutions. The frequent *coups d'état* in Latin America without fundamental changes in the conception of government are well known. The relative quality and transmissibility of ideologies also will influence the process of mobilization. The influence of Marxist ideology on revolutionary movements in many developing countries is a prime example.

Suppression of what were considered basic human rights contributed to the outburst of the Hungarian Revolution. (Part IV.1, Polanyi) In the contest between capitalist and communist ideologies for the allegiance of the Third World, the persistence of a counter-revolutionary mentality may only hasten the pace of revolutionary change. (Part IV.2, Heilbroner) Due to the serious problems confronting these countries and the rapid increase in their population, there is no time for slow evolution. Communist ideology seems to be able to force the pace of necessary change.

Fourth, leadership and organization must be considered in assessing the chances of a revolution. In a situation of increasing chaos and disorder, a charismatic leader might inspire loyalty toward himself as the new source of authority. (Part IV.3, Willner) However, his appeal will depend on his ability to draw upon the myths and sacred symbols of his culture and to translate them into revolutionary terms.

The rise of charismatic leaders such as Lenin and Mao greatly facilitated the success of the Russian and the Chinese revolutions.

In the development of revolutionary organizations the existence of sectarian associations is of vital importance. By themselves these associations provide a source of psychological support and act as nurseries for the growth of revolutionary ideology. Generally, sectarian associations develop from conflicts with outsiders, and in time they crystallize into permanent, disciplined, and structured organizations with positive goals. These associations are formed by the workers, the youth, the frontiersmen, or the marginal groups, and they can be classified into gangs and sects. (Part IV.4, Lang) The gang is more active and worldly, whereas the sect is more passive and transcendental. The gang serves as a nucleus in the initial stage of revolutionary organization.

The organization of guerrillas is an important process in the revolutionary struggle. Reliable information on the study of guerrillas is hard to come by. One researcher has analyzed data gathered from a variety of guerrilla movements during the last thirty years.[15] He found that only a small segment of the population was involved in guerrilla movements, and most of them were local young people. The participation of these people depended upon a set of motivating conditions. So long as the need for individual advancement was met by the revolutionary movement, coercion and propaganda from the revolutionaries were strong and effective. If governmental oppression was intolerable, guerrilla activities remained at a high level. But as soon as the guerrillas suffered repeated military setbacks, disillusionment set in. In that case a policy of leniency on the part of the government helped to disorganize and in the end even disband the guerrilla forces.

The fifth influence relates to the way social controls are used. The effectiveness of social controls depends on the resources available to the controlling group and the way these resources are employed. For instance, in the unsuccessful Russian Revolution of 1905, the military forces available to the Czarist government were effectively employed. Consequently the revolution was suppressed. In the 1917 Revolution the Czarist government could not use its available forces to advantage, and this facilitated the success of the revolution.

In the exercise of social controls a variety of options may be employed by the government, ranging from suppression of acts of hostility to the opening of channels for normative change as a way of reducing sources of strain. (Part IV.5, Smelser) Persistent and effective suppression might stamp out a revolutionary movement altogether, or turn it into a passive movement. But if suppression is followed by erratic, hesitant, and inconsistent governmental policies, the revolutionary movement might revive.

Armed forces are indispensable instruments of social control. During a period of growing conflicts and disorder armies are brought in by the government or set themselves up as the arbiter of policies. (Part IV.6, Chorley) With recent technological developments military power has played an increasingly decisive role in revolution. No revolution can be successful without at least the tacit support of the armed forces. However, guerrilla warfare may wear out the army, as happened during the Chinese Revolution of 1949 and the Cuban Revolution of 1959. By pinning down government forces in static positions and by controlling and regimenting population in large areas, guerrilla forces gradually can turn a war of attrition in their favor.[16]

Even if all circumstances favor a revolution it does not mean that no alternative is possible. During the process of mobilization the opportunities for reaction, reform, or breakdown of the government often increase. For instance, massive and direct foreign military intervention might change the situation and reduce the probability of revolution; the United

States' intervention in the Vietnam Revolution and Russia's intervention in the Hungarian Revolution are cases in point.

### Consequences of Revolution

Although revolutions aim at implementing basic changes, their success does not mean that the desired changes actually occur. Many of the problems that existed before the revolution will continue to confront the newly established revolutionary regime. The revolution itself probably will br ng about a host of new problems. The policies of the newly established revolutionary regime will be affected by the circumstances that had existed before the revolution as well as by circumstance created by the revolution. For instance, in a comparative study of the English, American, French, and Russian Revolutions, Brinton observed that the problems of reconstruction were so great that the moderates among the revolutionaries were soon superseded by radicals who set up a centralized regime of their own and eliminated all opposition. (Part V.1, Brinton) In the case of China, the Republican government that replaced the Manchu monarchy could not achieve political unity after the 1911 Revolution. Consequently the nation became militarily fragmented, and there was a period of chaotic rule by warlords. (Part V.2, Wilbur)

Economic backwardness aggravated the problem of post-revolutionary reconstruction in Soviet Russia. Hence force was used in the collectivization of agriculture as a means of promoting rapid industrialization. (Part V.3, Kirchheimer) In the case of France, after 1789 the lack of unified and centralized leadership among the revolutionaries kept the post-revolutionary reconstruction from moving toward a radicalized stage of development.

After the revolution the problem of leadership remains serious. Leadership qualities required for revolutionary success may be quite different from leadership qualities required in the organization of post-revolutionary government and the bureaucratization of its administration. (Part V.4, Weber) This seems to be the situation in China at the present time. Mao's advocacy of the doctrine of permanent revolution, his role in the "Great Leap Forward" and the Cultural Revolution, and the difficulties his government has encountered in convening the National People's Congress and in the selection of a successor, all indicate the problem of leadership in the post-revolutionary period.

The direction of post-revolutionary development seems to correlate somewhat with the type of authority present in the pre-revolutionary era.[17] When the revolutionary struggle is directed against alien authority (imperialism), the direction of change moves toward the founding of a new political community based on nationalism. When the revolutionary struggle is directed against loosely organized and ineffectual authority (anarchy), the direction of change points toward the establishment of a strongly centralized government. When the revolutionary struggle is against arbitrary authority (tyranny), the direction of change turns toward the formation of a constitutional system of government. When the revolutionary struggle is against hereditary authority (monarchy), the direction of change veers toward the extension of the common rights of the citizenry. But empirical cases often combine several developments, and it is difficult to determine the strength of all the factors involved. Besides, there are other factors that influence political developments. Therefore the "type of authority" should be regarded as only one of many factors that influence the direction of a political development.

### Psychological Factors in Revolution

Up to now we have been dealing with sociological factors in revolution. Hopefully the materials presented will contribute to an understanding of the nature, circumstances, and problems of revolution on a sociological level. However, there are certain psychological factors that merit brief consideration.[18] In social psychology a number of theories have been advanced as explanations of human aggression and rebelliousness. One such theory is developed in terms of relative deprivation. According to this theory people rebel not as a result of absolute, but of relative deprivation. (Part VI.1, Gurr) Absolute deprivation of the masses may lead to a state of general lethargy in which the bulk of the population merely accommodate themselves to poverty with varying degrees of fatalism. Relative deprivation, however, will lead to frustration and aggression. The greater the intensity and scope of relative deprivation, the higher will be the probability for collective political violence. Another theory suggests that childhood love or hate for parents is a source of repressed feelings for which collective activism and protest movements provide outlets. (Part VI.2, Smelser)

The degree of violence varies considerably from revolution to revolution. Some of the factors accounting for this variation are obviously sociological. But the degree of revolutionary violence also may be attributed to certain psychological factors. On the basis of his biographical research Wolfenstein[19] finds that Gandhi ascribed the death of his father and mother to his own unfilial behavior. This belief developed into a sense of active guilt that subsequently reflected itself in his renunciation of masculinity and of all forms of aggression. Nasser, on the other hand, had hardly a trace of active guilt in his personality. He identified with a courageous and patriotic uncle who had been strongly anti-British. However, in his dealings with the British government, Nasser's masculinity was tempered by his understanding of the British way of governing. He realized that the use of force against the British might not be in the best interests of his country.

Lenin identified himself with the masculinity of his father and brother; the latter was executed by the Czar for his revolutionary activities. Lenin's masculinity was externalized in his aggression against the Czarist government. He held up the Czar as a symbol of evil and advocated the use of violence as an instrument of revolution. This type of analysis is interesting, but it should be regarded as being no more than suggestive at this stage.

The ability of revolutionaries to mobilize the masses is a crucial factor in the outcome of a revolution. In this connection three types of theories have been advanced as explanations of crowd formation.[20] (Part VI.3, Turner) Contagion theories explain crowd formation in terms of such psychological mechanisms as imitation, suggestion, emotional contagion, and identification. In the interactions of these mechanisms dissemination, anonymity, and attention concentration evolve to neutralize ordinary behavior anchorages. Convergence theories explain crowd formation on the basis of the aggregation of people who share the same predispositions and preoccupations. Emergent norm theories explain crowd formation in terms of relevant norms that arise in specific situations and affect crowd behavior.

**Summing Up**
I have attempted to arrange various points of view on revolution into a coherent taxonomy. As given in the table of contents, this taxonomy includes six parts. The subject matter of definitions and classifications appears in Part I. In Parts II, III, and IV, the necessary and sufficient conditions of revolution are analyzed to show that when a society develops to a high level of specialization, its structures and functions become rigidly integrated and resistant to change. This is especially true when a society's value system is oriented in support of a highly centralized system of government with no channels for group representations or redress of grievances. When changes do occur in economic, educational, or religious spheres as a result of internal or external pressures, the rigidity of the system may generate an intensification of conflicts between those who want to change

and those who want to maintain the status quo. If these conflicts continue and there are no opportunities for the discontented to emigrate or for the government to insulate them, open political struggle eventually may take place. In this situation revolutionaries with a viable ideology and strong organization and leadership might succeed in over-throwing the government, especially if the government is hesitant or unable to use force effectively. After a revolution a host of reconstruction problems has to be reckoned with, and these are discussed in Part V. Finally, in Part VI, a number of psychological factors are introduced to stimulate interest in the subject by raising such questions as why men revolt, why some revolutions are more violent than others, and what mechanisms are used in the mobilization of the masses in crowd situations. It is hoped that this book of readings will provide a basis for more systematic research into the etiology of revolution.

## NOTES

1. Jules Michelet, *History of the French Revolution* (Chicago: University of Chicago Press, 1967).
2. Edmund Burke, *Reflections on the Revolution in France* (New York: Gateway Editions, 1955).
3. Chalmers Johnson, *Revolution and the Social System* (Palo Alto: Hoover Institution Studies: 3, Stanford University, 1964), pp. 26-31.
4. Samuel P. Huntington, *Political Order in Changing Society* (New Haven: Yale University Press, 1968), pp. 266-277.
5. M.D. Sahlins and E.R. Service, "The Law of Evolutionary Potential," in *Evolution and Culture* (Ann Arbor: University of Michigan Press, 1960), pp. 94-99, 103-110.
6. Lyford P. Edwards, *The Natural History of Revolution* (Chicago: University of Chicago Press, 1927), pp. 1-15.
7. R.W. McColl, "A Political Geography of Revolution: China, Vietnam, and Thailand," in *Journal of Conflict Resolution*, Vol. 11, No. 2 (1967): pp. 153-167.
8. See the following literature for discussions on the functions of Economy: Talcott Parson, Neil Smelser, *Economy and Society*

(London: Routledge and Kegan Paul, 1957), pp. 13-28; Karl Polanyi and others, ed. "Ch. 15: Parsons and Smelser on the Economy," in *Trade and Market in the Early Empires* (New York: Free Press, 1957), pp. 307-319; K. Polanyi, "Ch. 13: The Economy as Instituted Process," *Trade and Market in the Early Empires*, pp. 243-270; N. J. Smelser, "A Comparative View of Exchange Systems," *Economic Development and Cultural Change*, 7 (1959) 173-182; N. J. Smelser, *The Sociology of Economic Life* (Englewood Cliffs: Prentice-Hall, 1963), pp. 32-37.

9. See the following literature for discussions on the functions of religion: Thomas G. O'Dea, *The Sociology of Religion* (Englewood Cliffs: Prentice-Hall, 1966), Ch. 1 and 2; Clifford Geetz, "Religion as a Cultural System," in *Reader in Comparative Religion: An Anthropological Approach*, edited by W. A. Lessa and E. Z. Voget (New York: Harper and Row, 1965), pp. 204-216.

10. See the following literature for discussions on the functions of education: A. H. Halsey, "Ch. 7: The Sociology of Education," in *Sociology: An Introduction*, edited by Neil J. Smelser (New York: John Wiley and Sons, 1967), pp. 381-434.

11. W. F. Ogburn, "Cultural Lag as Theory," in *Sociology and Social Research*, Vol. 41 (1957): pp. 167, 169-174.

12. See "Ch. 4: Social Structure and Organizations," by Arthur L. Stinchcombe, in *Handbook of Organizations*, ed. by James G. March (Chicago: Rand McNally & Co., 1964), pp. 169-196.

13. Alexis de Tocqueville, Part II: Ch. 1: "Why Feudalism Had Come to be More Detested in France Than in Any Other Country," in *The Old Regime and the French Revolution* (New York: Doubleday Anchor Books, 1955), pp. 22-32.

14. D. T. Campbell, "Variation and Selective Retention in Socio-cultural Evolution," in *Social Change in Developing Areas,* ed. by H. R. Barringer and others (Cambridge, Massachusetts: Schenkman Publishing Company, 1965), pp. 26-35.

15. A. R. Molnar, "Factors Related to Revolutionary Warfare," in *Strategies of Revolutionary Warfare*, ed. by J. M. Tinker and others (New Delhi: S. Chand and Company, 1969), pp. 23-42.

16. A. T. Rambo, "The Concept of Revolutionary Warfare," in *Strategies of Revolutionary Warfare*, ed. by J. M. Tinker and others (New Delhi: S. Chand and Company, 1969), pp. 5-6, 8-9, 12-18.

17. William Kornhauser, "Rebellion and Political Development," in *Internal War: Problems and Approaches*, ed. by Harry Eckstein (New York: Free Press, 1964), pp. 142-156.

18. The need for studying both sociological and psychological variables has been pointed out in "Social and Psychological Dimensions of Collective Behavior," in *Essays in Sociological Explanation* by Neil J. Smelser (Englewood Cliffs: Prentice-Hall, 1968), pp. 92-121.

19. E. V. Wolfenstein, *Violence or Nonviolence: A Psychoanalytic Exploration of the Choice of Political Means in Social Change*, Research Monograph Number 20 (Princeton: Center of International Studies, 1965), pp. 1-2, 5, 40-43.
20. Also see "Collective Behavior: An Examination of Some Stereotypes," by Carl J. Couch, *Social Problems*, 15 (1968): pp. 310-322, for some interesting comments on popular conceptions of characteristics of crowds.

# PART I

# Definitions and Classifications
of Revolution

# 1.

# CURRENT DEFINITIONS OF REVOLUTION

Dale Yoder

The term "revolution" is one of the most used and, one suspects, one of the most misused of words. Both within and without the literature of the social sciences it has acquired a variety of meanings which make it as adaptable to personal purposes as is the chameleon's skin. In general parlance it carries connotations and significances which involve the deepest fears as well as the highest hopes. To some it represents the most formidable danger threatening modern civilization; to others, the only gleam of hope in a present world of darkness. So general is the popular belief that revolution is a calamity of the direst order and a thing to be avoided at any cost that the newspapers of the day regularly refer to it as the one outstanding catastrophe which faces modern nations. The most effective means for opposing any present-day social movement is to brand it as "revolution" or to suggest that it is a step in that direction.

On the other hand and at the same time, the stories of successful revolutionary changes are the most cherished traditions of our society. To the Protestants, the Reformation represents the beginning and the guiding beacon of their faith. To the citizen of the United States, the traditions of the Revolutionary

Reprinted with permission of the University of Chicago Press from the *American Journal of Sociology*, vol. 32, 1926. Copyright 1926 by Dale Yoder.

War are among those which are most carefully implanted in the minds and hearts of each succeeding generation. At the same time, the word "revolution" suggests violence, bloodshed, disaster. These two contradictory conceptions give rise to such striking anomalies as that of a modern newspaper which in perfect seriousness presents in one editorial column a denunciation of the friendship of Americans with Russian revolutionists while in an adjacent column it carries an equally vituperous harangue against the slipshod Americanism which permits the schools to neglect a proper emphasis upon the virtues of the revolutionary heroes who embodied the "spirit of seventy-six."

Confusion of thought, which results from a failure to define terms carefully, is to be expected in popular speech and the lay press. But it is more or less remarkable that among those who attempt to speak in the terminology appropriate to scientific investigation and description, the concept is manipulated rather than defined. It is used to describe any sort of change, from a change in the location of sovereignty, a purely political phenomenon, to a change in the social processes underlying and supporting the fundamental structural elements of society: the political, economic, religious, and other institutions.

Burns, in commenting upon the necessity of some uniformity in usage, within the scientific field at least, suggests that the present diversity in meanings is due to the fact that the term is used to express the temper of the writer rather than to describe objective reality. He says:

> The word "revolution" may have many meanings, and for the purposes of controversy it can be usefully employed by the same persons in contradictory senses. Thus the professed opponents of all revolution can take it for granted that it involves the cutting of throats and at the same time the control of society by intellectual fanatics. The professed revolutionary can also do a little to confuse the issue by calling on us to shoot capitalists and at the same time to love our enemies.[1]

The most striking difference in the various conceptions of revolution displayed by scientific writers is in the extent of the field of behavior which they include within their usage of the term. To one group revolution is a very narrowly restricted phenomenon observable only occasionally and in a particular aspect of social life, the political phase. By far the majority of those who have described revolutions in their writings have used the term in that sense—to describe a change in the location of sovereignty. Bodin is given the credit for such a restricted usage. In his attempt to describe a revolutionary process, a sequence of stages in revolutionary behavior, he carefully specified that the thing of which he was speaking was a political reversal.[2] The precedent thus established has been widely followed by others who have written on the same and kindred subjects.

Small, for instance, explaining that the sociological interest in revolutions consists in tracing the relationship which exists between the behavior characteristic of such phenomena and the fundamental human interests, suggests that the student take as a subject for examination the French Revolution.[3] Adams, although he styles his analysis of the revolutionary process *The Theory of Social Revolutions,* is clearly using the term to describe the same political phenomena to which Bodin had reference. He makes repeated references to the French Revolution in illustration of the principles he seeks to elaborate, and is clear cut in his declaration that revolutions are problems of administrative adjustment and readjustment. His major emphasis is placed upon the economic causes which appear to him to underlie all such disorders, but when he speaks of revolution he has in mind political change—nothing more.[4]

Sorokin, similarly, although he relates revolution to a wide variety of psychological, neurological, and endocrinal manifestations, sees all of these as the accompaniments of the political upheaval.[5] Ross takes a position similar to that of Adams in tracing the causes of revolution to economic changes, and he restricts his usage of the term to its political connotations.[6] Martin presents a suggestive analysis of the crowd activity which prepares for, leads up to, carries on, and emerges from revolutions, using the term in its political sense. Although he mentions the Reformation as a revolution, his description proceeds in terms of the political aspects of that movement.[7] In this restricted sense the concept is used by various other writers, including Dewe,[8] Edwards,[9] Webster,[10] the Pauls,[11] and Spargo.[12]

To another group of writers in the same field this usage is too narrow. Revolution to this second group may be political, but the political revolutions are but one of a number of types. The term includes religious, economic, industrial, political, and other forms of upheaval and disorder. Both Le Bon and Ellwood have specifically stated that in their conceptions of the term there is ample room for types of revolution other than the political. In both cases, it is true, all of the behavior which they have selected as characteristic of that in revolution and all of the material upon which they have based their analyses has been selected from the political forms, and that fact does much to add to the confusion involved in defining the term. But each has stated a broader definition of it. Le Bon, in his introductory statements in *The Psychology of Revolutions*, extends his usage to include "all sudden transformations, or transformations apparently sudden, whether of beliefs, ideas, or doctrines."[13]

How broad his conception is may be gathered from the following criticism which he makes of those who hold to the strictly political aspects:

> The sudden political revolutions which strike the historian most forcibly are often the least important. The great revolutions are those of manners and thought. The true revolutions, those which transform the destinies of people, are most frequently accomplished so slowly that the historians can hardly point to their beginnings. Scientific revolutions are by far the most important.[14]

Ellwood, especially in his later writing on the subject, has expressed a similar idea of the numerous forms of phenomena which the term "revolution" includes. In his earlier statements he was rather specific in declaring that the phenomenon to which he referred in his use of the term was not "any sudden social or political change from *coups d'état* or 'palace revolutions' to mutations in fashions or industrial changes due to great inventions." "Rather," he says, "we are now using the term in its strictly political sense. As Bodin long ago pointed out, the mark of revolution in this sense is a change in the location of sovereignty."[15] This statement may be taken to indicate that he recognized that the term could be used in other senses, and his more recent definition makes clear that he has come to that conclusion. Revolution is simply abrupt, violent social change. It is one of the two great classes of change with which the social scientist is called upon to deal. His continued use of political revolutions as examples of such changes suggests that he considers such movements one of the several forms.

> Almost any observer would say, at the present time, that the problems of our human world are problems of unity and change, and he would probably add that the changes that we are forced to deal with in practical human affairs are of two types, gradual changes which may be called "growth," and abrupt, violent changes, which might be called "revolutions."[16]

There is another and more inclusive sense in which the term is used in this literature—a conception which includes in revolution not alone political phenomena, or economic, political, religious, and other phenomena, as various forms of revolution, but which makes the concept involve all of these aspects of social life. According to this conception, which, it should be remarked, is not clearly defined by more than one or two writers, the change which is revolutionary is basic, underlying. It involves the elementary aspects of the social structure, the institutions, and it is a change so inclusive that the whole social life of the group is disorganized. The fact that revolutions appear to be political or religious or economic arises, according to this viewpoint, because the overt aspects of the change are most striking in relation to some one element of the social organization. Considered as a whole, however, the revolution affects all parts of society and includes the underlying and perhaps less obvious changes as well as those which are superficial, obvious, and spectacular.

A suggestion of this idea appears in the statements of a number of writers, but their general use of the term is such as to raise the query whether or not they are clearly aware of the implications of their own language. Such, for instance, is the usage of Professor Sumner. In one place, he describes revolution as a change in the mores of a group, obviously a phenomenon of the underlying social structure:

In higher civilizations crises produced by the persistency of old mores after conditions have changed are solved by revolution or reform. In revolutions the mores are broken up. . . . A period follows in which there are no mores. The old are broken up; the new are not formed.[17]

But in another statement, he describes the sudden developments of transportation which have brought the urban and rural districts into closer communication as the greatest revolution of all time. In the same connection he uses the term in its political sense and suggests that the underlying social changes are its causes.

The cheapening of transportation between the great centers of population and the outlying masses of unoccupied land is the greatest fact of our time, and it is the greatest economic and social revolution which has ever taken place.[18]

The French Revolution was due to the fact that a great change had come about in the distribution of economic power between the classes and in the class mores which correspond to economic power.[19]

Similarly, Parsons appears to have a conception of the breadth of changes which occur either in or before revolution, but his usage of the term "unrest" makes it impossible to determine whether he considers such wide changes an essential part of revolution or simply an inevitable causal situation with respect to it.[20] A similar statement may be made with regard to Finney. It is difficult to ascertain whether he sees revolution as including the various changes in the social life of a group or whether it is his idea that the revolution merely occasions such a widespread series of changes, that such changes are results of revolution.[21]

Hyndman has made the most explicit statement of this viewpoint which sees revolution as an inclusive social process involving all the aspects of group life in a sudden more or less violent change. He dignifies some aspects of that change more than others, for he places especial emphasis upon the economic changes in revolution. But he is clear in his insistence that the revolution is not complete, the conception of revolution is inadequate, unless it includes change in all the various aspects of social existence.

There are thus two sides to every great change in the conduct of human affairs. First, and most important in all progressive societies, is the economic development itself, which, up to the present era, has been for the most part unconscious, so far as the mass of the people and even the most capable brains of the time were concerned. Next to the growth of economic forms comes the mental appreciation of them, which enables the community, led by its clearest thinkers, to comprehend what is taking place.[22] . . . Revolution, in its complete sense, means a thorough economic, social, and political change in any great community.[23]

Such are the generally expressed conceptions of the term "revolution." To some it is an exclusively political change, a shifting in the location of sovereignty. To others it is a change in any of several aspects of the life of society, and it takes its particular form according to the institution with which it is most obviously associated. To still others it is an extensive and inclusive social change affecting all the various aspects of the life of a society, including the economic, religious, industrial, and familial as well as the political.

This confusion in the use of the concept seems to result from the fact that none of the writers has considered revolution in its entirety, has given attention to all of its ramifications at one time. There are changes in society that are inclusive, that are broad and deep, that affect basic attitudes supporting the social structure, the mores, folkways, customs, and conventions as well as the institutions of the group. It is to these changes in the social attitudes which underlie and support the social structure, which determine the complex of habits and senti-ments that alone make any social order a possibility, that the concept "revolution" may be properly applied.

Social life is a process in which change is continual. The situations in which societies find themselves are in a continuous state of flux as inventions, discoveries, and the contributions of other cultures disorganize and reorganize the material environ-ment. The organized group which is to continue its existence and maintain its status must be in a state of regular and con-tinual readjustment to the changing situation. The successful adjustments to new situations are passed on from generation to generation as folkways and mores. The gradual and usually unconscious organization of these behavior patterns gives the institutional basis peculiar to any society. In a relatively static social order these institutional patterns enable the society to meet the exigencies of the various crises that arise. They are, therefore, carefully guarded and inculcated through tradition in each succeeding generation, and they take on, as time passes, a high degree of emotional approval.

But as the conditions basic to social life change, there comes a time when the old folkways, the old institutions, are unable to meet the demands of the new situation. They may become things of positive disutility to the group. To a portion of the group members they are no longer positive values. Sometimes they are modified through a redefinition of the situation, and the group sets about to devise new mechanisms to permit and facilitate its continued existence and to maintain or improve its status, or they fall into disuse and pass out of the culture complex as new behavior adjustments are found more advantageous. This gradual and non-spectacular accommodation of a group to the changing conditions of its life we define as normal social change.

Occasionally, however, for one reason or another, there are groups within the society which desire to preserve the old order, the traditional institutions, the time-tried folkways, mores, conventions, and customs, even though the behavior they define is inadequate in the present situation. So long as such a group has power to enforce the old definitions, the new problems remain unsolved, organized society is unable so to change as to make life tolerable to all of its individual members. The old institutions and customs fail to serve the needs of the society and its members and prevent the introduction of such new elements of social structure as the situation demands. They have then not only ceased to be positive values to the members of the group; they have become of distinctly negative value. In such a situation there is discontent, unrest becomes general, individuals become disorganized. The unrest is inchoate, unorganized, without head or objective; the group members do not see the forces that are at work. As time goes on they attribute their discomfort to that portion of the social order in which the maladjustment is most obvious. Thus, the resulting disorder may be political, religious, or economic as the discomfort is most easily attributed to one of these phases of the social organization by the crowds which center their attack upon one of these aspects.

It is this violent attack which the writers on the subject have called "revolution," and it is because this overt act is directed toward some particular part of the social structure that they have assumed that revolutions are political or religious or economic. But the real revolution occurs far below the surface of the social life. It is the change in the attitudes of the citizenry toward the underlying basis of the institutions or customs which have come to stand in the way of a tolerable life-experience. The real revolution is the change in the social attitudes and values basic to the traditional institutional order. The political, religious, industrial, or economic changes are but overt manifestations of the deeper change which has previously taken place.

## NOTES

1. C. D. Burns, *The Principles of Revolution,* p. III.
2. Jean Bodin, *The Six Books of The Commonwealth,* pp. 406-7.
3. A. W. Small, *General Sociology,* pp. 515 ff.
4. Brooks Adams, *The Theory of Social Revolutions.*
5. Pitirim A. Sorokin, *The Sociology of Revolution.*
6. E. A. Ross, *Principles of Sociology, Russia in Upheaval, Russian Bolshevik Revolution, Russian Soviet Republic, Social Revolution in Mexico.*
7. Everett Dean Martin, *The Behavior of Crowds,* esp. pp. 184 ff.
8. Rev. J. A. Dewe, *The Psychology of Politics and History.*
9. Lyford Patterson Edwards, "The Mechanics of Revolution," *St. Stephen's College Bulletin,* LXIX, No. 2.
10. Mrs. Nesta Webster, *World Revolution and The French Revolution.*
11. Eden and Cedar Paul, *Creative Revolution.*
12. John Spargo, *The Psychology of Bolshevism.*
13. Gustave Le Bon, *The Psychology of Revolutions,* p. 25.
14. *Ibid.,* p. 25.
15. C. A. Ellwood, *Sociology in Its Psychological Aspects,* p. 163.
16. C. A. Ellwood, *The Psychology of Human Society,* pp. 20-21.
17. W. G. Sumner, *Folkways,* p. 86.

18. W. G. Sumner, *Essays*, p. 167.
19. *Ibid.*, p. 167.
20. P. A. Parsons, *An Introduction to Modern Social Problems*, pp. 235 ff.
21. Ross L. Finney, *Causes and Cures for the Social Unrest*, pp. 35-37.
22. Henry M. Hyndman, *The Evolution of Revolution*, pp. 11-12.
23. *Ibid.*, p. 12.

## 2.

# REVOLUTION — TYPOLOGY AND PROCESS

**George Pettee**

In order to discuss revolutions more clearly it is essential to define some classes. For initial purposes the following types serve fairly well to separate likes from unlikes.

A type that may be called the private palace revolution occurred many times in earlier history, but is less common today. The story told by Shakespeare of the murder of Duncan by Macbeth, and Macbeth's succession, is an illustration. It was conducted within one building; it involved very few people; the public had no information of it until after the fact. The general cultural circumstances were permissive, but the causes lay within the personalities of Macbeth and his wife.

Another type is the public palace revolution. These have occurred many times from our oldest to our most recent history. The event is more elaborate and much larger in scale than in the private type. Typically, there may be movements of troops about a city and a small battle at the palace. The public knows that something is going on, but it did not initiate the event, and takes little part in it. The causation is involved with economic and political issues, but at the level of organized factions. It is not linked to major economic and social contradictions. The new rulers are not altogether outsiders to the

Reprinted from Carl J. Friedrich, editor, *Revolution: Nomos VIII* (New York: Atherton Press, 1966). Copyright 1966 by Atherton Press. Reprinted by permission of the author and Aldine, Atherton, Inc.

prevailing ruling class; and the new regime and old regime are not very different. Although the term *coup d'état* is used rather loosely, its most frequent and significant manifestations belong to this public palace revolution type. One need not look far away in time for good examples. They have occurred in Korea, in Vietnam, in Iraq, in Syria, in Brazil, and in several other countries.

Next in significance, of the recognized types, is the rebellion of an area against rule by the government of another country. Such a movement arises from large-scale social factors, involves large-scale military action, or at least the realistic threat of such action, and strong popular support. It is generally regarded as right and just. It reflects a considerable cultural advance by the rebellious people. A people submissive to foreign rule has become hostile to such rule, able to defy it, capable of expelling it, and to some unspecified degree, capable of providing a government for itself.

It is difficult to think of a case of rebellion that was not preceded either by the conquest of the rebellious people, or by true migratory colonization. Conquest is seldom mentioned in the context of revolution, yet it would seem as revolutionary, in the nonmilitary sense, for the conquered, as is rebellion for the liberated. Since history is predominantly told by the winners in such events, there is a bias here. We know of the conquest of Peru from Spanish sources rather than from Inca sources, and the violent revolution that was inflicted on the Incas passes as an incident of Spanish expansion. So for Clive in India, or Cecil Rhodes in South Africa. Yet these imposed revolutions are important, for they measure the condition of a people at one time as subjugable, just as their rebellion at a later time measures their emergence to a higher level of competence and activity.

The most important of the recognized types, however, is the type of which the French and the Russian Revolutions are the classic examples. They may be called the great national revolutions. One could almost regard one of them as a rebellion without spatial separation of the rebellious from the former rulers. Changes have occurred; a people that was subjugable has grown out of its passivity. A ruling class, separated from a formerly passive people by the privileges of power and property and culture, has remained isolated, has decayed in function, in leadership capacity, and in motivation toward measures needed for the growth and advancement of the society of community. Here we have a mass phenomenon, a people rejecting its government and the ruling class. It moves by plan, but the events constantly contradict the plans, and the results can be measured only long after the event. The social and political structure is drastically reorganized. Not every law is changed, but very great changes in the laws do occur, and public law is almost entirely changed. There is widespread violence, acute bitterness, brutality, and intense mass emotion. The process is in some respects like the business cycle, a mass action by a great number of individuals, with the course and outcome on a basis that is statistically and historically logical, *but not understood by the participants.*

There is one more class of historic event which is rarely mentioned in discussion of revolution, but which may deserve an important place in such a discussion. This I will call, for the sake of a label, a systemic revolution. The "system" referred to is not the internal social and political system; rather it is the system of state organization, the type state, for a wider human area than a single state.

Within Western history we have had several distinct state systems. In the earliest historical times there were tribes, and at quite an early time there were empires, originating in the Near or Middle East. Then there arose, in Greece and in nearby Asia Minor, and elsewhere about the Mediterranean littoral, the city-state. There were numerous examples of this type of political organization. The rise of the city-states reached a phase at which the Empire of Persia attempted to suppress the Greek cities. Persia was defeated. So for a time, some centuries before, and a little time after, there was the city-state system. Its strength, its progress, its growth, all led to conditions in which its supersession was inevitable. Great processes of change, with great wars and much violence, intervened between the time when the city-state flourished and the next time of stability, under the

Augustan settlement of the Roman Empire. Thucydides recognized these civil wars as the first great revolutionary wars. They came in series, because the sides did not well understand what they were fighting about. So there were several Peloponnesian Wars, followed by several Punic Wars, and several Roman "social wars."

The change from the state system at the time of Pericles to that at the time of Augustus stands as the first great systemic revolution of which we know much detail. The second is the one we call "the fall of Rome." The third, oddly, we know as "the Renaissance and the Reformation." The fourth we think of mainly by its wars, World War I and World War II.

For each of these it is easy to identify an *ancien régime*, and (except for the last case) easy to identify a postrevolutionary system. Each involved exceptionally severe wars, recognized later as of civil war character in many respects. Each was conducted to a great extent, including the conduct of its wars, under ideas and doctrines that had little relevance to its main political effect. Each affected a human area recognized as constituting a cultural community, though a larger and less intense one than has generally been organized as a single state (with the exception of the case of Rome). In each case, a state system stood as the political order for the larger community, as a single state may stand for a smaller and more closely knit area.

# PART II

# Preconditions to Revolution

# 1.

# STRUCTURAL CONDUCIVENESS

## Neil J. Smelser

What structural arrangements permit or encourage value-oriented movements rather than other kinds of outbursts? More particularly, to what degree is the value-system of a society differentiated from the other components of social action? What are the available means for expressing grievances? Among the several possible kinds of value-oriented responses, does a given social structure favor one or more kinds? Finally, what are the possibilities for communicating value-oriented beliefs among those who might be receptive to them?

*The Differentiation of the Value-system from Other Components of Action.* In a classic article on religious sects, Gillin observed that "religious sects will arise only when religion is the dominant interest. When political interest predominates, political parties will spring up."[1] This is a simple but forceful statement of a major dimension of structural conduciveness: the degree to which a value-system is differentiated from other components of action.

When values are not differentiated from norms, breaking a norm means more than merely trespassing on property, divorcing a spouse, or failing to display proper deference; it also involves defiance of a *general value*. As Bellah points out, this fusion of values and norms is

---

characterized by the comprehensiveness and specificity of . . . value commitments and by . . . consequent lack of flexibility. Motivation is frozen, so to speak, through commitment to a vast range of relatively specific norms, usually including those governing social institutions, are thoroughly integrated with a religious system which invokes ultimate sanctions for every infraction. Thus changes in economic or political institutions, not to speak of family and education, in traditional societies tend to have ultimate religious implications. Small changes will involve supernatural sanctions.[2]

Because of this lack of differentiation, specific dissatisfactions with any social arrangements eventually become religious protests, or, more generally, protests against values. For instance, if interest on loans is defined as sinful rather than merely economically unsound, controversy over interest becomes a religious conflict rather than a matter of economic policy.[3] In a theocratic setting objections against artistic and architectural styles become moral and theological matters, rather than mere matters of taste; under such conditions esthetic criticism is not differentiated from moral outrage. . . .

In the major Western revolutions of modern times, the degree to which protests became religious depends largely on the differentiation of religious and political issues. Trotsky, in comparing the British and French revolutions, remarked:

> In the middle of the seventeenth century the bourgeois revolution in England developed under the guise of a religious reformation. A struggle for the right to pray according to one's own prayer book was identified with the struggle against the king, the aristocracy, the princes of the church, and Rome. The Presbyterians and Puritans were deeply convinced that they were placing their earthly interests under the unshakable protection of the divine Providence. The goals for which the new classes were struggling commingled inseparably in their consciousness with texts from the Bible and the forms of churchly ritual. . . .
>
> In France, which stepped across the Reformation, the Catholic Church survived as a state institution until the revolution, which found its expression and justification for the tasks of the bourgeois society, not in texts from the Bible, but in abstractions of democracy.[4]

The leaders of newly established revolutionary regimes frequently define the world in undifferentiated value terms, and thus make it probable that any opposition *to the new regime*

will be expressed in value-oriented terms.[5] An example of the
transformation of protest into a challenge against the legitimacy
of a revolutionary regime is seen in the Kronstadt Revolt of
1921 in the Soviet Union. The Petrograd workers' economic
demands gradually crystallized into political opposition. The
government, itself consolidating its newly gained power, took
an intransigent stand against the protest and denounced it as
"Menshevik" and "Socialist Revolutionary," and hence counter-
revolutionary.[6] Leaders of successful value-oriented revolutionary
movements, because of their undifferentiated definition of the
social and political situation, have a great potential for breeding
new revolutions.

*The Availability of Means to Express Grievances.* To summarize the above: If a social situation is defined entirely in
value-oriented terms, every protest is necessarily value-oriented.[7]
This kind of conduciveness, however, never exists in pure form;
other conditions of conduciveness also determine in part why
a value-oriented movement arises, rather than some other type
of outburst. Among the most important of these conditions is
the availability of means to express protest or grievances among
a population suffering from any kind of strain.

Many religious sects, observed Gillin, arise among "lower
classes which have been shut out from any part in the socializing
process."[8] Shutting out may appear in several guises. Worsley
notes three types of political situations in which millenarian
movements arise:

> [Millenarian movements] occur, firstly, among people living in
> the so-called "stateless" societies, societies which have no overall
> unity, which lack centralized political institutions, and which may
> lack specialized political institutions altogether. They have thus
> no suitable machinery through which they can act politically as
> a unified force when the occasion arises, except on a temporary,
> localized or *ad hoc* basis. They often have no chiefs, no courts of
> law other than the council of elders or of prominent or wealthy
> men, no policy, no army and no administrative officials. . . .
> The second major type of society in which millenarian cults
> develop is the agrarian, and especially feudal, State. Such societies,
> of course, have indeed an elaborate formal hierarchical organization
> unlike stateless peoples, but the cults arise among the lower orders
> —peasants and urban plebians—in opposition to the official

regimes. These groups, like stateless Melanesians, lack any overall political organization.

There is a third type of social situation in which activist millenarian ideas are likely to flourish. This is when a society with differentiated political institutions is fighting for its existence by quite secular military-political means, but is meeting with defeat after defeat. . . . Again, when the political structure of a society is smashed by war or other means, or fails to answer the needs of a people who wish to carry on the struggle, then a prophetic, often millenarian, leadership is likely to emerge.[9]

Value-oriented beliefs, then—and here we lump millenarian beliefs with all other value-oriented beliefs—arise when alternative means for reconstituting the social situation are perceived as unavailable. In terms of our scheme of analysis, this unavailability has three main aspects: (*a*) The aggrieved group in question does not possess facilities whereby they may reconstitute the social situation; such a group ranks low on wealth, power, prestige, or access to means of communication. (*b*) The aggrieved group is prevented from expressing hostility that will punish some person or group considered responsible for the disturbing state of affairs. (*c*) The aggrieved group cannot modify the normative structure, or cannot influence those who have the power to do so.[10]

This closing-off of the means of reconstituting the social order can be illustrated in the following situations in which value-oriented beliefs typically congeal:

(1) The politically disinherited.[11] By this we mean especially the "lower orders" of society, including "discontented peasants" and the "jetsam of the towns and cities."[12]

Recent migrants to American cities are especially prone to join value-oriented protest movements. According to a number of studies, such migrants participate minimally in the organized political, social, and recreational activities of the city.[13] This isolation, combined with the general "cultural shock" of migration, makes for the clustering of value-oriented religious sects among recent migrants to cities.[14] Among recent Negro migrants, who suffered the same disadvantages plus the hardships of racial discrimination, the clustering of such value-oriented movements is also pronounced.[15]

(2) The colonially dominated. In colonial societies the dominant power imposes both conditions of strain and conditions of conduciveness for value-oriented movements on the native population. Thus R. Kennedy, in listing "the outstanding universal characteristics of colonialism all over the dependent areas of the world," notes the following consequences of colonialism:

> the color line; political and economic subordination of the native population; poor development of social services, especially education, for natives; and rigid social barriers between the ruling class and the subject people. These are the elements of which the colonial system is constructed....[16]

The Dutch system of indirect rule in Indonesia, which developed through the nineteenth century, not only permitted exploitation of the natives by Indonesian aristocrats and Chinese merchants, but also created a more authoritarian social structure than existed before the Dutch initiated this system of rule.[17] The resulting politico-economic controls ruled out much peaceful reform activity, and thus set the stage for the development of a series of value-oriented outbursts which culminated in the movement for national independence. Finally, the religious secessionist movements in South Africa also reflect the lack of political representation of the large Bantu population.[18]

(3) Persecuted minorities. Like colonial populations, persecuted minorities are under strain but do not have access to avenues for relieving the sources of strain. Historically the Jews provide the best example of a minority which, under periods of persecution, turn to value-oriented movements of a millenarian sort.[19]

(4) Governmental inflexibility. Analytically similar to the strong, unresponsive colonial power is the domestic government which, through autocracy or incapacity, displays rigidity in the face of demands for reform by groups in the population. Virtually every major ideological revolution in the West has been preceded by a period of governmental inflexibility in the face of rapid social change, inflexibility "effected through manipulation of the agencies of social control, such as government, religion, and education."[20] In a classic work, Sorokin maintains

that one of the major "causes" of revolution is repression of major instincts in the population.[21] Similarly, Brooks Adams observes that "most of the worst catastrophes of history have been caused by an obstinate resistance to change when resistance was no longer possible."[22]

. . . When avenues for influencing political authorities are absent, blocked, or atrophied, value-oriented beliefs begin to flourish. This is seen in Tocqueville's penetrating remarks on the shifting state of public opinion in France during the eighteenth century. The rise of the generalized ideals of liberty and a new society, he maintained, were preceded by a period of moderate agitation by the economists and physiocrats. These agitators

> conceived all the social and administrative reforms effected by the Revolution before the idea of free institutions had once flashed upon their minds. . . . Their idea . . . was not to destroy but to convert the absolute monarchy. . . . About 1750 the nation at large cared no more for political liberty than the economists themselves. . . . People sought reforms, not rights.[23]

Only *after* these demands for reform were thwarted by governmental indifference, monarchical ineffectiveness, and the destruction of the Parliaments, did grievances begin to be defined in terms of the values—liberty, the natural state of man, etc.— which later became the basis for the French Revolution. . . .

(5) Inflexibility in new revolutionary regimes. One basis for this inflexibility lies in the tendency for newly legitimized governments to define all protest in value-oriented terms. In addition, the social disorganization created by the revolutionary upheaval keeps the level of strain high. Frequently, also, the pressure to mobilize the local population is great because of revolutionary involvement in foreign and civil wars. And finally, because the machinery of social order under a new revolutionary government is uninstitutionalized, it is often applied with a heavy hand to "compensate" for its lack of established legitimacy. These several factors combine to result in a reign of terror after a revolutionary overthrow.[24] The typical effect of this terror is to freeze the channels for expressing grievances. The

period of terror, itself the product of a successful value-oriented movement, frequently breeds a set of conditions that are structurally conducive for the rise of new value-oriented beliefs.

(6) The breakdown of party systems. Hertzler has characterized the pre-revolutionary party situation as follows:

> . . . Italy, just prior to the dictatorship, had fifteen parties; Germany thirty-eight; and Poland, thirty. A multiple-party system raises unsurmountable barriers to the pursuance of a firm, consistent, stabilized executive policy. As a result of such *Zersplitterung* there is government by blocs and groupments, and even the best of coalitions, when they can be achieved, lack unity, force, and decisiveness and have difficulty in winning the support necessary to carry on public affairs in a confidence-producing manner.[25]

The failure of parties is conducive to the rise of value-oriented beliefs; it is also conducive to the transformation of these beliefs in revolutionary direction because one or more of the fragmented groups is likely to encourage illegal use of violence, or the groups are likely to deadlock so that the government cannot act forcefully.[26]

The common feature of all these examples is that a part of the population finds itself under strain and unable to find means of remedying the situation. It is without facilities for organized action on its own; it cannot attack or expel the persons or agencies considered responsible for its difficulties; and it does not have access to those who could initiate normative changes. These conditions apply whether the group be a permanently dispossessed segment of society, a colonially dominated people, a population under an inflexible system of authority, or a persecuted minority. Under such conditions—combined with other determinants—people begin to redefine the fundamental values of the entire system in which they find themselves. . . .

*The Insulation and Isolation of Value-oriented Movements.* Under certain circumstances, one means of expressing grievances is to initiate a value-oriented movement itself. The ease with which such a movement may be accommodated—either through isolation to another geographical setting or through insulation within a society—determines in part whether such value-oriented movements will arise. . . .

Two outstanding examples of accommodating movements through insulation are (1) The monastic order which is contained within the church. This has been a dominant method of accommodation in the Catholic Church.[27] (2) Denominationalism, which is the dominant method of accommodation in American and British Protestantism.[28] When imported into a colonial area through missionary activity, denominationalism frequently produces a rash of secessionist sects and cults. This effect is very marked among the South African Bantu, in which the Protestant pattern of denominationalism has combined with the indigenous tradition of Bantu kraal-splitting.[29] The effects of institutionalizing denominationalism can also be seen in contemporary Japan. The postwar Japanese constitution—which guaranteed greater religious freedom than before—has permitted the emergence of many pre-war schismatic bodies as independent sects. Before 1945 "those bodies which were not branches of established religions existed precariously . . . and were harassed by the police if their policies were believed to be in opposition to State Shinto and acknowledged standards of patriotism."[30] A final example of insulation: The spread of Christianity in its first centuries depended in part on "the religious policy of Rome, which furthered the interchange of religions by its toleration, hardly presenting any obstacles to their natural increase or transformation or decay, although it would not stand any practical expression of contempt for the ceremonial of the State-religion."[31] The institutionalized insulation of value-oriented movements constitutes, then, a set of conditions which is conducive to the rise of value-oriented movements.

One way of safeguarding the political integrity of the constituted authorities of any system is to permit the insulated development of value-oriented movements. One of the consequences of denominational pluralism in the Anglo-Saxon tradition is to permit a value-oriented movement (religious schism) to develop without challenging the legitimacy of the political constitution. In this way religious conflict is segregated from political conflict, and value-conflict at lower political levels (i.e., the political organization of the churches) is segregated from value-conflict at higher political levels (i.e., state and federal government).[32]

Even if insulation is not possible, a sect may sometimes with-draw to an area which is more tolerant of its peculiarities. North America, with its wide open spaces and its tradition of religious toleration, has been the haven for groups which found a hostile reception in their countries of origin. The English Puritans, the Doukhobors, and the Amana settlers are but a few of the groups which have sought isolation in North America.[33] Even within this country religious groups under attack (e.g., the Mormons) have been able to withdraw to distant geographical areas.[34] Finally, the possibility of emigrating to set up expatriate communities in other lands is yet another way of removing potential value-oriented challenges to the legitimacy of a political system.[35]

*Possibilities of Communication.* As in all collective behavior, the spread of a value-oriented movement depends on the possi-bility of disseminating a generalized belief. One of the "essential preliminary conditions" for revolutions, for instance, is "a high development of traffic and a widespread similarity of thought."[36] The actual method by which communication is carried—mouth to mouth, the press, etc.—varies from situation to situation,[37] but *some* channels of communication must be available. Con-sider the following examples:

(1) In addition to the spread of Judaism, which anticipated and prepared the way for Christianity, the latter was facilitated by the following historical developments, according to Harnack:

(a) The *Hellenizing* of the East and (in part also) of the West, which had gone on steadily since Alexander the Great: or, the *comparative unity of language and ideas which this Hellenizing had produced.* . . .
(b) The *world-empire of Rome* and *the political unity* it secured for the nations bordering on the Mediterranean. . . .
(c) The exceptional facilities, growth, and security of *international traffic* [roads, trade, etc.] . . .[38]

(2) Colonial powers often consolidate communication patterns in colonial areas which foster the spread of value-oriented beliefs such as nationalism. This consolidation is facilitated by estab-lishing countrywide trading and communication patterns, im-posing a common language, centralizing a colonial area politi-

cally, using mass media, and attempting to convert the population to a common religion.[39]

(3) A high rate of internal migration usually occasions widespread strain in a society, as we shall see. In addition, however,
it facilitates the development of collective movements. In India,
for instance, rapid urbanization creates conditions whereby

> . . . large numbers of rootless, crowded, and often unmarried urban
> workers are easily provoked to violence and readily organized by
> political groups. [In addition,] the continued ties between the
> urban worker and the rural area to which he returns for births,
> weddings, and funerals, and in which he settles when he has suffi-
> cient income, serve to bring urban political ideas and organization
> to the rural areas.[40]

# NOTES

1. J.L. Gillin, "A Contribution to the Sociology of Sects," *American
   Journal of Sociology,* Vol. 16 (1910-11), p. 246. Cf. Linton's remark
   that "a devout society will turn to (magical-revivalistic) nativism . . .
   long before a skeptical one will." "Nativistic Movements," *American
   Anthropologist,* Vol. 45 (1943), p. 239.
2. R.N. Bellah, "Religious Aspects of Modernization in Turkey and
   Japan," *American Journal of Sociology,* Vol. 164 (1958), p. 1.
   Bellah treats such societies as manifesting "prescriptive" values
   as discussed by Becker in "Current Sacred-Secular Theory and
   Its Development," in H. Becker and A. Boskoff (eds.), *Modern
   Sociological Theory* (New York, 1957).
3. For the long process by which the control of interest changed
   from the religious to the secular sphere, cf. R.H. Tawney, *Religion
   and the Rise of Capitalism* (New York, 1924).
4. *History of the Russian Revolution* (Ann Arbor, 1957), Vol. 1, pp.
   14-15. The secular character of the French Revolution should not,
   however, be overemphasized. For the strong conditioning effect
   which the Catholic Church had on the ideals of the eighteenth
   century philosophers and revolutionaries, cf. Tocqueville, *The
   Old Regime and the Revolution* (New York, 1856), pp. 184-186.
5. Bellah, "Religious Aspects of Modernization in Turkey and Japan,"
   *op. cit.,* p. 2.
6. R.F. Daniels, "The Kronstadt Revolt of 1921: A Study in the

Dynamics of Revolution," *American Slavic and East European Review,* Vol. 10 (1951), p. 241.

7. Cf. Bellah: "The new movement must take on a religious (i.e., value-oriented) coloration in order to meet the old system on its old terms." "Religious Aspects of Modernization in Turkey and Japan," *op. cit.,* p.2.

8. "A Contribution to the Sociology of Sects," *op. cit.,* p. 239.

9. P.M. Worsley, *The Trumpet Shall Sound* (London, 1957), pp. 227-228. For a contrast between the political situation of medieval peasantry—among whom millenarian movements were conspicuously lacking—and that of the urban masses in medieval times—among whom millenarian movements flourished—cf. Cohn, *The Pursuit of the Millennium* (New York, 1961), pp. 25-29.

10. In terms of the table of components of action, this means that the aggrieved group feels itself powerless to reconstitute the Facilities, Mobilization, and Normative components. Under such circumstances, attention turns to the highest level, namely reconstitution of the Value component.

11. In one sense all six examples just enumerated are instances of politically disinherited peoples (e.g., natives in a colonial setting, middle classes blocked by aristocratic inflexibility, etc.). We consider the examples separately to elucidate the many different kinds of social settings in which this political condition may occur.

12. Worsley, *The Trumpet Shall Sound,* pp. 225-226. Worsley limits the second category to the towns and cities of feudal societies, but as the following examples show, the generalization applies to migrants in modern American cities as well.

13. H.W. Beers and C. Heflin, "The Urban Status of Rural Migrants," *Social Forces,* Vol. 23 (1944), pp. 32-37; B.G. Zimmer, "Participants of Migrants in Urban Structures," *American Sociological Review,* Vol. 20 (1955), pp. 218-224; G.C. Leybourne, "Urban Adjustments of Migrants from the Southern Appalachian Plateaus," *Social Forces,* Vol. 16 (1937-38), pp. 238-246.

14. Holt, "Holiness Religion: Cultural Shock and Social Reorganization," *American Sociological Review,* Vol. 5 (1940), pp. 746-747.

15. Fauset, *Black Gods of the Metropolis* (Philadelphia, 1944), pp. 87-88, 107-108; E.D. Beynon, "The Voodoo Cult among Negro Migrants in Detroit," *American Journal of Sociology,* Vol. 43 (1937-38), pp. 897-898; H.M. Brotz, "Negro 'Jews' in the United States," *Phylon,* Vol. 13 (1952), pp. 325-326; Parker, *The Incredible Messiah* (Boston, 1937), p. 34.

16. R. Kennedy, "The Colonial Crisis and the Future," in R. Linton (ed.), *The Science of Man in the World Crisis* (New York, 1952), p. 311. The several colonial powers—British, French, Dutch, Americans, Belgians, Portuguese, Japanese, etc.—varied as to the

extent to which they imposed these consequences. Pp. 320 ff.

17. Kahin, *Nationalism and Revolution in Indonesia* (Ithaca, 1952), pp. 4-13.

18. M. Wilson, "The Beginning of Bantu Nationalism," in A. Locke and B.J. Stern (eds.), *When Peoples Meet* (New York, 1946), pp. 516-521; also B.G.M. Sundkler, *Bantu Prophets in South Africa* (London, 1948), pp. 296-296. For similar reflections on the origin of the Mau Mau in Kenya, cf. A. Rosenstiel, "An Anthropological Approach to the Mau Mau Problem," *Political Science Quarterly,* Vol. 68 (1953), pp. 427-428.

19. N. Cohn, "Medieval Millenarism and its Bearing on the Comparative Study of Millenarian Movements," Paper delivered at the Conference on Religious Movements of a Millenarian Character, under the auspices of the Editorial Committee of Comparative Studies in Society and History at the University of Chicago, April 8-9, 1960 (mineographed), pp. 2-3; J. Kastein, *The Messiah of Ismir* (New York, 1931), pp. 3-36; K.S. Pinson, "Chassidism," *Encyclopaedia of the Social Sciences,* Vol. 3, pp. 354-355. For a brief study of the revival of two Japanese cults at the Tule Lake wartime segregation center at the California-Oregon boundary, cf. M.K. Opler, "Two Japanese Religious Sects," *Southwestern Journal of Anthropology,* Vol. 6 (1950), pp. 69-78.

20. Ellwood, *The Psychology of Human Society* (New York, 1925), pp. 251-252, 254-256. See also Ellwood, "A Psychological Theory of Revolutions," *American Journal of Sociology,* Vol. 11 (1905-06), pp. 53-55.

21. *The Sociology of Revolution* (Philadelphia, 1925); the second "cause" consists of the ineptitude of the ruling classes in repressing these instincts, which we shall discuss under the heading of social control.

22. *The Theory of Social Revolutions* (New York, 1914), p. 133; also pp. 204-206. For similar statements of the inflexibility of ruling groups before revolutionary movements, cf. Edwards, *The Natural History of Revolution* (Chicago, 1927), p. 9; Trotsky, *History of the Russian Revolution,* Vol. III, pp. 173-174; Reeve, *The Natural Laws of Social Convulsion,* Vol. III, p. 502; Turner and Killian, *Collective Behavior,* pp. 503-504. Almost identical observations have been made by scholars of dictatorships—which are frequently a byproduct of revolutionary convulsion. Cf. J.O. Hertzler, "The Causal and Contributory Factors of Dictatorship," *Sociology and Social Research,* Vol. 24 (1939-40), pp. 10-11; D. Spearman, *Modern Dictatorship* (New York, 1939), p. 16; A. Carr, *Juggernaut* (New York, 1939), pp. 482-484; Kellett, *The Story of Dictatorship from the Earliest Times Till To-Day,* pp. 7-8.

23. *The Old Regime and the Revolution,* pp. 194, 196-197, 200.

24. Brinton, *The Anatomy of Revolution* (New York, 1958), pp. 185-213; J. Burckhardt, *Force and Freedom* (New York, 1943), pp. 279-287.

25. "The Causal and Contributory Factors of Dictatorship," *Sociology and Social Research,* Vol. 24 (1939-40), p. 12.

26. Cf. Roberts, *The House that Hitler Built* (London, 1939), pp. 35-36; Abel, *Why Hitler Came to Power* (New York, 1938), p. 127; E. Colton, *Four Patterns of Revolution* (New York, 1935), p. 81; A. Rossi (*pseud.*) *The Rise of Italian Fascism 1918-1922* (London, 1938), pp. 21 ff.

27. Cutten, *The Psychological Phenomena of Christiantiy,* pp. 148-150; P. Meadows, "Movements of Social Withdrawal," *Sociology and Social Research,* Vol. 29 (1944-45), pp. 47-50.

28. For commentary on American denominationalism, particularly as experienced by immigrant groups, cf. Niebuhr, *The Social Sources of Denominationalism* (Hamden, Conn., 1954), pp. 201-210, and Handlin, *The Uprooted* (New York, 1951), pp. 110-116. For a brief account of a period of vigorous sect-formation within this setting during the first half of the nineteenth century, cf. Sears, *Days of Delusion* (Boston, 1924), pp. xviii-xix.

29. Sundkler, *Bantu Prophets in South Africa,* pp. 170, 295.

30. L.C. May, "The Dancing Religion: A Japanese Messianic Sect," *Southwestern Journal of Anthropology,* Vol. 10 (1954), p. 119.

31. A. Harnack, *The Expansion of Christianity in the First Three Centuries,* Vol. I (New York, 1904), p. 22.

32. The institutionalization of this system of denominational pluralism also accounts for various areas of "touchiness" in the American political scene. The Catholic Church, for instance, is likely to be regarded as suspect first because as an organization it does not draw the line between religion and politics to nearly the degree to which it is drawn in the dominant religious tradition of the country, and second, because it does not permit denominationalism within its own ranks. On these two grounds the Catholic Church is likely to be regarded as out of keeping with the American religious tradition. Another instance of touchiness concerns the famous court case of the constitutionality of the refusal of the Jehovah's Witnesses to salute the American flag. While in itself the issue does not seem enormous, it assumed great significance in the American setting because it marked a symbolic crossing of the line which separates value-oriented movements in the religious sphere from their possible political implications.

33. W.B. Silbie, *Nonconformity: Its Origin and Progress* (London 1912), pp. 43-44; H.B. Hawthorn (ed.), *The Doukhobors of British Columbia* (Vancouver, 1955), p. 23; B.M.H. Shambaugh, *Amana That Was and Amana That Is* (Iowa City, 1932), pp. 41-5, 63. For a brief description of the appropriateness of the American

social setting for the Owenite experiments in the first half of the nineteenth century, cf. Bassett, "The Secular Utopian Socialists," in Egbert and Persons (eds.), *Socialism and American Life* (Princeton, 1952), p. 167.

34. T.F. O'Dea, *The Mormons* (Chicago, 1957), pp. 41-75.
35. The American political expatriate communities in cities like Paris, London, and Rome are functionally equivalent to sects which have been effectively isolated from the possibility of challenging the legitimacy of the political authority.
36. Burckhardt, *Force and Freedom* (New York, 1943), pp. 268-269.
37. For a contrast between the communication patterns of the mid-seventeenth and mid-nineteenth centuries, and their implications for the development of revolutions in those periods, cf. Merriman, *Six Contemporaneous Revolutions* (Oxford, 1938), p. 211.
38. *The Expansion of Christianity in the First Three Centuries*, pp. 19-21.
39. Kahin, *Nationalism and Revolution in Indonesia* (Ithaca, 1952), pp. 37-41; Coleman, *Nigeria; Background to Nationalism* (Berkeley, 1958), pp. 63-65. Coleman also points out (p. 413) that the British emphasis on "freedom of speech, of press, of assembly, and of movement, including the freedom to study abroad" has facilitated the development of nationalism in the Gold Coast and Nigeria. For an analysis of the ways in which the Japanese occupation during World War II fostered cultural unity, especially in Indonesia, cf. W.H. Elsbree, *Japan's Role in Southeast Asian Nationalist Movements 1940 to 1945* (Cambridge, Mass., 1953), pp. 120, 165-167. Among the factors which encouraged the spread of Peyotism and other nativistic movements among the American Indians in the late nineteenth and early twentieth centuries were the development of intertribal councils, the juxtaposition of reservations, the ease of travel, the use of English rather than sign language for intertribal communication, and the use of the white media of communication, especially the mails. Slotkin, *The Peyote Religion* (Glencoe, Ill., 1956), pp. 18-19.
40. Weiner, "The Politics of South Asia," in Almond and Coleman (eds.), *Politics of the Developing Areas* (Princeton, 1960), p. 174.

# 2.

# POLITICAL CHANGE IN TRADITIONAL POLITIES

Samuel P. Huntington

Traditional political systems come in varied shapes and sizes: village democracies, city-states, tribal kingdoms, patrimonial states, feudal polities, absolute monarchies, bureaucratic empires, aristocracies, oligarchies, theocracies. The bulk of the traditional polities which have faced the challenges of modernization, however, can be subsumed under two broad categories familiar in political analysis. "The kingdoms known to history," observed Machiavelli, "have been governed in two ways: either by a prince and his servants, who, as ministers by his grace and permission, assist in governing the realm; or by a prince and by barons, who hold their positions not by favour of the ruler but by antiquity of blood." Machiavelli cited the Turks as an example of the former, and the French polity of his day as an example of the latter. Mosca drew a somewhat similar distinction between bureaucratic and feudal states. The "feudal state" was "that type of political organization in which all the executive functions of society—the economic, the judicial, the administrative, the military—are exercised simultaneously by the same individuals, while at the same time the state is made up of small social aggregates, each of which possesses all the organs that are required for self-sufficiency." In the bureaucratic state, on the other hand, "the central power conscripts a considerable portion of the social wealth by taxation and uses it first to maintain a military establishment and then to support a more or less extensive number of public services." In a similar manner, Apter distinguishes between hierarchical and pyramidal authority structures.[1] The key element in all these distinctions is the extent to which power is concentrated or dispersed. The two historical traditional polities which are most representative of these two types are the bureaucratic empire, on the one hand, and the feudal system, on the other.

In the centralized, bureaucratic state, the king possesses, as Machiavelli says, "more authority" than he does in the dispersed feudal state. In the former he directly or indirectly appoints all the officials, while in the latter office and power are hereditary within an aristocratic class. The bureaucratic state, consequently, is characterized by considerable social and political mobility—those from the lowest orders may reach the highest offices—while the feudal state is more highly stratified and only rarely do men pass from one *Stand* to another. In the bureaucratic state, "there is always a greater specialization in the functions of government than in a feudal state."[2] The bureaucratic state thus tends toward the separation of functions and the concentration of power while the feudal state tends toward the fusion of functions and the division of power. In the bureaucratic state all land is often in theory owned by the king and in practice he exercises primary control over its disposition. In the feudal state land ownership is usually dispersed and hereditary; its control is in large part beyond the influence of the monarch. In the bureaucratic polity the king or emperor is the sole source of legitimacy and authority; in the feudal polity he shares this legitimacy with the nobility whose sources of authority over their subjects are independent of the monarch's authority over them. The essence of the bureaucratic state is the one-way flow of authority from superior to subordinate; the essence of the feudal state is the two-way system of reciprocal rights and obligations between those at different levels in the social-political-military structure. Clearly all the traditional political systems known to history cannot be squeezed into these two categories. Yet, all traditional polities are characterized by a greater or lesser centralization of power, and the mere fact that these categories have constantly reappeared in political analysis suggests that they do have a general relevance and validity. . . .

"A bureaucratic state," Mosca argues, "is just a feudal state that has advanced and developed in organization and so grown more complex"; bureaucratic states are characteristic of societies at higher "levels of civilization," feudal states, of societies at more primitive levels of civilization.[3] This relation between political form and level of development seems reasonable enough. In contrast to feudal polities, bureaucratic systems do manifest more differentiated political institutions, more complicated administrative structures, greater specialization and division of labor, more equality of opportunity and social mobility, and greater predominance of achievement criteria over ascriptive ones. All these features presumably reflect a higher level of political modernization than is found in dispersed or feudal polities. At the same time, the centralization of power in the bureaucratic polity enhances the capability of the state to bring about modernizing reforms in society.

Yet the equation of modernity with centralization and the ability to innovate policy is incomplete at best. In fact, the more "modern" a traditional polity becomes in this sense, the more difficulty it has in adapting to the expansion of participation which is the inevitable consequence of modernization. The power which is sufficiently concentrated in the monarchy to promote reform may become too concentrated to assimilate the social forces released by reform. Modernization creates new social groups and new social and political consciousness in old groups. A bureaucratic monarchy is quite capable of assimilating individuals; more than any other traditional political system it provides avenues of social mobility for the intelligent and the artful. Individual mobility, however, clashes with group participation. The hierarchy and centralization of power which makes it easier for the monarchy to absorb individuals also creates obstacles to the expansion of power necessary to assimilate groups. . . .

In addition, the inability of the monarchy to adapt to broadened political participation eventually limits the ability of the monarch to innovate social reforms. The effectiveness of the monarch depends upon his legitimacy and the decline in the latter erodes the former. The success of his reforms diminishes the monarch's impetus to innovate policy and increases his concern for the preservation of his institution. A gap opens between the increasingly modern society and the traditional polity which gave it birth; able to transform the society, but unable to transform itself, the monarchial parent is eventually devoured by its modern progeny.

Many societies offer evidence of the contrast in the ability to expand participation satisfactorily between those traditional polities in which power was highly centralized and which consequently had the capacity for policy innovation and those in which power was dispersed and which consequently possessed less of such capacity. In the western world, as we have seen, the centralization of power and modernizing reforms occurred earlier on the Continent than they did in England, and earlier in England than they did in America. In the eighteenth century the French centralized despotism was viewed as the vehicle of reform and progress; only conservatives such as Montesquieu could see advantages in what was generally held to be the corrupt, disorganized, fractionated and backward English political system. Yet the centralization of power under traditional auspices also worked to obstruct the expansion of political participation, while the polities where power remained dispersed were better able to assimilate rising social classes into the political system. So also, in America the centralization of power was even less advanced than in England and the expansion of political participation proceeded even more rapidly and smoothly. Thus, the polities which were less modern politically in the seventeenth and eighteenth centuries came to be more modern politically in the nineteenth century.

A similar difference in evolution exists between China and Japan. In the mid-nineteenth century, authority and power were far more centralized in China than in Japan: one was a bureaucratic empire, the other still essentially feudal. Japanese society was highly stratified and permitted little social mobility; Chinese society was more open and permitted the movement of individuals up and down the social and bureaucratic ladder. In Japan heredity was, in Reischauer's phrase, "the basic source of authority," while in China it played a much smaller role, and advancement in the bureaucracy was based on an elaborate system of examinations.[4] As Lockwood suggests, an observer of 1850 asked to judge the potential for future development of the two countries "would have placed his bet unhesitatingly on China." Politically,

> the feudal heritage of Japan . . . tended to conserve political power in the hands of a self-conscious warrior caste, [whose] traditional skills and habits of domination over an unfree people were dubious assets for modernization, to say the least. . . . By comparison, China alone among the Asian peoples brought to the modern world a tradition of egalitarianism, of personal freedom and social mobility, of private property freely bought and sold, of worldly pragmatism and materialism, of humane political ideals sanctioned by the right of rebellion, of learning as the key to public office.[5]

The same feudal system, however, which made Tokugawa Japan seem so backward compared with Ch'ing China also furnished the social basis for the expansion of political participation and the integration of both the traditional clans and the newer commercial groups into the political system. In Japan the "potential leadership, because of feudal political institutions, was much more widespread, not only among the 265 'autonomous' *han* but even among the various social groups with their differing functions in society. If one geographical area or sector of Japanese society failed to respond adequately to the crisis created by Western pressures, another one would; in fact, this is what happened."[6] The gap between the symbolic end of feudalism (1868) and the organization of the first modern political party (1881) was sufficiently brief so that the latter could be built on the wreckage of the former. Thus, in Japan the broadening and institutionalizing of political participation went on simultaneously with the introduction of modernizing policy innovations. In China, on the other hand, Confucian values and attitudes delayed the conversion of the political elite to the cause of reform, and, once it was converted, the centralization of authority precluded the peaceful assimilation of the social groups produced by modernization.

The patterns of evolution in Africa do not seem to differ significantly from those of Europe and Asia. Ruanda and Urundi, for instance, were two traditional societies of similar size, similar geography, similar economies, and similar ethnic make-up of about 85 per cent Bahutu tribesmen and about 15 per cent Watutsi warriors who comprised the political and economic elite. The principal differences between the two kingdoms were in the distribution of power and the flexibility of social structure. The *mwami* or king of Ruanda "was an absolute monarch who governed through a highly centralized organization and by principles that enabled him effectively to control his militarily powerful feudatories." In Urundi, on the other hand, the king shared power with the royal clan or *baganwa*, whose members "were by hereditary right the ruling class of Urundi." In Ruanda the king might make grants of land to members of the royal family, but they "had no special rights or powers." The *baganwa* of Urundi, however, could appoint their own subordinates "to lead their personal armies and to administer their lands." Not infrequently these personal armies, in typical feudal fashion, would be used against the king. Thus, while the king of Urundi was in theory absolute, in practice he was "with respect to the *baganwa* virtually *primus inter pares* in a decentralized state." The systems of royal marriage and of inheriting the throne tended to "consolidate royal power" in Ruanda but contributed to "weakening royal power" in Urundi. Similarly the foreign wars which were typical of Ruanda also "consolidated the royal power by increasing the royal treasury and thus putting at the king's disposal new lands, cows, and other goods for distribution to his successful feudatories."[27] In Urundi, in contrast, civil wars among the rival princes helped to reduce royal authority.

While Ruanda was, in some respects, more conservative and traditional than Urundi, clearly it was also more centralized and bureaucratic while Urundi was more dispersed and feudal. The receptivity of the two societies to social-economic change reflected these differences. The Ruandans demonstrated "greater intellectual quickness for 'book-learning' " and greater "interest in and ability to learn European ways—in the school system, in religious instruction, and in response to economic or political reforms proposed by the Europeans." The Ruandans appraised "European culture as holding out to them the opportunity to increase their prestige and power, and they tend to act to make it as much as possible their own." For the Rundi, on the other hand, "the new institutions and ways seem to be received as new impositions from above, accepted out of necessity rather than welcomed or pursued, avoided as far as possible." These differences in receptivity to change were found in large measure to be the result of the difference between "a strongly centralized and a decentralized political system."[8]

The ability to expand political power and to assimilate groups into the political system, however, would appear to vary in just the reverse way between the two systems. In the more modern and "progressive" Ruanda the process of political change involved a violent revolution in 1959, in which the previously subordinate Hutu turned on their Watutsi rulers, slaughtered several thousand of them, ousted the *mwami*, established a Hutu-dominated republic, and drove some 150,000 Tutsi into exile. As in Russia, China, and the Ottoman Empire, the centralized monarchy in Ruanda was replaced by a single-party regime. In late 1963 raids by Watutsi guerrillas across the borders into Ruanda provoked another savage tribal massacre in which the Hutu apparently killed over 10,000 more of the Tutsi remaining within their borders, floating their bodies down the Ruzizi River to Burundi and hacking and maiming thousands of others. Kigali, the capital of Ruanda, was reported to be pervaded with the stench of human flesh. "In a few weeks," one European resident observed, "Ruanda slipped back 500 years."[9] The centralized, hierarchical, more open traditional Ruandan political system was thus able to adapt to social and economic reforms but was clearly unable to provide for the peaceful absorption of the previously excluded social groups into the political system. The result was bloody revolution and conflict in which about half the Watutsi population of over 400,000 had by 1966 been either killed or forced into exile. . . .

Thus, the evidence is fairly conclusive that the more pluralistic in structure and dispersed in power a traditional political system, the less violent is its political modernization and the more easily it adapts to the broadening of political participation. These conditions make possible the emergence of a modern, participant political system which is more likely to be democratic than authoritarian. Paradoxical as it may seem, dispersed or feudal traditional systems characterized by rigid social stratification and little social mobility more often give birth to modern democracy than do the more differentiated, egalitarian, open, and fluid bureaucratic traditional systems with their highly centralized power. The experience of seventeenth- and eighteenth-century Europe is reproduced in twentieth-century Asia and Africa. Those traditional systems which are most modern before the expansion of political participation have the greatest difficulty in dealing with the consequences of that expansion.

## NOTES

1. Niccoló Machiavelli, *The Prince and The Discourses* (New York, The Modern Library, 1940), p. 15; Gaetano Mosca, *The Ruling Class* (New York, McGraw-Hill, 1939), pp. 80 ff.; David E. Apter, *The Politics of Modernization* (Chicago, University of Chicago Press, 1965), pp. 81 ff. See also S.N. Eisenstadt, "Political Struggle in Bureaucratic Societies," *World Politics, 9* (Oct. 1956), 18-19, and *The Political Systems of Empires* (New York, Free Press, 1963), pp. 22-24.
2. Mosca, p. 83.
3. Mosca, p. 81.
4. Edwin O. Reischauer, *The United States and Japan* (rev. ed. Cambridge, Mass., Harvard University Press, 1957), p. 157.
5. William W. Lockwood, "Japan's Response to the West: The Contrast with China," *World Politics, 9* (1956), 38-41.
6. Edwin O. Reischauer and John K. Fairbank, *East Asia: The Great Tradition* (Boston, Houghton Mifflin, 1960), pp. 672-73. For an analysis along somewhat similar lines attempting to explain why England and Japan developed economically more rapidly than France and China, see Robert T. Holt and John E. Turner, *The*

*Political Basis of Economic Development* (Princeton, N.J., Van Nostrand, 1966), passim, but esp. pp. 233-91.

7. Ethel M. Albert, "Socio-political Organization and Receptivity to Change: Some Differences Between Ruanda and Urundi," *Southwestern Journal of Anthropology, 16* (Spring 1960), pp. 54-60. See also René Lemarchand, "Political Instability in Africa: The Case of Ruanda and Burundi" (unpublished paper), p. 34. On the traditional system in Ruanda in general, see Jacques Maquet, *The Premise of Inequality in Ruanda* (London, Oxford University Press, 1961).

8. Albert, pp. 66-67, 71-73.

9. *New York Times*, January 22, 1964, p. 2, Feb. 9, 1964, p. 1; *Newsweek, 63* (Feb. 24, 1964), 51.

# PART III

# Increasing Contradictions and Conflicts in Society

# 1.

# STABILITY AND INSTABILITY: A NOTE IN COMPARATIVE POLITICAL ANALYSIS

## Taketsugu Tsurutani

Within the context of comparative political analysis, consensual society is deemed stable.[1] The most fundamental as well as general source of stability is the existence of consensus, viz., a tacit agreement, engendered by a homogeneous political culture, between the government and the governed as well as among groups within the governed, concerning the broad goal of society within a given time context and the means to implement its attainment.[2] Put differently, there exists, in consensual society, uncoerced adherence to a mutually accepted set of procedures for decision-making deemed necessary and appropriate by both the government and the governed for order, progress, and general well-being,[3] for the resolution of issues and conflicts arising out of the public at large, and for the elicitation and promotion of societal goals.[4] The idea of political legitimacy as well as of governmental efficiency is implicit in such voluntary harmony. . . . [5]

Two conceptual categories of analysis contained in consensus require immediate elucidation. Society's goal is one of the following: maintenance of the *status quo*, restoration of the *status quo ante*, and pursuit of a *status nuovo*. Every authoritative political decision is made for the purpose of one of these three goals.

Reprinted with permission of the author and publisher from the *Journal of Politics*, Vol. 30 No. 4, 1968. Copyright 1968 by Taketsugu Tsurutani.

That any of these goals, when it becomes the goal of society officially projected and pursued by the regime, encounters opposition of one kind or another is unavoidable.[6] Consensus does not and need not signify unanimity. Existence of consensus means simply that there is an adequately broad harmony in society enabling mutually accepted and regular processes of government,[7] and that whatever opposition may arise in society against the goal or a policy can be either effectively restrained, or integrated into consensus by accommodation and compromise without, in either case, disrupting the normal processes of government. To state the same idea somewhat differently, consensus exists because the government is both responsive and responsible to the governed and because the governed have an implicit trust in the probity of the government. The government does not pursue the kind of goal that the governed are not willing or cannot be induced to pursue. There is perceptually an identity of interest between the government and the governed. Consensual society, therefore, is not necessarily a so-called democratic republic. A monarchy may very well be consensual if there is this fundamental mutual harmony between the ruler and the ruled. So can aristocratic polity be consensual. So-called authoritarian society can, for the same reason, be consensual if it enjoys general approval, tacit or otherwise, of the people at large.[8] Popular participation as such in politics does not necessarily make for democracy, let alone consensus. Conversely, neither consensus nor democracy requires universal popular participation as the *sine qua non*.[9]

Responsiveness and responsibility of the government to the governed (the idea central to political philosophy since antiquity that the ruler must govern in the interest of the ruled in order to enjoy the latter's genuine support) are relevant also to the problem of the means for the attainment of the goal. Every authoritative decision concerning means for the pursuit of the goal affects some group or groups in society directly or perceptively (e.g., higher income taxes for the promotion of general welfare). For this reason, in consensual society, every significant policy must be based on at least general acquiescence or grudging acceptance, if not altogether enthusiastic, support of the governed.[10] The means in this regard signify authoritative elicitation, utilization, and allocation of resources, tangible and intangible, material or human, that are needed to implement the goal desired. This category includes, among others, general support for the goal; material, technological, and human resources; and social cultural value systems that may be conducive to such uses of resources as will enable smooth and economical implementation of necessary steps to attain the goal. Crucial importance of this category consists in the fact that means for the attainment of the goal always signify sacrifices of resources that could otherwise be consumed for immediate or short-run psychic and appetitive gratifications.

From the above consideration of goal and means in relation to consensus emerges a third category of analysis, viz., the concept of balance between what the goal demands by way of tangible and intangible sacrifices and the ability to meet that demand. In consensual society there is a reasonable or tolerable (i.e., in the eye of the society 'at large) balance between the two. Else, consensus would seriously decline. The Great Society as a national goal demands various kinds of sacrifices on the part of the governed, but, not only have the Americans by and large accepted the desirability of the goal, but there apparently exist in America adequate amounts as well as kinds of means to meet that demand. Suppose that the same goal were projected and pursued in, say, Portugal or the Philippines. There would clearly be a critical lack of means, especially material means, to meet its demand. To be sure, material and other shortcomings for a certain goal may at times and even for a period of time be or in fact are compensated for by highly electrifying enthusiasm, fanaticism, or religious devotion generated by charisma and/or skillful manipulation on the part of the regime of real or fancied crises, fear, hatred, ignorance, ambition, and illusion of the masses in society. "Superhuman" efforts of society may thus be induced and heightened by the consummate skill in propaganda, indoctrination, and other forms of manipulation of symbols, thereby apparently overcoming the otherwise insurmountable shortcomings in certain material and other resources. This may be termed a principle of compensatory mobilization.[11] It is often applied in situations of extraordinary crisis, especially of crisis that is perceived as threatening the identity and/or existence of society. In such a situation as this, there does indeed exist consensus in society— a form of hyperactive consensus, feverish and intoxicating. This feverishness is the very core of the compensatory mobilization, and its duration depends upon the manipulative skill of the political leadership.

The presumed balance between goal and means generated and maintained by the application of the principle of compensatory mobilization cannot last indefinitely, however, for the basic imbalance between goal and means is bound to overwhelm the temporary efficacy of compensatory mobilization. The demise of Juan Peron, Sukarno, or Ahmed Ben-Bella may be explained by this sequence of phenomena. In the end, therefore, there must be some tolerable approximation of balance between the goal desired and the means available for the attainment of the goal if consensus is to be maintained. In other words, there ought to be a viable equilibrium between the sacrifices that the goal desired demands for its realization on one hand and, on the other, the extent of sacrifices of tangible and intangible resources that the governed are willing and able or can be induced to undergo for the attainment of the goal. That government is responsive as well as responsible which can maintain some approximation of this necessary balance.

A fourth category of analysis necessarily involved in the consideration of the nature of consensus and stability is the idea of tension as the phenomenon of imbalance between goal and means. Tension, in short, signifies decline of consensus, and if it becomes pervasive, it will cause serious erosion or disappearance of that fundamental mutual harmony between the government and the governed discussed earlier, and emergence of mutual distrust and fear between the government and the governed. Tension, therefore, spells insecurity in the relationship between the government and the governed, hence political instability in society. When it becomes such that the normal and accepted processes of government become disrupted and/or impotent, tension will·lead the government, if it is strong enough, to resort increasingly to the use of coercion for its own safety and for the pursuit of the goal. If, on the other hand, the government is not sufficiently strong, the situation will lead to political fragmentation where no meaningful goal may be projected and pursued.[12]

The idea of consensus which necessarily presupposes the acceptance of and adherence to a certain set or sets of values concerning political, social, and human relationships implies the rejection of certain other sets of values. It implies a certain notion of probity or standard of behaviour on the part of both the government and the governed. Deviation is that which detracts from what is considered by the existing consensus to be proper and desirable. Some cases of deviant behaviour may be condoned or tolerated; others are suppressed or persecuted. Whether a particular deviant act is tolerated or suppressed depends upon the nature and the extent of consensus that prevails in a given society. (For example, even the draft-card burner has some chance of a fair hearing in America, but the same deviant act may be punished with dispatch and severity in another consensual society.)

Consideration of whether or not an act of deviation is to be condoned leads to a concept of tolerance. In consensual society, the degree of tolerance is high for two reasons: (1) few individuals or groups care to act deviantly because of the existence of consensus,[13] and (2) few deviant acts threaten the stability of society, again for the same reason. . . .

There is an important point to the nature of consensus. Inasmuch as the government, in consensual society, is responsive to, hence responsible to and representative of,[14] the diversity of community interests, there is little dogma or doctrinaire rigidity in the political system, and different views within the outer limits of consensus are constantly expressed by representative members of the participating groups concerning politically relevant decisions to be made. . . .

In a society of oppression, on the other hand, the regime must be oppressive simply because the goal it pursues is not adequately supported by the public at large and by necessary material and human resources. Since it does not enjoy adequate consensus of society, it cannot but be rigid in its responsiveness to public demands and needs, for to allow itself to become amendable to interests of the variety of groups and segments in society is tantamount to discarding the goal it insists on pursuing. Its allegiance is owed not to the governed but to the central theoretical/ideological rationale of the avowed goal.[15] As resistance to the pursuit of the goal becomes more intense, the regime's adherence to the pursuit of the goal becomes more obstinate and doctrinaire. Tension in society grows in intensity. Under the circumstances, fewer and fewer acts of deviation from the central norm of the ideology and the dictate of the goal will be tolerated until the slightest deviation from them will be regarded as heretic, dangerous, hence deserving of suppression. Dogmatism is by its very nature incompatible with diversity and freedom. Dogma is its own criterion. Thus, once established for the dogged pursuit of the goal that far exceeds the limits of means (same, in this context, as authority exceeding the limits of assent[16]), the oppressive regime by its own logic cannot but be inflexible, rigid, and dictatorial. Suppression of freedom which generates various demands and claims, therefore, is an inevitable consequence. Hence, further aggravation of tension and instability....[17]

Lack of a meaningful goal signifies an absence of effective political leadership in society. Take, for example, the Fourth Republic of France. The reputed competence of the French bureaucracy and the relative functional efficacy of the parliamentary committee system notwithstanding, a general overview of the total picture of the politics of the *Quatrieme Republique* leads to a conclusion that there existed no clear center of political power. Instead, there were too many small pockets of power for effective final and authoritative decision-making to be feasible. These numerous, fragmented pockets of power tended to cancel one another out, and each of them was led, not on the basis of any particular political goal or principle, but rather by leaders of comparative longevities in legislative service with the exception, perhaps, of M. Pierre Mendes-France. The power of the politically influential in French politics, therefore, seems to have been not that of decision-making, but rather that of preventing any coherent final authoritative decision-making. The apparent authority of the Gaullist regime in the Fifth Republic must be viewed against this sharply contrasting background. . . .

The second context in which the situation of imbalance . . . arises is one in which an increase in the extent of popular participation in decision-making processes is not accompanied by its necessary corollary, viz., a sense of common citizenship and responsibility. This is what Huntington means when he says that equality of political participation must grow together with the "art of associating together." But in many a developing nation today, "The rates of mobilization and participation are high; the rates of organization and institutionalization are low"[18] Under such circumstances, "Rapid increases in mobilization and participation, the principal political aspects of modernization, undermine political institutions. Rapid modernization, in brief, produces not political development, but political decay."[19] A majority of developing nations today seem to be plagued by this problem, thereby undermining the possibility of coherence, authority, and effectiveness of government. This phenomenon gives rise to deepening fragmentation of society. . . .

From the discussion above of stability and two types of instability, a variety of observations can be inferred. Of these, two may be stated with a degree of relevance and empirical validity. One is that the propensity of many a newly developing nation to resort to an actually or potentially oppressive system, at least at some points during the process of "nation-building", is largely a necessary response to the otherwise insoluble phenomenon of continuing, often worsening, internal fragmentation. To offset the glaring lack of a genuinely congruent political culture and consensus as well as some of the material means for purposes of pursuing the goal of modernization, such a nation as this finds it necessary to apply the principle of compensatory mobilization. . . .

The second tentative observation is that the regime of oppression, once the efficacy of compensatory mobilization has declined, will eventually confront the choice of either continuing, at the risk of its own overthrow, the practice of now naked oppression, or of allowing the natural tendency toward a lessening of tension without, in the meantime, permitting such tendency to undermine its authority in the eyes of the masses.[20] In the latter case, care must be taken by the regime not to alienate itself from the process of relaxation. Menderes' regime in Turkey and Rhee's in South Korea, it seems, chose the first alternative, thereby spelling their own downfalls. (In the case of South Korea, Rhee's demise promptly led the nation into the situation of fragmentation where it remained until the rise of General Park.) The Soviet Union and many of the East European nations seem to have opted for the second alternative, and, at least thus far, with fair degrees of success.

Perhaps the most crucial question to be asked concerning the basic problem that developing nations face is about the timing of the relaxation of tension. Since the propriety of such relaxation presupposes social discipline of a sufficient degree to render it truly meaningful in terms of promoting political development, premature concession to the tendency toward relaxation, especially when the community never had a consensual tradition before the establishment of the oppressive political regime, could prove disastrous. Where there is no tradition of consensus and a unifying political culture embedded in society, the first task of the nation-building leaders is to enforce the necessary discipline upon society before any meaningful effort might be made to engender viable consensus. This, of course, is easier said than done, since there is the ever-present danger, even natural proclivity, of such a regime becoming a permanent institution of oppression, thereby preparing the grounds for an eventual upheaval, be it a revolution or a *coup d'etat*, which may produce another, equally or more oppressive regime, or pervasive fragmentation. While emergence of consensus, in a situation where none has existed before, seems to be predicated upon engenderment and enforcement of certain discipline, the enforcement of discipline, when the regime is capable, is far easier than the fostering of consensus for the purpose of which it must be effectuated.

## NOTES

1. There is an abundance of literature on this particular matter among which, to mention but a few outstanding works, are: Gabriel Almond, "Comparative Political Systems," *Journal of Politics*, XVIII, 3 (August 1956); Gabriel Almond and Sidney Verba, *The Civic Culture* (Princeton, N.J.: Princeton University Press, 1963); Carl J. Friedrich, *Man and His Government: An Empirical Theory of Politics* (New York: McGraw-Hill, 1963); Samuel H. Beer and Adam B. Ulam (eds.), *Patterns of Government* (New York: Random House, 1958); and William C. Mitchell, *The American Polity* (New York: The Free Press of Glencoe, 1962).

2. This requires not only a vertical harmony and communication between the government and the governed, but, perhaps more significantly, also a sufficient horizontal agreement and mutual communication among various groups in society. This consideration is of utmost importance since consensual society is characterized by a network of legitimate (i.e., acceptable to or acquiesced in by all significant groups concerned) relationships both horizontally and vertically. The critical nature of this problem in developing nations is summarized in Fred R. von der Mehden, *Politics of the Developing Nations* (Englewood Cliffs, N. J.: Prentice-Hall, 1964). For detailed empirical investigations of the problem, one of the best is still Gabriel Almond and James Coleman (eds.), *The Politics of the Developing Areas* (Princeton, N.J.: Princeton University Press, 1960). See also Gabriel Almond and G. Bingham Powell, Jr., *Comparative Politics: A Developmental Approach* (Boston and Toronto: Little, Brown, 1966).

3. Cf. Reinhard Bendix, *Nation-Building and Citizenship: Studies of Our Changing Social Order* (New York, London, and Sidney: Wiley, 1964), pp. 19-21.

4. "The essence of the integrative relationship is seen as *collective action to promote mutual interest.*" Philip E. Jacob and Henry Teune, "The Integrative Process: Guidelines for Analysis of the Bases of Political Community" in Philip E. Jacob and James V. Toscano (eds.), *The Integration of Political Communities* (Philadelphia and New York: Lippincott, 1964), p. 5.

5. For the necessary combination of legitimacy and efficiency for stable society, see, for example, S. M. Lipset, *Political Man* (Garden City, N. Y.: Doubleday, 1960), ch. iii, as well as Chalmers Johnson, *Revolutionary Change* (Boston and Toronto: Little, Brown, 1966), ch. ii, especially p. 28.

6. It is probable also that a rationally determined policy results in an irrational or nonrational outcome, thereby subverting the goal. Cf. Mitchell, *op. cit.*, pp. 371-372.

7. See, for example, Friedrich, *op. cit.*, pp. 239-241.
8. Friedrich, *op. cit.*, ch. 10, especially pp. 188-191.
9. For the thesis that there is no positive correlation between participation and consensus, see, for example, Aristotle, *Politics*, Bks.
   V-VI; Harold Lasswell, Daniel Lerner, and Easton Rothwell, *The
   Comparative Study of Elites* (Stanford University Press, 1952);
   Lester G. Seligman, "Elite Recruitment and Political Development,"
   *Journal of Politics*, XXVI, (August 1964); and Samuel P. Huntington, "Political Development and Political Decay," *World Politics*,
   XVII, 3 (April 1965).
10. The role of indifference or apathy does not lend itself to neat
    quantification. Its theoretical relevance to political stability, how-
    ever, has been subjected to some interesting studies. Bernard R.
    Berelson, in one of the now classics in the study of voting behaviour,
    argues that indifference provides some sort of cushion for tension
    generated by overparticipation on the part of some politically
    active groups in society as well as "maneuvering room for political
    shifts necessary for a complex society in a period of rapid change.
    Compromise . . . is more often induced by indifference. Some
    people are and should be highly interested in politics, but not
    everyone is or needs to be. Only the doctrinaire would deprecate
    the moderate indifference that facilitates compromise." Berelson,
    "Democratic Practice and Democratic Theory" in Leonard J. Fein
    (ed.), *American Democracy: Essays on Image and Realities* (New
    York: Holt, Rinehart, Winston, 1965), p. 191. S. M. Lipset, on
    the other hand, recognizes the danger that is latent in indifference
    or apathy, namely, the danger of susceptibility of the apathetic
    and the indifferent to extremism in times of crisis. (Lipset, *op. cit.*,
    pp. 103-105, 115-116). Both arguments seem valid, however, since
    each assumes a particular type of context for its validity. What is
    desirable or even promotive in one context is not necessarily so in
    the other.
11. Such mobilization is compensatory, and not substitutive, in that
    it can furnish only what may appear equivalent in value to what
    is lacking but not what can fulfill the function of what is lacking.
    The payment from the insurance company for the loss of an
    arm, for example, is compensatory, but not substitutive.
12. What is significant here, and difficult to explicate, is the relativity
    of tension. Diagramatic illustrations and their discussions below
    will, hopefully, clarify the matter. Tension as such is germane,
    as Davies notes, to every society, for politics is at once the condi-
    tion, the result, and the method of the resolution of conflict.
    Within certain limits, therefore, tension and consensus are not
    mutually exclusive. Also, see James Davies, *Human Nature in
    Politics* (New York and London: Wiley, 1963), p. 65; Lewis A.

Coser, *The Functions of Social Conflict* (Glencoe, Ill.: The Free Press, 1956); and Irving L. Horowitz, *Three Worlds of Development* (New York: Oxford University Press, 1966), esp. pp. 372-379.

13. "In a well-governed State there are few punishments, not because there are many pardons, but because there are only a small number of criminals." Jean-Jacques Rousseau, *The Social Contract* (New York: Hafner, 1947), p. 32.

14. "Representativeness" is relevant only valuationally and attitudinally, and not in terms of personnel composition of the government leadership. Sociological variables concerning political elites are less pertinent in relation to policies made than are often felt. "Democracy" in personnel compositions of political elites is no guarantee for "democracy" in governance. See, among various works on political elites that are significant in this regard, Karl Deutsch and Lewis Edinger, *Germany Rejoins the Powers* (Stanford, 1959); W. L. Guttsmann, *The British Political Elite* (London, 1963); Dwaine Marvick (ed.), *Political Decision-Makers* (Glencoe, 1961); Harold Lasswell and Daniel Lerner (eds.), *World Revolutionary Elites* (Cambridge, Mass., 1965); Maurice Duverger, *Political Parties* (New York, 1963).

15. This is relevant to what Friedrich calls "convictional ground" for the doctrinaire devotees. Cf. Friedrich, *Man and Government*, p. 240.

16. Cf. Bertrand de Jouvenel, *Sovereignty: An Inquiry into the Political Good* (Chicago: University of Chicago Press, 1963), p. 33 and T. D. Weldon, *The Vocabulary of Politics* (Baltimore: Penguin, 1960), pp. 51-53.

17. The problem of delineation of consensual society from oppressive society is difficult. Theoretically, the delineation should be achieved by means of quantification. This writer limits himself, however, to offering a set of phenomena that would suggest the direction in which a quantificatory device might be formulated. Society of oppression is to be characterized by one or more of the following phenomena: policy of terror; systematic arrest, imprisonment and/or execution of significant persons such as famous writers, scientists, scholars, political leaders, military officers, and government officials; sustained government action against specific groups in society; clandestine, sporadic, and largely futile nature of resistance against the regime; and isolation and suddenness of revolts without significant prior indications thereof. Cf. Taketsugu Tsurutani, *Tension, Consensus, and Political Leadership: A New Look into the Nature and Process of Modernization* (Unpublished PhD dissertation, University of Wisconsin, 1966), chs. xii and xx. For an example of recent attempts quantitatively to identify stability and instability, see Ivo Feierabend *et al.*, *Dimensions of Political Unrest*, a paper presented at the 20th Annual Meeting of the

Western Political Science Association, March 25, 1966, at the University of Nevada, Reno, Nevada.

18. Huntington, *op. cit.*, p. 386. Also see Robert Lane, *Political Life* (Glencoe, Ill.: The Free Press, 1959), pp. 341-343 and James Coleman, "Conclusion" to Almond and Coleman (eds.), *op. cit.*

19. Huntington, *op. cit.*, p. 386. See also Lipset, *op. cit.*, pp. 318-322.

20. "Either suppression amounts to complete nonrecognition and exclusion of opposition, in which case revolutionary changes of the Hungarian type are virtually bound to occur; or suppression of opposition is coupled with a careful and continuous scrutiny of the embryonic manifest interests of the potential opposition, and changes are introduced from time to time which incorporate some of these interests." Ralf Dahrendorf, *Class and Class Conflict in Industrial Society* (Stanford University Press, 1959), pp. 224-225.

# 2.

# VIETNAM: THE ORIGINS OF REVOLUTION

## John T. McAlister

In administering their territorial acquisition, the French created a state in which colonial administration virtually supplanted indigenous politics. Obviously, the primary French concern was to prevent Vietnamese opposition from threatening their colonial rule. Although they could not stop rebellion entirely, the French did neutralize it through military and administrative control. Yet the effect of these preventives was to eliminate all but the most circumscribed and stylized political activity. In becoming the country's incumbent government, the French suppressed the energies that had gone into centuries of political conflict among the Vietnamese. Almost no legitimate channels for political expression existed; the politics of the Vietnamese became synonymous with sedition in French Indochina. Unintentionally, however, Vietnamese political energies were enlarged by the unexpected social consequences of colonial programs. Ultimately, when French strength wavered in the 1940's, pent-up political energies erupted in a revolution that no amount of French force could subdue.[1]

### Partitionment as a Suppressive Measure

The suppression of Vietnamese political life was begun by the administrative partitioning of the country. It occurred initially

Reprinted with permission of The Center of International Studies, Princeton, from *Vietnam: The Origins of Revolution (1885-1946)*, originally published by Alfred A. Knopf and Co. Copyright 1968 by John T. McAlister.

through the uneven pattern of French military occupation. Viet Nam would have been occupied all at once but for the limits on French resources imposed by other foreign commitments. A combination of far-flung imperial ambitions and domestic counterpressures made the French occupation a piecemeal affair. By the treaty of June 1862, the southernmost portion of Viet Nam—called Cochinchina by its French occupiers—came under French control. The central and northern parts of the country, known to the French as Annam and Tonkin, did not become parts of the French Empire until more than twelve years after Cochinchina was occupied. Annam, the former Chinese name for Viet Nam—a term considered derogatory by the Vietnamese—and Tonkin were acquired through treaties of 1884-85 with the Vietnamese government at Hue and the Chinese at Peking.[2] The resulting fragmentation of the country was perpetuated by a colonial mythology which regarded Viet Nam not as one country but as three: Annam, Tonkin, and Cochinchina. Even the name Viet Nam, with which the country had been baptized by Gia Long in 1802, was outlawed and uttered only as a rallying cry of revolutionaries.[3]

Partitioning Viet Nam into three parts aided the security of France's colonial state against countrywide uprisings. Administrative barriers were imposed to discourage the Vietnamese from unifying their potential resources against the French. Such obstacles helped to perpetuate the traditional pressures of regionalism and parochialism that had previously limited Vietnamese political unity. Prior to French intervention administrative regions (known as *ky* in Vietnamese) had existed, and the tripartite subdivision roughly approximated the territories of the three *ky*. But under the Vietnamese these regions were apparently intended, especially in Gia Long's regime, to promote the unity of a disparate and difficult-to-administer country. With the French, however, the three countries, or *pays* in the French language, appeared as manifestations of the well-worn technique, "divide and rule."[4]

Of course, administrative subdivisions alone could not ensure political impotence among the Vietnamese. But new and more important bases for disunity were created through separate French policies and programs for each administrative region. Perhaps the sharpest of these regional differences was between Cochinchina and the other two *pays*. Partly because it was occupied more than two decades before the rest of Viet Nam and partly because it was ruled as a colony of France with fewer treaty or legal restraints, Cochinchina developed after a distinctive pattern.

## Patterns of Administration

A difference in public administration was one of the more significant aspects of this distinctiveness. In Viet Nam, as elsewhere, the selection and training of civil servants is a key political act indicating where power lies. Originally, the French Navy expected to govern Cochinchina through the existing mandarinal administration. But after the French occupation, local officials fled northward into central Viet Nam, leaving the French with the task of administering the territory directly. Because the number of French personnel was limited, it became necessary to recruit another cadre of Vietnamese to consolidate French colonial control. Chosen without regard to traditional criteria and trained in the French language and procedures, a totally new kind of Vietnamese official appeared. Enjoying a status of authority and prestige by virtue of their loyalty to the alien rule, these new Vietnamese officials were committed to France even before the whole of Viet Nam had come under French control.[5]

By contrast, when occupied two decades later, the other areas of Viet Nam were administered indirectly through the traditional bureaucracy, the mandarinate. Although some mandarins resisted the French, there existed no sanctuary where the majority of them could flee. Moreover, in Annam and Tonkin France's occupation was in theory a "protection" of Viet Nam's traditional government. In principle, the continuation of the mandarinate was sanctioned by treaty. Despite its treaty commitments, however, France actively interfered with the administration of these "protectorates" in order to insure the perpetuation of its colonial rule. Instead of abolishing the mandarinate outright, the French sought to decrease .its continuity with traditional politics and to increase its bureaucratic capacities to fulfill colonial programs. Entrance examinations for the mandarinate which tested Confucian learning were discontinued in Tonkin in 1915 and in Annam in 1918. Classical knowledge also lost more of its relevance for social mobility as political opportunities developed, such as the ones offered by the University of Hanoi which opened in 1918 to train limited numbers of Vietnamese for technical specialties and administration. During the 25 years before revolution broke out, the distinction between direct and indirect rule became virtually meaningless except in a legal sense.[6]

Even though administrative personnel throughout Vietnam were eventually trained in essentially the same manner, definite regional differences persisted. By the time direct rule was considered for the whole of the country, Cochinchina already had more than half a century of experience with its effects. The French-oriented functionaries of Cochinchina contrasted with the curious mixture of administrative personnel in Tonkin and Annam. In these protectorates were the older mandarins, submissive to the French yet loyal to the traditional monarchy. Alongside them were the younger, Western-trained administrators whose loyalties were uncertain. When the revolution occurred, these administrative elites formed only a portion of the political leadership of the country, yet they had a substantial impact on the course of events through their attempts to lead the various regions in separate directions.[7] And until the revolution broke out, their diversity was a guarantee that they would not unite their energies against French rule.

## Regional Differences

Differences in administration, despite their significance in shaping a potential political leadership along regional lines, were overshadowed by social and economic changes in creating new bases for regionalism. Rather than being randomly distributed, these changes were clustered regionally. Industrial development in the north and plantation agriculture, along with a vast increase in cultivatable land in the Mekong Delta in the south, produced conspicuous regional peculiarities in Vietnamese society. What industrial labor force there was in Viet Nam was concentrated in the north, while a previously nonexistent class of Vietnamese absentee landowners arose in Cochinchina as a result of land development.[8]

From these clustered changes came regional identities which were often stronger, especially in Cochinchina, than any lingering feelings for a unified and independent Viet Nam. Of all the regions, the south was more susceptible to such changes. It had been settled by the Vietnamese for less than a century before French occupation occurred. The Vietnamese people and their traditions had not yet been firmly implanted before they came under the forceful influence of France. Consequently, Cochinchina became known as the most Gallicized area of colonial Viet Nam, while Annam—which on the whole had had the least amount of social change—was known as the most traditional area of the country. Although Tonkin, the administrative and academic center of all Indochina, underwent substantial social change, it nonetheless retained a close identification with Vietnamese traditions.

Colonially induced regionalism that tended to reinforce cultural differences developed during the Vietnamese southward migration. Parochial characteristics have become convenient symbols of regional identity. One of the most easily noticed has been the difference in dialect and pronunciation in the Vietnamese language between north and south. The southern tongue is a less inflected, flatter, and softer way of speaking a language common to all Vietnamese,[9] but it is thought by northerners to be a less proper, provincial accent. In addition, village customs and family structure in the less densely populated Mekong Delta have been more informal and less rigid than traditional practices which originated in the thickly settled Red River Delta homeland of the Vietnamese.[10] These characteristics have made the southerners more amenable to change, yet have given them less stability during the uncertainty of social change. Speaking a parochial tongue and showing less respect for traditions, southerners have been looked down upon by northerners as being less cultivated. In turn, northerners have been thought by their more gregarious southern brethren to be overly formal and haughty. Eventually such popular conceptions limited the possibilities for cooperation among the Vietnamese and affected their potential for common action.

Symbolizing the changes that gave regionalism a new emphasis in Viet Nam were the superficial contrasts that developed between the regional centers of Hue, Hanoi, and Saigon. In Annam, Hue—the center of the country—remained virtually unchanged except for its increasing impotence and its irrelevance to the changes occurring elsewhere. It continued to be a small, sedate town where the archaic imperial court of Viet Nam periodically performed Confucian rituals amid the decaying monuments of the vestigial Nguyen dynasty. Court mandarins presided over a government that had been the first to unite Viet Nam, yet which, by the beginning of the twentieth century, lacked all but the anachronistic vestiges of power.

To the north, Hanoi became a mandarin-controlled, red brick administrative city, built on the ruins of an ancient Vietnamese capital. In the period after 1920, here were found the new men of Vietnamese politics; the recently trained administrators who, despite uncertain political loyalties, helped carry the burden of administering Indochina. In the little more than two decades between the beginning of their recruitment in the 1920's and the outbreak of revolution in 1945, these administrators did not develop a close identification with French interests; their opportunities were too restricted for that. When the revolution arrived they went along, taking their administrative talents with them. At the other end of the country in Cochinchina were the Francophile Vietnamese who had found wider opportunities through French colonialism. It was they who supported France when the challenge came. Saigon—their "Paris of the Orient—emerged from a marsh, through an elaborate French construction program, to become a gleaming commercial port city which often reminded visitors of a provincial town in the south of France.

**New Problems Emerge**
Besides reinforcing old—mainly regional—tensions, French colonial policies created new ones. Although colonially sponsored social change became clustered regionally it was not planned that way. A reinforced regionalism was a byproduct of changes that resulted from programs directed toward other, primarily economic, purposes. In broad outline, these changes

occurred from the creation of an export economy in primary products—mainly rice and rubber but some minerals—with a protected market for French-manufactured imports; the introduction of taxation in money to finance expenditures of the colonial budget; and the expansion of primary education. While these changes held out the promise of modernization, they were insufficient to achieve that goal. They left Viet Nam halfway between the traditional and modern worlds. Viet Nam's colonial economy was vulnerable to fluctuations in international commodity and monetary markets and did not possess the institutional structure for sustained economic growth. It lacked a self-generating industrial sector able to absorb the people drawn into the towns in the hope of gaining access to the monetary economy.[11]

Under the impetus of colonial programs, wide segments of Vietnamese society were moving away from traditional and toward modern ways of life. Such a movement has been described by Karl Deutsch "as the process in which major clusters of old social, economic, and psychological commitments are eroded or broken and people become available for new patterns of socialization and behavior."[12] Two distinct stages are implied in this process. The first stage involves "the uprooting or breaking away from old settings, habits, and commitments," while the second stage is concerned with "the induction of the mobilized persons into some relatively stable new patterns of group membership, organization, and commitment."[13] During the colonial era in Viet Nam the first stage was fairly widespread, but the second touched the mobilized population only slightly. The Vietnamese were only partially mobilized. They had moved away from traditional lives, but they had not been reintegrated into a new pattern, nor had the institutions for this reintegration been established.

Viet Nam's halfway house on the road to modernization was neither stable nor tension-free. Many Vietnamese were caught between the deterioration of old commitments—to the village and the clan—and the lack of or the uncertainty of new commitments to factory, foremen, teachers, work groups, classmates, and the like. Voluntary associations so closely identified with social integration in highly mobile, modern societies did not come easily to the Vietnamese. They fell back upon fictive or real kinship identities and secret societies. Moreover, there was little hope of reintegration through the institutions of the colonial state; it sought only to keep tensions arising out of the imbalances of Vietnamese society from erupting out of control.

Potential reintegration through economic growth was restricted by the mercantilist system of colonial trade in which the colonies were supposed to absorb the exports of French industry while supplying tropical products in return. Unfettered, indigenous economic development would have reduced the need for French imports into Viet Nam, and therefore had to be controlled. Politics also could not play its potentially conciliatory role, much less act as a force for reintegration. The colonial bureaucracy absorbed most of the functions of Viet Nam's political life down to the village. The role that mandarinal recruitment had once played in institutionalizing political power, conciliating tensions, and integrating farflung villages into a centralized political system was neglected. The colonial administration could fulfill none of these functions; instead, it became a training ground for a new type of bureaucratically competent Vietnamese elite. In the uncertainty of the colonial world the understandable anxiety of these new bureaucrats for prestige and occupational mobility outweighed their concern for the problems of politics of the country and generated another set of tensions.

## Destruction of Traditional Political System

The existence of unreconciled tensions was nothing new to Viet Nam. Prior to the French intervention the Vietnamese political capacity for resolving conflict was conspicuously poor; violence and internal warfare were endemic. Yet, on occasions when unity had been achieved, determined efforts were made to institutionalize political power. France was both capable of quelling violence and eager to do so, but she gave little attention to the long-range consequences of holding power by force rather than through institutionalized compliance. Political, as distinct from administrative, institutions were not a part of the French colonial state, except for high-level advisory councils composed of a small number of French and Vietnamese in each of the three *pays* of Viet Nam.[14] While the French administrative structure was suppressing a traditional system of politics with its own unique criteria for mobility and power based on Confucian concepts, it was establishing a system with little mobility and almost no power for indigenous participants. At the time that social change was occurring more rapidly than ever, no legitimate channels for expressing or reconciling social tension were permitted to a people with a long tradition of lively political life. In destroying the old structures of politics and neglecting to create new ones, France was undermining its own interests in Viet Nam.

The destabilizing effects of French colonialism had several important consequences in developing the potential for revolution in Viet Nam. At the lowest level of the institutional hierarchy, the Vietnamese village was no longer the vital cohesive force it had once been. These qualities were lost to it largely because the French had violated the anonymity of the villagers and the autonomy of the village. This occurred through three major reforms: "(1) The institution of regular registration of births and deaths, which permitted the composition of more accurate tax rolls; (2) the imposition of tighter French control over the Council of Notables, particularly in tax and budgetary matters; and (3) the substitution of election for co-optation of council members. The first two of these reforms undermined the patriarchal system by curtailing the considerable administrative—and consequently financial—latitude with which the councils of notables had been accustomed to function. The third reform encouraged the taxpayers to look after their own affairs."[15] By weakening traditional village leadership and promoting the legal autonomy of the individual villagers without establishing new forms of political organization to encompass these relationships, the French were inviting the disintegration of the Vietnamese social system.

Perhaps the most important change in creating the potential for revolution in Viet Nam was the formation of new sets of elites. These elites emerged from French colonial institutions which were bringing Viet Nam into closer contact with the modern world. Besides the administrative cadre, this elite included people who were naturalized as French citizens, those who received French education, those who became commercial entrepreneurs and property owners, and finally those members of the traditional elite who adapted their talents to qualify for colonial elite status. Although by definition these elites had more opportunities than did the mass of the population, still, their social and occupational mobility was limited. Restrictions arose because the institutions into which they were mobilized were circumscribed by the confines of the colonial society. Moreover, most of the important positions in these institutions were held by Frenchmen. Vietnamese did not receive opportunities commensurate with their expectations, especially in having access to positions of authority.[16] For the French to have shared such power would have required the creation of a mutually beneficial relationship with the Vietnamese to protect France's colonial interests. Such a political relationship or community of interest the French conspicuously failed to create.

Under the impact of French colonialism Viet Nam became "a nation off balance."[17] Social changes had been induced by colonial programs, but there was hardly a harmonious relationship between the new society and the old Viet Nam. These changes had "dislocated the traditional mode of life and produced a poorly integrated society in which a small, urban-oriented Westernized elite was largely alienated from the bulk of the village based population."[18] Although harmony had been intermittent in traditional Viet Nam, it seems to have been a widely shared ideal, especially in the life of the villages. The basis for this harmony had been a structure of authority based on Confucian precepts and buttressed by strong patrilineal kinship ties. The social changes wrought during colonial rule were undoubtedly unnecessary if Viet Nam were to participate in the interdependent life of the modern world. However, too little attention was given to the effects of this process on the structure of authority or popular compliance. Since the village has been and continues to be the foundation of Vietnamese society, the deterioration of its resilience was certain to have a strong impact on the stability of the society as a whole. Because the villages lay outside the modern sector that France was creating in the urban centers, this social instability was not apparent. French administration, commerce, and military force provided a veneer of stability on a society halfway between the traditional and the modern worlds.

Despite the instability emergent in Vietnamese society during colonial rule, revolution might never have occurred. Although rebellions broke out periodically, they were usually localized affairs and rarely threatened to overwhelm the colonial regime. Before 1940, a force of only 10,776 regular French troops, 16,218 men of the indigenous militia, and 507 French police agents were sufficient to keep order among 19 million Vietnamese.[19] In 1954, 200,000 French and African troops and 225,000 indigenous troops were forced to surrender after seven years of revolutionary war.[20] Initially, rebellions against French rule were led by men loyal to the imperial government at Hue; later rural uprisings became virtually leaderless protests of discontented peasants. However, in the early 1930's a new type of leadership appeared to take advantage of incipient rebellion. Paradoxically, the rural areas did not produce these leaders; they came from the French schools and bureaucracy in the urban centers. They were part of the modern elite that France had created to facilitate the development of a colonial economy and administration. Yet this elite had not been assimilated into the world they were being asked to create. Their lack of a stake in the colonially created world induced many French-trained Vietnamese to seek the fulfillment they had come to expect through rebellion against France.

Not surprisingly, the rebellions led by the new French-trained elites were no more successful than previous traditionalist uprisings. Gradually it became clear that the old-style Vietnamese rebellion could not affect French power. A more comprehensive, structured, and enduring movement was required. When the Japanese wartime occupation broke the French hold on Viet Nam, a small but strategic portion of this frustrated elite went into action. They had learned that only a broad-scale revolution could achieve the objectives they sought.

# NOTES

1. Virginia Thompson: *French Indochina* (London: George Allen and Unwin; 1937) is the standard work in English on the French colonial regime.
2. In hopes of maintaining their autonomy, the Vietnamese tried to play off the Chinese against the French. See Hall: *A History of South East Asia,* pp. 569-71. Also see Cho Huan-Lai: *Les origines du conflict franco-chinois à propos du Tonkin jusqu'en 1883* (Paris: Jouve: 1935). A documentary history of the French conquest is Georges Taboulet: *La geste française en Indochine: Histoire par les textes de la France en Indochine des origines à 1914* (2 vols., Paris: Adrien Maisonneuve: 1955-6).
3. Jean Chesneaux: *Contribution à l'histoire de la nation viêtnamienne* (Paris: Editions Sociales; 1955), p. 7.
4. Hoang Van Chi: *From Colonialism to Communism: A Case History of North Vietnam* (New York and London: Frederick A. Praeger; 1964), pp. 10-13.
5. Paul Isoart: *Le phénomène national viêtnamien,* (Paris: Librairie Générale de Droit et de Jurisprudence; 1961), pp. 126-37.
6. Joanne Marie Coyle: "Indochinese Administration and Education: French Policy and Practice, 1917-1945" (unpublished Ph.D. dissertation, Fletcher School of Law and Diplomacy, Tufts University, 1963), pp. 54ff.; see also Ray Jumper: "Vietnam: The Historical Background," in George McTurhan Kahin, ed.: *Government and Politics of Southeast Asia.* 2nd edn. (Ithaca, N.Y.; Cornell University Press; 1964), pp. 383-4.
7. Harry J. Benda has discussed these regional distinctions among political elites in Viet Nam in his perceptive essay "Political Elites in Colonial Southeast Asia: An Historical Analysis," *Comparative Studies in Society and History,* Vol. VII, No. 3 (April 1965), pp. 233-51, especially pp. 248-9.
8. A sharp critique of French colonial policies in promoting social disequilibrium and regionalism is Chesneaux: *Contribution à l'histoire de la nation viêtnamienne,* pp. 158-82.
9. Laurence C. Thompson: *A Vietnamese Grammar* (Seattle: University of Washington Press; 1965) is a text which uses the northern pronunciation, which it describes as "the most widely accepted as a sort of standard." Robert B. Jones, Jr., and Huynh Sanh Thong: *Introduction to Spoken Vietnamese* (Washington: American Council of Learned Societies; 1957) uses the southern pronunciation and gives a comparison with the northern style.
10. Gerald C. Hickey: *Village in Vietnam* (New Haven, Conn.; Yale University Press; 1964), pp. 280-2.
11. Donald Lancaster: *The Emancipation of French Indochina*

(London: Oxford University Press, under the auspices of the Royal Institute of International Affairs; 1961), pp. 65-8.

12. Karl W. Deutsch: "Social Mobilization and Political Development," *The American Political Science Review*, Vol. LV, No. 3 (September 1961), p. 493.

13. Ibid.

14. Isoart: *Le phénomène national viêtnamien*, pp. 191-219, presents a detailed account of the structures of the French colonial state.

15. Paul Mus: "The Role of the Village in Vietnamese Politics," *Pacific Affairs*, Vol. XXII, September 1949, p. 266.

16. In 1935 all the schools of the University of Hanoi, with the exception of law and medicine, were closed because of "intellectual unemployment." Joanne Marie Coyle: "Indochinese Administration and Education: French Policy and Practice, 1917-1945," p. 82.

17. Paul Mus: "Viet Nam: A Nation Off Balance," *Yale Review*, Vol. XLI (Summer 1952), pp. 524-33.

18. Jumper: "Vietnam: The Historical Background," p. 383.

19. *Annuaire statistique de l'Indochine*, 1936-1937, pp. 25, 241.

20. Henri Navarre: *Agonie de l'Indochine* (1953-1954). Rev. ed. (Paris: Plon; 1956), p. 46.

# 3.
# THE ECONOMIC INCENTIVE

## Lyford P. Edwards

Without adopting too rigidly the doctrine of economic determinism, it may be stated with a considerable degree of assurance that no great historical revolution has ever succeeded without the assistance of the economic incentive. Human cupidity must be appealed to in order to arouse the energy, the aggressiveness, and the sustained interest of masses of people—without which no revolution can succeed. This is true of the most idealistic, religious revolutions no less than of the most frankly economic ones. Revolution involves the disintegration of society. The evils of this disintegration are so many and so obvious that men are willing to incur them only under stress of the strongest incentives. Whatever may be thought about the power of different incentives, it must be admitted that the economic incentive is not the weakest one.

Although the economic incentive may not assume formal and recognized importance until a relatively late period of pre-revolutionary development, it seems probable that it is the earliest in point of origin of all the revolutionary incentives. In its first form it is negative—mere discontent on the part of the repressed class at their own economic condition. In every society there is discontent at poverty and envy of the

Reprinted with permission of the University of Chicago Press from *The Natural History of Revolution*, by Lyford P. Edwards. Copyright 1927 by Lyford P. Edwards.

rich by the poor. At the earliest stage at which any revolutionary symptoms are observable it does not appear that the envy of the repressed class for their oppressors is in any degree unusual. But it soon becomes very evident and continually increases, reaching its highest point early in the revolutionary outbreak. Before that time it is changed into, or perhaps reinforced by, hatred of the repressors. With this hatred comes the determination to confiscate the wealth of the repressors at the first opportunity. Even fairly reliable statistics on this matter are unavailable except in France and Russia. But it is at least a curious coincidence that in those two countries the peasants owned almost exactly one-third of the agricultural land at the outbreak of the revolutions. In both cases they had been adding largely to their holdings during the generation or two preceding the revolutions. In both cases, also, their eagerness to own the land increased by what it fed on. The greater the amount of land they got into their possession, the stronger was their desire for more. In both cases this "hunger for land" which animated the peasantry seems to have been the ultimate power which determined the success of the revolutions and defeated the forces of reaction.

The peasants, being activated only by the economic motive, do not bother themselves with any aspects of revolution except those connected with their fight to get the land. As soon as they get it, they are willing to allow any form of control to step in which does not imperil their new property rights. But any form of reaction which seems, even in the remotest degree, to threaten their acquisitions is absolutely prohibited.

It should not be inferred that the economic incentive to revolution is merely base and selfish. At its worst it is a desire for a better economic order. It is at the same time, and perhaps mainly so, a desire for status. The repressed class who desire more property seek it not merely as a material value, but because it is a symbol which confers prestige. The property they wish to seize is in the hands of owners, some of them mere parasites, whose ownership of property is detrimental to the welfare of everybody but themselves. Indeed, in a larger social sense, it may be, and often is, argued that the confiscation of the property of the repressors is not only beneficial to the society as a whole, but is beneficial to the repressors themselves, who, so far as they survive, are forced to become productive laborers—a change of condition which may fairly be interpreted as an ethical advance even if it involves a lowering of their social status. An idle and luxurious countess, forced by a revolution to take up stenography or dressmaking for a living, does not occupy so prominent a social position as formerly, but there is no doubt about the fact that she is a more useful member of society. She earns her keep—which is more than she ever did before.

Even though the confiscation of the property of the parasitic repressors may be and is regarded by the revolutionists as essentially just and moral, it can be made to seem so only by a revision of the ethical code prevailing in the older order of society.

This revision of the morals of ownership is one of the most interesting of the pre-revolutionary processes. This justification is invariably a reassertion and application of the principle that the only ultimately valid title to ownership is that the owner can do more for the general welfare by his ownership than can anyone else. On this principle, if any change of ownership, by confiscation or otherwise, promotes the general welfare, it is morally and socially justifiable and will ultimately prevail. That it will prevail in spite of all legal, ethical, and religious codes teaching the contrary, and in spite of any amount of physical force used to back up such codes, is an article of revolutionary faith. The greater the physical force used to back up any system of property not based on the social utility principle, the greater the ferocity of the revolution, if it occurs, by which that system of property is destroyed.

A very simple case of the pre-revolutionary revision of the morals of property will illustrate the process. A Russian peasant by hard work and extreme thrift has been able to purchase one-third enough land to enable him to live decently according to his standard. He desires to own three times as much land as he has. The man from whom he has to get it is a grand duke who rents the land to the peasant and perhaps squanders the rent upon an actress of dubious morals in Moscow or Paris. The peasant finds the price of land to be such that even by the hardest labor and most extreme economy he can never obtain the land he so eagerly desires and which he needs to maintain a decent standard of living. Dull as he is, this fact sets him to thinking, and presently there dawns on his mind the question of the justification of ownership. Why should the grand duke own so many thousands of acres while he, the peasant, owns less than a score? The grand duke does no work on the land. He rarely even visits his large property. More than likely he never does any work of any kind. Yet he lives in luxury because he owns the land. He, the peasant, works hard every day, but is poor because he does not own the land. His priest teaches him that it is the "will of God" that the grand duke should own the land. It is also obvious to the peasant that soldiers will come and kill him if he tries to take any of the grand duke's land without paying whatever price the grand duke asks. In spite of all this, the peasant gradually works out in his mind the idea that the land should belong to him because he works on it and makes it productive. After a while he goes a step farther in his reasoning. If the land should belong to him and his fellow-peasants, then the grand duke is a robber for keeping the land. This idea that the grand duke is a robber, holding land that rightly belongs to the peasants, becomes firmly fixed after a time and colors all the peasant's thinking. He has never so much as heard the name of the French philosopher, Proudhon, yet in his own particular case of the grand duke and the land he has arrived at the same conclusion as that famous man: "La propriété c'est le vol." If his village priest were more informed, he could tell the peasant that this same idea that "property is robbery" was held by Christianity in its great early days, and that the peasant had rediscovered the teaching of the most holy saints and doctors of the church—St. Jerome, for example, or St. Chrysostom, whose icons are in all the churches. The peasant hears nothing of all this. But presently he does hear, from his cousin who works in a factory in Moscow, that the great Prince Peter Kropotkin in the Czar's very palace had said that peasants should have the land and have it without payment. The Czar put him in prison but he has escaped out of Russia, and there are many other great ones who want the peasant to have the land. This fires the peasant's imagination. He begins to dream of a day when somehow, with the aid of people in the great city who think as he does, he will be able to get his land from that big robber the grand duke and no soldiers will come to kill him for it. If only there is a chance that the soldiers will not come he will run the risk and take the land.

This, or something very like this, was the actual mental process that went on in the heads of millions of illiterate Russian peasants in the generations preceding the Revolution. Without knowing anything about socialism, syndicalism, anarchism, or any other radical theory whatever, the peasant was prepared by 1917 to act with any revolutionary group in the cities, if only they would help him get the land he wanted. He was psychologically ready to take his part in the Revolution. Of the broad purposes, the philosophical and political theories, of the revolutionary leaders in the cities, he neither knew nor cared to know anything. All he wanted was the land, and he was ready to help the devil himself in order to get it.

The growth of the economic incentive is not essentially different in other cases. A wider perspective, a more far-reaching series of calculations, are involved in the other forms of the incentive, but the main idea of justifying confiscation on the basis of the utility theory of ownership is common to all of them.

A Russian workingman, cousin of our peasant, was employed in a factory in Moscow. He belonged to a labor union (*sub rosa*). He had taken part in a strike. He read socialist pamphlets. Without being affiliated with any revolutionary movement himself, he knew several workingmen who were, and he was in sympathy with them. His hours of work were long, his pay was small, and the conditions under which he worked and lived were bad. Still he had a much more interesting and varied life than his cousin the peasant. He was better educated; he could read and write. He took a newspaper and knew in a vague and hazy way something of what was going on in the country. He was thoroughly familiar with the peasant belief that the grand dukes and other aristocrats were robbers, holding land which by right belonged to the peasants. Indeed, his father had come to Moscow from a peasant village not so many years before, and he had a host of relatives who were peasants whom he visited from time to time. He believed, as much as if he were a peasant, that the peasants should own the land, and he inevitably applied the peasant idea of land ownership to the factory in which he worked. The two cases seemed to him to be much alike. None of the owners of the factory worked in it. Even the manager was just a hired man. The owners got a great deal of money every year from his labor and that of his fellow-workmen—none of whom owned any of the factory. It seemed to him that the factory should belong to the man who worked in it and made it produce goods. Of the financial end of the business, of bank loans and credits, of the complicated operations of the purchasing and sales departments, he saw nothing and knew next to nothing. He did not think they were very important. He thought that the man who worked in the factory did all the labor of producing the goods. He knew, indeed, that the factory had to have a manager, but the present manager, or some other, could manage for him and the other workers as easily as for the absent owners. These absent owners were robbers of the workers. He had no sympathy with them. He hated them. He had never seen one of them, but he knew they lived comfortably on the product of his labor. They had no connection with the factory, except to take all the profit it made. The factory and the profit it made should belong to the men who worked in it and made it productive. This idea became as firmly fixed in his mind as the similar idea about land in the mind of his peasant cousin. The absent owners never thought of presenting their side of the case to him—a mere workingman! So they held possession of the factory by mere legal title. He was eager to seize "his" factory and to dispossess the robber owners. He knew that the great Prince Peter Kropotkin believed as he did about the factory and the land. He told his cousin how the Czar had put the Prince in prison and how the Prince had escaped. Perhaps some day, with the help of the Prince and the other sympathetic great ones, he could get possession of the factory. Only the soldiers of the Czar prevented him. If those soldiers could by any means be kept away he could do it, and he was eager for the chance to do it. If he and his fellow-workmen could once get hold of the factory, they would have short hours and good pay and would be comfortable and happy.

It is very easy to point out the crudity, the simplicity, and the impracticability of such ideas. The important point is that these ideas, or others very like them, did actually develop in the minds of millions of Russian workingmen during the two or three generations before the Revolution. The workingmen in the cities, like the peasants in the country, were psychologically ready for the Revolution. Indeed, the workingmen were better prepared; they were better educated and more alert mentally. City life had freed them from many of the superstitions and traditions which held back the peasants. When, therefore, bold and capable revolutionary leaders pointed out to the city workers how by organizing soviets and going on a general strike, they could render the soldiers helpless and thus get possession of the factories they so eagerly desired, the workingmen were fully prepared and eager to play their part.

In the period preceding the French Revolution the peasants developed the same "hunger for land" which has been noted in Russia. The mental process was essentially the same, and by 1789 the enormous mass of the peasants were ready and eager to confiscate the estates of the nobles and the church. They felt perfectly justified on the basis of their utility theory of property.

The French bourgeoisie present the same phenomenon in a slightly different aspect. In their case it was property right in government which was the issue. These people, the bankers, the merchants, the trades people, and the business class generally were the prime movers in the Revolution. The economic incentive in their case took the form of a desire to get control of the government and the law, particularly the administrative positions, with the idea of using such control for the furthering of their business enterprises. Authority under the ancient régime was in the hands of aristocrats who felt only contempt for the commercial classes. These aristocrats neither knew nor cared anything about business enterprise. As a result, French trade and commerce were being hampered by all sorts of obsolete internal tariffs, customs duties, regulations, rules, and restrictions which were at once burdensome and absurd. A total reconstruction of the system of government and law was necessary if the commercial development of the country was not to be strangled. The enormous sums of public money squandered on mistresses and palaces were needed for roads and bridges, docks and harbors, and a hundred other public improvements essential to the prosperity of the business class.

The French bourgeoisie did not promote the Revolution from any desire to confiscate property. On the contrary, they were believers in the "sacredness" of property. They consented to the confiscation of the lands of the nobles and the church but only to gain the support of the peasants, without which any revolution must have been a failure. Neither did the bourgeoisie, for the most part, expect to make any money directly by gaining control of the government. What they wanted was to get the management of public affairs and the control of public expenditure in their hands, so that they could use these agencies to promote private business enterprise. They were quite sure of their ability to make plenty of money, if only the government and the law were so administered as to be a help instead of a hindrance to private business. They had an indirect, but quite real and urgent, financial interest in overthrowing the old order. The old order prevented them in a thousand ways from getting rich by their own efforts in trade and commerce, so they hated it with a deadly hatred. They were as willing to bring on the Revolution for their own financial reasons as the peasants were in order to get the land.

It is to be noted that the Industrial Revolution had not made any appreciable progress in France up to 1789. There was little large-scale manufacturing. The modern factory-worker had not yet appeared. The city workers were still in the stage of handicraft production. They were without any organization for their own economic betterment, and they gained little or nothing financially from the great Revolution.

The economic incentive to revolution in the case of the American colonists was practically identical with the one which motivated the French bourgeoisie. In the theory of that time, colonies existed only for the benefit of the mother-country. They were not to be allowed to engage in any industry or commerce except such as might tend to the *aggrandizement* of the parent-state. The British Parliament was supreme over the colonies, and acted on the colonial theory current at the time. No goods could be imported into the colonies, or exported from them, except in British ships. Tobacco, turpentine, and other principal colonial products could be shipped to no country except Great Britain. Various kinds of manufactures were interfered with whenever such manufactures seemed to threaten the home trade. These restrictions were so burdensome that many persons of the first importance in society engaged in smuggling, which was very common. It is noteworthy that several such smugglers became prominent revolutionists. Samuel Adams was one; John Hancock, another.

Under such circumstances it was natural that the business men of the American colonies should wish to be free from British rule—and most Americans had a great deal of the business man in their makeup. What they resented, far more than stamp taxes or a duty on tea, was the fact that their financial welfare was always subordinated to that of English business men. The uncertainty of their position angered them. They could never be sure that a carefully built-up business would not be wiped out overnight by the act of a Parliament three thousand miles away. If they only had the government entirely in their own hands, all this vexation and uncertainty would be done away with and a thousand avenues to wealth, closed under colonial government, would open to them. In short, they had the strongest and most imperative economic incentive to revolution.

The economic incentive which drove the English Puritans to revolution had both a positive and a negative aspect. During the period preceding the Revolution, the English middle class were not only well to do, but were daily increasing in prosperity. They were making great improvements in banking methods, commercial organization, shipping, navigation, colonies, fisheries, and the technique of foreign trade. Every such improvement increased their wealth. But the government hindered them in innumerable ways. Usury laws, burdensome duties, monopolies given to court favorites, interference with their right of free contract—all of these things, and many others like them, hindered the middle class in making money. They did make money in spite of all their hindrances, but they were acutely aware that they could make much more money if these hindrances were removed. Then there was a greater danger in prospect. The Stuart kings had inherited a strongly autocratic monarchy from the Tudors. They were striving to make this autocracy absolute. If they succeeded, as appeared not improbable, every man's property would be at the king's mercy. The king openly proclaimed that it was, or should be, at his disposal. Already he was levying tonnage, poundage, customs duties of various kinds, benevolences, forced loans, and other taxes without consent of Parliament. The amount so raised was not excessive but the principle was exceedingly dangerous. Richelieu had already succeeded in making the French monarchy a despotism, and the English monarchy was apparently headed in the same direction.

So the English middle class were inspired by fear, the most potent form of fear to a commercial class—the fear of unlimited future raids on their pocket-books by an absolute monarch. They were thus driven to revolution by the two most compelling of economic incentives—the prospect of great gain and the fear of great loss. Without disparaging in any way the strong religious motives which animated the Puritans, it may be stated that the great struggle of Parliament against king was a pecuniary, as much as a religious, conflict.

The great point of contrast between the French and English revolutions is in the matter of peasant participation. The peasants were an extremely important factor in the French Revolution. It was their revolutionary spirit which made that Revolution a success. In the Puritan Revolution the peasants scarcely appear at all. It was strictly a struggle between the king and the middle class. The reasons for this are too numerous to give in detail. The mass of the English peasants were mere agricultural day laborers, ignorant and poor. There was no great class of independent, landowning peasants such as formed the backbone of the Revolution in France. Then the English landlords, unlike their French compeers, lived on their estates. They knew their peasants personally and, on the whole, were kindly and considerate masters. In times of distress they were liberal in their charities to the unfortunate. Then the great growth of industry and commerce which marked the period opened up many opportunities for employment in the cities, and the English peasant was free to leave the land if he thought he saw an opportunity to better his condition. The English peasant was poor but he was not harassed and irritated by the *gabelle*, the *taille*, and the numerous other feudal dues which so embittered the peasants of France. From such causes as these, it came about that the English peasants took almost no part in the Puritan Revolution. They hated both the royal and parliamentary military forces as thieves, marauders, and disturbers of the countryside. They showed their hatred, where they could, by impartially clubbing to death on the field of battle the wounded soldiers of both armies indiscriminately.

The workingmen in the cities for the most part sided with the Parliament and served in its armies. But the Industrial Revolution was still in the future. The city workers were without effective organization or group coherence. They hardly appear as an independent factor in the situation. Neither they nor the peasants gained any economic advantage from the Revolution.

# 4.

# TOWARD A THEORY OF REVOLUTION

James C. Davies

In exhorting proletarians of all nations to unite in revolution, because they had nothing to lose but their chains, Marx and Engels most succinctly presented that theory of revolution which is recognized as their brain child. But this most famed thesis, that progressive degradation of the industrial working class would finally reach the point of despair and inevitable revolt, is not the only one that Marx fathered. In at least one essay he gave life to a quite antithetical idea. He described, as a precondition of widespread unrest, not progressive degradation of the proletariat but rather an improvement in workers' economic condition which did not keep pace with the growing welfare of capitalists and therefore produced social tension.

> A noticeable increase in wages presupposes a rapid growth of productive capital. The rapid growth of productive capital brings about an equally rapid growth of wealth, luxury, social wants, social enjoyments. Thus, although the enjoyments of the workers have risen, the social satisfaction that they give has fallen in comparison with the increased enjoyments of the capitalist, which are inaccessible to the worker, in comparison with the state of development of society in general. Our desires and pleasures spring from society; we measure them, therefore, by society and not by the objects which serve for their satisfaction. Because they are of a social nature, they are of a relative nature.[1]

Reprinted with permission of the author and publisher from the *American Sociological Review*, Vol. 27 No. 1, 1962. Copyright 1962 by James C. Davies.

Marx's qualification here of his more frequent belief that degradation produces revolution is expressed as the main thesis by de Tocqueville in his study of the French Revolution. After a long review of economic and social decline in the seventeenth century and dynamic growth in the eighteenth, de Tocqueville concludes:

> So it would appear that the French found their condition the more unsupportable in proportion to its improvement. . . . Revolutions are not always brought about by a gradual decline from bad to worse. Nations that have endured patiently and almost unconsciously the most overwhelming oppression often burst into rebellion against the yoke the moment it begins to grow lighter. The regime which is destroyed by a revolution is almost always an improvement on its immediate predecessor. . . . Evils which are patiently endured when they seem inevitable become intolerable when once the idea of escape from them is suggested.[2]

On the basis of de Tocqueville and Marx, we can choose one of these ideas or the other, which makes it hard to decide just when revolutions are more likely to occur—when there has been social and economic progress or when there has been regress. It appears that both ideas have explanatory and possibly predictive value, if they are juxtaposed and put in the proper time sequence.

Revolutions are most likely to occur when a prolonged period of objective economic and social development is followed by a short period of sharp reversal.[3] The all-important effect on the minds of people in a particular society is to produce, during the former period, an expectation of continued ability to satisfy needs—which continue to rise—and, during the latter, a mental state of anxiety and frustration when manifest reality breaks away from anticipated reality. The actual state of socio-economic development is less significant than the expectation that past progress, now blocked, can and must continue in the future.

Political stability and instability are ultimately dependent on a state of mind, a mood, in a society. Satisfied or apathetic people who are poor in goods, status, and power can remain politically quiet and their opposites can revolt, just as, correlatively and more probably, dissatisfied poor can revolt and

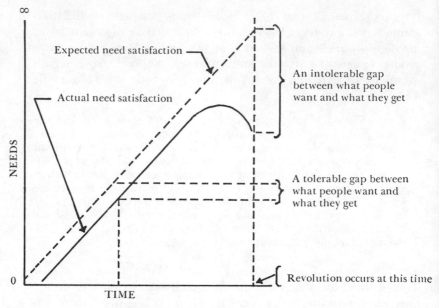

**Figure 1. Need Satisfaction and Revolution**

satisfied rich oppose revolution. It is the dissatisfied state of mind rather than the tangible provision of "adequate" or "inadequate" supplies of food, equality, or liberty which produces the revolution. In actuality, there must be a joining of forces between dissatisfied, frustrated people who differ in their degree of objective, tangible welfare and status. Well-fed, well-educated, high-status individuals who rebel in the face of apathy among the objectively deprived can accomplish at most a coup d'état. The objectively deprived, when faced with solid opposition of people of wealth, status, and power, will be smashed in their rebellion as were peasants and Anabaptists by German noblemen in 1525 and East Germans by the Communist élite in 1953.

Before appraising this general notion in light of a series of revolutions, a word is in order as to why revolutions ordinarily do not occur when a society is generally impoverished—when, as de Tocqueville put it, evils that seem inevitable are patiently endured. They are endured in the extreme case because the physical and mental energies of people are totally employed in the process of merely staying alive. The Minnesota starvation studies conducted during World War II[4] indicate clearly the constant pre-occupation of very hungry individuals with fantasies and thoughts of food. In extremis, as the Minnesota research poignantly demonstrates, the individual withdraws into a life of his own, withdraws from society, withdraws from any significant kind of activity unrelated to staying alive. Reports of behavior in Nazi concentration camps indicate the same preoccupation.[5] In less extreme and barbarous circumstances, where minimal survival is possible but little more, the preoccupation of individuals with staying alive is only mitigated. Social action takes place for the most part on a local, face-to-face basis. In such circumstances the family is a—perhaps the major—solidary unit[6] and even the local community exists primarily to the extent families need to act together to secure their separate survival. Such was life on the American frontier in the sixteenth through nineteenth centuries. In very much attenuated form, but with a substantial degree of social isolation persisting, such evidently is rural life even today. This is clearly related to a relatively low level of political participation in elections.[7] As Zawadzki and Lazarsfeld have indicated,[8] preoccupation with physical survival, even in industrial areas, is a force strongly militating against the establishment of the community-sense and consensus on joint political action which are necessary to induce a revolutionary state of mind. Far from making people into revolutionaries, enduring poverty makes for concern with one's solitary self or solitary family at best and resignation or mute despair at worst. When it is a choice between losing their chains or their lives, people will mostly choose to keep their chains, a fact which Marx seems to have overlooked.[9]

It is when the chains have been loosened somewhat, so that they can be cast off without a high probability of losing life, that people are put in a condition of proto-rebelliousness. I use the term proto-rebelliousness because the mood of discontent may be dissipated before a violent outbreak occurs. The causes for such dissipation may be natural or social (including economic and political). A bad crop year that threatens a return to chronic hunger may be succeeded by a year of natural abundance. Recovery from a sharp economic dislocation may take the steam from the boiler of rebellion.[10] The slow, grudging grant of reforms, which has been the political history of England since at least the Industrial Revolution, may effectively and continuously prevent the degree of frustration that produces revolt.

A revolutionary state of mind requires the continued, even habitual but dynamic expectation of greater opportunity to satisfy basic needs, which may range from merely physical (food, clothing, shelter, health, and safety from bodily harm) to social (the affectional ties of family and friends) to the need for equal dignity and justice. But the necessary additional ingredient is a persistent, unrelenting threat to the satisfaction of these needs: not a threat which actually returns people to a state of sheer survival but which puts them in the mental state where they believe they will not be able to satisfy one or more basic needs. Although physical deprivation in some degree may be threatened on the eve of all revolutions, it need not be the prime factor, as it surely was not in the American Revolution of 1775. The crucial factor is the vague or specific fear that ground gained over a long period of time will be quickly lost. This fear does not generate if there is continued opportunity to satisfy continually emerging needs; it generates when the existing government suppresses or is blamed for suppressing such opportunity.

## The Russian Revolution of 1917

In Russia's tangled history it is hard to decide when began the final upsurge of expectations that, when frustrated, produced the cataclysmic events of 1917. One can truly say that the real beginning was the slow modernization process begun by Peter the Great over two hundred years before the revolution. And surely the rationalist currents from France that slowly penetrated Russian intellectual life during the reign of Catherine the Great a hundred years before the revolution were necessary, lineal antecedents of the 1917 revolution.

Without denying that there was an accumulation of forces

over at least a 200-year period,[11] we may nonetheless date the final upsurge as beginning with the 1861 emancipation of serfs and reaching a crest in the 1905 revolution.

The chronic and growing unrest of serfs before their emancipation in 1861 is an ironic commentary on the Marxian notion that human beings are what social institutions make them. Although serfdom had been shaping their personality since 1647, peasants became increasingly restive in the second quarter of the nineteenth century.[12] The continued discontent of peasants after emancipation is an equally ironic commentary on the belief that relieving one profound frustration produces enduring contentment. Peasants rather quickly got over their joy at being untied from the soil after two hundred years. Instead of declining, rural violence increased.[13] Having gained freedom but not much free land, peasants now had to rent or buy land to survive: virtual personal slavery was exchanged for financial servitude. Land pressure grew, reflected in a doubling of land prices between 1868 and 1897.

It is hard thus to tell whether the economic plight of peasants was much lessened after emancipation. A 1903 government study indicated that even with a normal harvest, average food intake per peasant was 30 per cent below the minimum for health. The only sure contrary item of evidence is that the peasant population grew, indicating at least increased ability of the land to support life, as the following table shows.

The land-population pressure pushed people into towns and cities, where the rapid growth of industry truly afforded the chance for economic betterment. One estimate of net annual income for a peasant family of five in the rich blackearth area in the late nineteenth century was 82 rubles. In contrast, a "good" wage for a male factory worker was about 168 rubles per year. It was this difference in the degree of poverty that produced almost a doubling of the urban population between 1878 and 1897. The number of industrial workers increased almost as rapidly. The city and the factory gave new hope. Strikes in the 1880s were met with brutal suppression but also with the beginning of factory legislation, including the require-

## Table 1. Population of European Russia
### (1480-1895)

|  | Population in Millions | Increase in Millions | Average Annual Rate of Increase* |
|---|---|---|---|
| 1480 | 2.1 | — | — |
| 1580 | 4.3 | 2.2 | 1.05% |
| 1680 | 12.6 | 8.3 | 1.93% |
| 1780 | 26.8 | 14.2 | 1.13% |
| 1880 | 84.5 | 57.7 | 2.15% |
| 1895 | 110.0 | 25.5 | 2.02% |

* Computed as follows: dividing the increase by the number of years and then dividing this hypothetical annual increase by the population at the end of the preceding 100-year period.

Source for gross population data: *Entsiklopedicheskii Slovar*, St. Petersburg, 1897, vol. 40, p. 631. Russia's population was about 97% rural in 1784, 91% in 1878, and 87% in 1897. See Masaryk, *op. cit.*, p. 162n.

ment that wages be paid regularly and the abolition of child labor. The burgeoning proletariat remained comparatively contented until the eve of the 1905 revolution.[14]

There is additional, non-economic evidence to support the view that 1861 to 1905 was the period of rising expectations that preceded the 1917 revolution. The administration of justice before the emancipation had largely been carried out by noblemen and landowners who embodied the law for their peasants. In 1864 justice was in principle no longer delegated to such private individuals. Trials became public, the jury system was introduced, and judges got tenure. Corporal punishment was alleviated by the elimination of running the gauntlet, lashing, and branding; caning persisted until 1904. Public joy at these reforms was widespread. For the intelligentsia, there was increased opportunity to think and write and to criticize established institutions, even sacrosanct absolutism itself.

But Tsarist autocracy had not quite abandoned the scene. Having inclined but not bowed, in granting the inevitable emancipation as an act not of justice but grace, it sought to maintain its absolutist principle by conceding reform without accepting anything like democratic authority. Radical political and economic criticism surged higher. Some strong efforts to raise the somewhat lowered floodgates began as early as 1866, after an unsuccessful attempt was made on the life of Alexander II, in whose name serfs had just gained emancipation. When the attempt succeeded fifteen years later, there was increasing state action under Alexander III to limit constantly rising expectations. By suppression and concession, the last Alexander succeeded in dying naturally in 1894.

When it became apparent that Nicholas II shared his father's ideas but not his forcefulness, opposition of the intelligentsia to absolutism joined with the demands of peasants and workers, who remained loyal to the Tsar but demanded economic reforms. Starting in 1904, there developed a "League of Deliverance" that coordinated efforts of at least seventeen other revolutionary, proletarian, or nationalist groups within the empire. Consensus on the need for drastic reform, both political and economic, established a many-ringed circus of groups sharing the same tent. These groups were geographically distributed from Finland to Armenia and ideologically from liberal constitutionalists to revolutionaries made prudent by the contrast between their own small forces and the power of Tsardom.

Events of 1904-5 mark the general downward turning point of expectations, which people increasingly saw as frustrated by the continuation of Tsardom. Two major and related occurrences made 1905 the point of no return. The first took place on the Bloody Sunday of January 22, 1905, when peaceful proletarian petitioners marched on the St. Petersburg palace and were killed by the hundreds. The myth that the Tsar was the gracious protector of his subjects, however surrounded he might be by malicious advisers, was quite shattered. The reaction was immediate, bitter, and prolonged and was not at all confined to the working class. Employers, merchants, and white-collar officials joined in the burgeoning of strikes which brought the economy to a virtual standstill in October. Some employers even continued to pay wages to strikers. University students and faculties joined the revolution. After the great October strike, the peasants ominously sided with the workers and engaged in riots and assaults on landowners. Until peasants became involved, even some landowners had sided with the revolution.

The other major occurrence was the disastrous defeat of the Russian army and navy in the 1904-5 war with Japan. Fundamentally an imperialist venture aspiring to hegemony over the people of Asia, the war was not regarded as a people's but as a Tsar's war, to save and spread absolutism. The military defeat itself probably had less portent than the return of shattered soldiers from a fight that was not for them. Hundreds of thousands, wounded or not, returned from the war as a visible, vocal, and ugly reminder to the entire populace of the weakness and selfishness of Tsarist absolutism.

The years from 1905 to 1917 formed an almost relentless procession of increasing misery and despair. Promising at last a constitutional government, the Tsar, in October, 1905, issued from on high a proclamation renouncing absolutism, granting law-making power to a duma, and guaranteeing freedom of speech, assembly, and association. The first two dumas, of 1906 and 1907, were dissolved for recalcitrance. The third was made pliant by reduced representation of workers and peasants and by the prosecution and conviction of protestants in the first two. The brief period of a free press was succeeded in 1907 by a reinstatement of censorship and confiscation of prohibited publications. Trial of offenders against the Tsar was now conducted by courts martial. Whereas there had been only 26 executions of the death sentence, in the 13 years of Alexander II's firm rule (1881-94), there were 4,449 in the years 1905-10, in six years of Nicholas II's soft regimen.[15]

But this "white terror," which caused despair among the workers and intelligentsia in the cities, was not the only face of misery. For the peasants, there was a bad harvest in 1906 followed by continued crop failures in several areas in 1907. To forestall action by the dumas, Stolypin decreed a series of agrarian reforms designed to break up the power of the rural communes by individualizing land ownership. Between these acts of God and government, peasants were so pre-occupied with hunger or self-aggrandizement as to be dulled in their sensitivity to the revolutionary appeals of radical organizers.

After more than five years of degrading terror and misery, in 1910 the country appeared to have reached a condition of exhaustion. Political strikes had fallen off to a new low. As the economy recovered, the insouciance of hopelessness set in. Amongst the intelligentsia the mood was hedonism, or despair that often ended in suicide. Industrialists aligned themselves with the government. Workers worked. But an upturn of expectations, inadequately quashed by the police, was evidenced by a recrudescence of political strikes which, in the first half of 1914—on the eve of war—approached the peak of 1905. They sharply diminished during 1915 but grew again in 1916 and became a general strike in February 1917.[16]

Figure 2 indicates the lesser waves in the tidal wave whose first trough is at the end of serfdom in 1861 and whose second is at the end of Tsardom in 1917. This fifty-six year period appears to constitute a single long phase in which popular gratification at the termination of one institution (serfdom) rather quickly was replaced with rising expectations which resulted from intensified industrialization and which were incompatible with the continuation of the inequitable and capricious power structure of Tsarist society. The small trough of frustration during the repression that followed the assassination of Alexander II seems to have only briefly interrupted the rise in popular demand for more goods and more power. The trough in 1904 indicates the consequences of war with Japan. The 1905-6 trough reflects the repression of January 22, and after, and is followed by economic recovery. The final downturn, after the first year of war, was a consequence of the dislocations of the German attack on all kinds of concerted activities other than production for the prosecution of the war. Patriotism and governmental repression for a time smothered discontent. The inflation that developed in 1916 when goods, including food, became severely scarce began to make workers self-consciously discontented. The conduct of the war, including the growing brutality against reluctant, ill-provisioned troops, and the enormous loss of life, produced the same bitter frustration in the army.[17] When civilian discontent reached the breaking point in February, 1917, it did not take long for it to spread rapidly into the armed forces. Thus began the

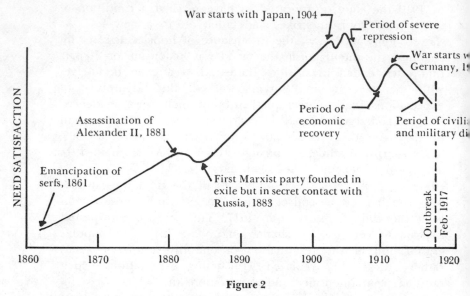

**Figure 2**

second phase of the revolution that really started in 1905 and ended in death to the Tsar and Tsardom—but not to absolutism —when the Bolsheviks gained ascendancy over the moderates in October. A centuries-long history of absolutism appears to have made this post-Tsarist phase of it tragically inevitable.

### The Egyptian Revolution of 1952

The final slow upsurge of expectations in Egypt that culminated in the revolution began when that society became a nation in 1922, with the British grant of limited independence. British troops remained in Egypt to protect not only the Suez Canal but also, ostensibly, to prevent foreign aggression. The presence of foreign troops served only to heighten nationalist expectations, which were excited by the Wafd, the political organization that formed public opinion on national rather than religious grounds and helped establish a fairly unified community— in striking contrast to late-nineteenth century Russia.

But nationalist aspirations were not the only rising expectations in Egypt of the 1920s and 1930s. World War I had spurred industrialization, which opened opportunities for peasants to improve, somewhat, their way of life by working for wages in the cities and also opened great opportunities for entrepreneurs to get rich. The moderately wealthy got immoderately so in commodity market speculation, finance, and manufacture, and the uprooted peasants who were now employed, or at any rate living, in cities were relieved of at least the notion that poverty and boredom must be the will of Allah. But the incongruity of a money-based modern semi-feudality that was like a chariot with a gasoline engine evidently escaped the attention of ordinary people. The generation of the 1930s could see more rapid progress, even for themselves, than their parents had even envisioned. If conditions remained poor, they could always be blamed on the British, whose economic and military power remained visible and strong.

Economic progress continued, though unevenly, during World War II. Conventional exports, mostly cotton, actually declined, not even reaching depression levels until 1945, but direct employment by Allied military forces reached a peak of over 200,000 during the most intense part of the African war. Exports after the war rose steadily until 1948, dipped, and then rose sharply to a peak in 1951 as a consequence of the Korean war. But in 1945 over 250,000 wage earners[18]—probably over a third of the working force—became jobless. The cost of living by 1945 had risen to three times the index of 1937.[19] Manual laborers were hit by unemployment; white collar workers and professionals probably more by inflation than unemployment. Meanwhile the number of millionaires in pounds sterling had increased eight times during the war.[20]

Frustrations, exacerbated during the war by German and thereafter by Soviet propaganda, were at first deflected against the British[21] but gradually shifted closer to home. Egyptian agitators began quoting the Koran in favor of a just, equalitarian society and against great differences in individual wealth. There was an ominous series of strikes, mostly in the textile mills, from 1946-8.

At least two factors stand out in the postponement of revolution. The first was the insatiable postwar world demand for cotton and textiles and the second was the surge of solidarity with king and country that followed the 1948 invasion of the

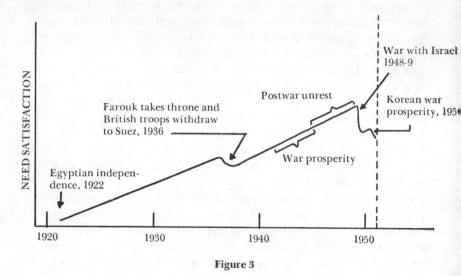

**Figure 3**

new state of Israel. Israel now supplemented England as an object of deflected frustration. The disastrous defeat a year later, by a new nation with but a fifteenth of Egypt's population, was the beginning of the end. This little war had struck the peasant at his hearth, when a shortage of wheat and of oil for stoves provided a daily reminder of a weak and corrupt government. The defeat frustrated popular hopes for national glory and—with even more portent—humiliated the army and solidified it against the bureaucracy and the palace which had profiteered at the expense of national honor. In 1950 began for the first time a direct and open propaganda attack against the king himself. A series of peasant uprisings, even on the lands of the king, took place in 1951 along with some 49 strikes in the cities. The skyrocketing demand for cotton after the start of the Korean War in June, 1950 was followed by a collapse in March, 1952. The uncontrollable or uncontrolled riots in Cairo, on January 26, 1952, marked the fiery start of the revolution. The officers' coup in the early morning of July 23 only made it official. . . .

## Some Conclusions

The notion that revolutions need both a period of rising expectations and a succeeding period in which they are frustrated qualifies substantially the main Marxian notion that revolutions occur after progressive degradation and the de Tocqueville notion that they occur when conditions are improving. By putting de Tocqueville before Marx but without abandoning either theory, we are better able to plot the antecedents of at least the disturbances here described.

Half of the general, if not common, sense of this revised notion lies in the utter improbability of a revolution occurring in a society where there is the continued, unimpeded opportunity to satisfy new needs, new hopes, new expectations. Would Dorr's rebellion have become such if the established electorate and government had readily acceded to the suffrage demands of the unpropertied? Would the Russian Revolution have taken place if the Tsarist autocracy had, quite out of character, truly granted the popular demands for constitutional democracy in 1905? Would the Cairo riots of January, 1952 and the subsequent coup actually have occurred if Britain had departed from Egypt and if the Egyptian monarchy had established an equitable tax system and in other ways alleviated the poverty of urban masses and the shame of the military?

The other half of the sense of the notion has to do with the improbability of revolution taking place where there has been no hope, no period in which expectations have risen. Such a stability of expectations presupposes a static state of human aspirations that sometimes exists but is rare. Stability of expectations is not a stable social condition. Such was the case of American Indians (at least from our perspective) and perhaps Africans before white men with Bibles, guns, and other goods interrupted the stability of African society. Egypt was in such a condition, vis-à-vis modern aspirations, before Europe became interested in building a canal. Such stasis was the case in Nazi concentration camps, where conformism reached the point of inmates cooperating with guards even when the inmates were told to lie down so that they could be shot.[22] But in the latter case there was a society with externally induced complete despair, and even in these camps there were occasional rebellions of sheer desperation. It is of course true that in a society less regimented than concentration camps, the rise of expectations can be frustrated successfully, thereby defeating rebellion just as the satisfaction of expectations does. This, however, requires the uninhibited exercise of brute force as it was used in suppressing the Hungarian rebellion of 1956. Failing the continued ability and persistent will of a ruling power to use such force, there appears to be no sure way to avoid revolution short of an effective, affirmative, and continuous response on the part of established governments to the almost continuously emerging needs of the governed.

To be predictive, my notion requires the assessment of the state of mind—or more precisely, the mood—of a people. This is always difficult, even by techniques of systematic public opinion analysis. Respondents interviewed in a country with a repressive government are not likely to be responsive. But there has been considerable progress in gathering first-hand data about the state of mind of peoples in politically unstable circumstances. One instance of this involved interviewing in West Berlin, during and after the 1948 blockade, as reported by Buchanan and Cantril. They were able to ascertain, however crudely, the sense of security that people in Berlin felt. There was a significant increase in security after the blockade.[23]

Another instance comes out of the Middle Eastern study conducted by the Columbia University Bureau of Applied Social Research and reported by Lerner.[24] By directly asking respondents whether they were happy or unhappy with the way things had turned out in their life, the interviewers turned up data indicating marked differences in the frequency of a sense of unhappiness between countries and between "traditional," "transitional," and "modern" individuals in these countries.[25] There is no technical reason why such comparisons could not be made chronologically as well as they have been geographically.

Other than interview data are available with which we can, from past experience, make reasonable inferences about the mood of a people. It was surely the sense for the relevance of such data that led Thomas Masaryk before the first World War to gather facts about peasant uprisings and industrial strikes and about the writings and actions of the intelligentsia in nineteenth-century Russia. In the present report, I have used not only such data—in the collection of which other social scientists have been less assiduous than Masaryk—but also such indexes as comparative size of vote as between Rhode Island and the United States, employment, exports, and cost of living. Some such indexes, like strikes and cost of living, may be rather closely related to the mood of a people; others, like value of exports, are much cruder indications. Lest we shy away from the gathering of crude data, we should bear in mind that Durkheim developed his remarkable insights into modern society in large part by his analysis of suicide rates. He was unable to rely on the interviewing technique. We need not always ask people whether they are grievously frustrated by their government; their actions can tell us as well and sometimes better.

In his *Anatomy of Revolution*, Crane Brinton describes "some tentative uniformities" that he discovered in the Puritan, American, French, and Russian revolutions.[26] The uniformities were: an economically advancing society, class antagonism, desertion of intellectuals, inefficient government, a ruling class that has lost self-confidence, financial failure of government, and the inept use of force against rebels. All but the last two of these are long-range phenomena that lend themselves to studies over extended time periods. The first two lend themselves to statistical analysis. If they serve the purpose, techniques of content analysis could be used to ascertain trends in alienation of intellectuals. Less rigorous methods would perhaps serve better to ascertain the effectiveness of government and the self-confidence of rulers. Because tensions and frustrations are present at all times in every society, what is most seriously needed are data that cover an extended time period in a particular society, so that one can say there is evidence that tension is greater or less than it was N years or months previously.

We need also to know how long is a long cycle of rising expectations and how long is a brief cycle of frustration. We noted a brief period of frustration in Russia after the 1881 assassination of Alexander II and a longer period after the 1904 beginning of the Russo-Japanese War. Why did not the revolution occur at either of these times rather than in 1917?

Had expectations before these two times not risen high enough? Had the subsequent decline not been sufficiently sharp and deep? Measuring techniques have not yet been devised to answer these questions. But their unavailability now does not forecast their eternal inaccessibility. Physicists devised useful temperature scales long before they came as close to absolute zero as they have recently in laboratory conditions. The far more complex problems of scaling in social science inescapably are harder to solve.

We therefore are still not at the point of being able to predict revolution, but the closer we can get to data indicating by inference the prevailing mood in a society, the closer we will be to understanding the change from gratification to frustration in people's minds. That is the part of the anatomy, we are forever being told with truth and futility, in which wars and revolutions always start. We should eventually be able to escape the embarrassment that may have come to Lenin six weeks after he made the statement in Switzerland, in January, 1917, that he doubted whether "we, the old [will] live to see the decisive battles of the coming revolution."[27]

## NOTES

1. The *Communist Manifesto* of 1848 evidently antedates the opposing idea by about a year. See Edmund Wilson, *To the Finland Station* (Anchor Books edition), New York: Doubleday & Co. (n.d.), p. 157; Lewis S. Feuer, *Karl Marx and Friedrich Engels: Basic Writings on Politics and Philosophy*, N. Y.: Doubleday & Co., Inc., 1959, p. 1. The above quotation is from Karl Marx and Frederick Engels, "Wage Labour and Capital," *Selected Works in Two Volumes*, Moscow: Foreign Languages Publishing House, 1955, vol. 1, p. 94.

2. A. de Tocqueville, *The Old Regime and the French Revolution* (trans. by John Bonner), N. Y.: Harper & Bros., 1856, p. 214. The Stuart Gilbert translation, Garden City: Doubleday & Co., Inc., 1955, pp. 176-177, gives a somewhat less pungent version of the same comment. *L'Ancien régime* was first published in 1856.

3. Revolutions are here defined as violent civil disturbances that cause the displacement of one ruling group by another that has a broader popular basis for support.

4. The full report is Ancel Keys *et al., The Biology of Human Starvation*, Minneapolis: University of Minnesota Press, 1950. See J. Brozek, "Semi-starvation and Nutritional Rehabilitation," *Journal of Clinical Nutrition*, 1, (January, 1953), pp. 107-118 for a brief analysis.

5. E. A. Cohen, *Human Behavior in the Concentration Camp*, New York: W. W. Norton & Co., 1953, pp. 123-125, 131-140.

6. For community life in such poverty, in Mezzogiorno Italy, see E. C. Banfield, *The Moral Basis of a Backward Society*, Glencoe, Ill.: The Free Press, 1958. The author emphasizes that the nuclear family is a solidary, consensual, moral unit (see p. 85) but even within it, consensus appears to break down, in outbreaks of pure, individual morality—notably between parents and children (see p. 117).

7. See Angus Campbell *et al., The American Voter*, New York: John Wiley & Sons, 1960, Chap. 15, "Agrarian Political Behavior."

8. B. Zawadzki and P. F. Lazarsfeld, "The Psychological Consequences of Unemployment," *Journal of Social Psychology*, 6 (May, 1935), pp. 224-251.

9. A remarkable and awesome exception to this phenomenon occurred occasionally in some Nazi concentration camps, e.g., in a Buchenwald revolt against capricious rule by criminal prisoners. During this revolt, one hundred criminal prisoners were killed by political prisoners. See Cohen, *op. cit.*, p. 200.

10. See W. W. Rostow, "Business Cycles, Harvests, and Politics: 1790-1850," *Journal of Economic History*, 1 (November, 1941), pp. 206-221 for the relation between economic fluctuation and the activities of the Chartists in the 1830s and 1840s.

11. There is an excellent summary in B. Brutzkus, "The Historical Peculiarities of the Social and Economic Development of Russia," in R. Bendix and S. M. Lipset, *Class, Status, and Power*, Glencoe, Ill.: The Free Press, 1953, pp. 517-540.

12. Jacqueries rose from an average of 8 per year in 1826-30 to 34 per year in 1845-49. T. G. Masaryk, *The Spirit of Russia*, London: Allen and Unwin, Ltd., 1919, Vol. 1, p. 130. This long, careful, and rather neglected analysis was first published in German in 1913 under the title *Zur Russischen Geschichts—und Religionsphilosophie.*

13. Jacqueries averaged 350 per year for the first three years after emancipation. *Ibid.*, pp. 140-141.

14. The proportion of workers who struck from 1895 through 1902 varied between 1.7 per cent and 4.0 per cent per year. In 1903 the proportion rose to 5.1 per cent but dropped a year later to 1.5 per cent. In 1905 the proportion rose to 163.8 per cent, indicating that the total working force struck, on the average, closer to twice than to once during that portentous year. In 1906 the proportion

dropped to 65.8 per cent; in 1907 to 41.9 per cent; and by 1909 was down to a "normal" 3.5 per cent. *Ibid.*, p. 175n.

15. *Ibid.*, p. 189n.

16. In his *History of the Russian Revolution*, Leon Trotsky presents data on political strikes from 1903 to 1917. In his *Spirit of Russia*, Masaryk presents comparable data from 1905 through 1912. The figures are not identical but the reported yearly trends are consistent. Masaryk's figures are somewhat lower, except for 1912. Cf. Trotsky, *op. cit.*, Doubleday Anchor Books ed., 1959, p. 32 and Masaryk, *op. cit. supra*, p. 197n.

17. See Trotsky, *op. cit.*, pp. 18-21 for a vivid picture of rising discontent in the army.

18. C. Issawi, *Egypt at Mid-Century: An Economic Survey*, London: Oxford University Press, 1954, p. 262. J. & S. Lacouture in their *Egypt in Transition*, New York: Criterion Books, 1958, p. 100, give a figure of over 300,000. Sir R. Bullard, editor, *The Middle East: A Political and Economic Survey*, London: Oxford University Press, 1958, p. 221 estimates total employment in industry, transport, and commerce in 1957 to have been about 750,000.

19. International Monetary Fund, *International Financial Statistics*, Washington, D. C. See monthly issues of this report, 1950-53.

20. J. and S. Lacouture, *op. cit.*, p. 99.

21. England threatened to depose Farouk in February 1942, by force if necessary, if Egypt did not support the Allies. Capitulation by the government and the Wafd caused widespread popular disaffection. When Egypt finally declared war on the Axis in 1945, the prime minister was assassinated. See J. & S. Lacouture, *op. cit.*, pp. 97-98 and Issawi, *op. cit.*, p. 268.

22. Eugen Kogon, *The Theory and Practice of Hell*, New York: Farrar, Straus & Co., 1950, pp. 284-286.

23. W. Buchanan, "Mass Communication in Reverse," *International Social Science Bulletin*, 5 (1953), pp. 577-583, at p. 578. The full study is W. Buchanan and H. Cantril, *How Nations See Each Other*, Urbana: University of Illinois Press, 1953, esp. pp. 85-90.

24. Daniel Lerner, *The Passing of Traditional Society*, Glencoe, Ill.: Free Press, 1958.

25. *Ibid.*, pp. 101-103. See also F. P. Kilpatrick & H. Cantril, "Self-Anchoring Scaling, A Measure of Individuals' Unique Reality Words," *Journal of Individual Psychology*, 16 (November, 1960), pp. 158-173.

26. See the revised edition of 1952 as reprinted by Vintage Books, Inc., 1957, pp. 264-275.

27. Quoted in E. H. Carr, *A History of Soviet Russia*, vol. 1, *The Bolshevik Revolution: 1917-23*, London: Macmillan, 1950, p. 69.

# 5.

# RELIGION IN REVOLUTION

## Charles Tilly

"Was the Vendean insurrection produced by plots and reactionary agitation against the established regime, or was it not the result of repeated vexations and increasingly tyrannical persecutions against the religious freedom of an entire people who, after trying by every legal means to obtain justice, finally grew tired of seeing its just demands trampled, and believed that the way to obtain justice from its executioners was to seize it by armed force?" That was the question of the Dom Chamard (1898:7). I hope there is no reader who wonders what choice the good Dom made between the alternatives he posed. He was only one of the thousands of interpreters of the Vendée—right down to Sunday preachers of the present day—who have made of the great counterrevolution the defense of wronged religion by an outraged, upright people. The explanation is too simple. But so is the debunker's claim that religious belief had nothing to do with it. The fact is that religious belief, organization, and affiliation all became consuming concerns of political life in southern Anjou during the early Revolution. Disagreements over religious issues contributed heavily to both the formation and the conflict of the major parties. To the extent that the rebellion of 1793 can be said to have had articu-

Reprinted with permission of the Harvard University Press from *The Vendée*, by Charles Tilly. Copyright 1967 by Charles Tilly.

lated aims and ideology, they were cast primarily in religious terms. Can this be very surprising, considering that peasants everywhere have so rarely been familiar with any systematic view of the world, or any rhetoric, that was *not* religious? The most important task of the present chapter is to show how response to the religious reforms of the Revolution helped define the positions of the parties of revolutionaries and counter-revolutionaries—Patriots and Aristocrats—and committed an ever larger portion of the population to one party or the other.[1]

### Ecclesiastical Politics and Political Ecclesiastics

Among the clergy, clear and irrevocable options for or against the Revolution took a long time to develop. While it is wrong to think of an abstract Public Opinion in southern Anjou as evolving from naïve enthusiasm for reform to massive enmity for the reformers, it is right to conceive of a substantial block of the lower clergy as veering from willing cooperation with the new regime to opinionated opposition to all its works and workers. From the beginning, priests played a significant political role.

There were many priests in southern Anjou, on both sides of the Layon, who saw the Revolution as a chance to right some wrongs of long standing, and even more who felt that some changes in the way France was governed would be timely. A number of curés and vicars (although theoretically barred from mixing in the affairs of the Third Estate) drafted their communities' Statements of Grievances in 1789. Some were articulate preachers of patriotism during the first year of the Revolution (see Port 1888: I, 102-107). The deputies of the clergy, Rabin, curé of Cholet, and Mesnard, curé of Martigné-Briand, were among the early migrants from the Assembly of the Clergy to the National Assembly. Numerous other priests became communal administrators, mayors, and even members of the departmental hierarchy. In short, the evidence available indicates no uniform or organized clerical resistance to the Revolution during its first year. . . .[2]

From the Estates General on, religious questions increasingly became political questions as well. One of the things that was revolutionary about the Revolution was that it made religious organization a matter of public policy. . . . The novel idea of the Constituent Assembly was that the internal organization and practice of the Church, from top to bottom, ought to be legislated to conform to the new political regime. And the consequence of the new idea was that civil authorities had to oversee the reform of the Church at all levels. Result: religious reform became a fundamental political issue.

The first drastic step the Assembly took to define the place of the Church in the new regime was to seize its properties (Nov., 1789). The sale of these properties, beginning a year or so later, marked the beginning of two related developments: 1) the *public* alienation of a substantial part of the clergy of southern Anjou from the Revolution, 2) the clear definition of prorevolutionary and antirevolutionary parties in southern Anjou.

We have already seen that the sales of church properties were a commercial success throughout southern Anjou. We have also seen that they meant a greater transfer of property, and benefits spread more widely through the population, in Val-Saumurois than in the Mauges, where a smaller amount of property was practically monopolized. Finally, we have seen some [not entirely conclusive] evidence that the sales in the Mauges were the occasion of resentment on the part of some of the peasantry toward the bourgeois doing the buying. So the bourgeois were condemned for taking part in what they saw as an excellent means of serving the nation and themselves at the same time.

The fact that they considered their purchases a patriotic duty, and the fact that they benefited particularly from the sales hardly distinguishes the merchants of Cholet or Chemillé from the bourgeois of the rest of France. But they benefited more exclusively than elsewhere, more so than in Val-Saumurois. Furthermore, they did so in the face of growing opposition, in which the parish priests played an important part.

Even the appearance of religious resistance to the sales was not peculiar to the Mauges, since some spokesmen of the clergy everywhere were denouncing them as illegal and immoral (Lefebvre 1954: 230; Sagnac 1898: 168). The peculiarity was the vigor, unanimity, and effectiveness of the campaign. It is crucial to recognize that open clerical condemnation of the sales did not begin until *after* the initial application of the other religious reforms.

### The Clergy's Choice

January, 1791, was a fateful month, for then the sales of church properties began through much of the Mauges, and the Civil Constitution of the Clergy was promulgated there as well. At the same time, parish priests began openly to preach opposition to the Revolutionary government's policies. An official of the District of St. Florent wrote on 29 January that "people are afraid that the oath for the clergy is going to cause trouble [with the sales of church property]; the country folk seem to be shaken by their curés" (A.D. M-et-L 2 Q 63). Around Maulèvrier, a few months later, several correspondents reported a "coalition" among the countrymen to oppose the sales, to resist the ousting of the priests who would not comply with the new laws, and to support the nobles (A.D. M-et-L 1 L 357).

The clergy of the Mauges rapidly became unanimous in their denunciation of purchasers of church properties. The *Journal des amis de la constitution* reported that the country priests had pronounced the buyers anathema. So long as people continued to come to them for confession, the curés held a weapon. The roving commissioners sent out by the department of Maine-et-Loire in mid-1791 reported that the commune of Chanteloup was disorganized, the municipality lacking necessary members, and that "difficulties in filling the offices resulted from the secret instructions given by the Refractory priests, threatening the buyers of the nationalized properties and the supporters of the Constitution with excommunication and refusal of absolution" (A.D. M-et-L 1 L 357 bis). The same report came from many another section of the Mauges. . . .

By this time, it is clear, the sale of church properties had become a burning political issue. By this time, it was correct to speak of an "ecclesiastical party" opposed to the supporters of the Revolution. By this time, the identification of Patriots, enforcers of religious changes, and purchasers of church properties in the Mauges was already established. . . .

## The Civil Constitution

While the machinery for the sales of church property was rumbling into motion, its designers in Paris were assembling a new system for the operation of religion throughout France: the Civil Constitution of the Clergy. During the first year of the Revolution, a number of moves of the new lawmakers had shaken the old position of the Church: abolition of the tithe, curtailment of other fiscal privileges, the guarantee of religious freedom by the Declaration of the Rights of Man, the abolition of religious orders, and the confiscation of church lands. The clergy had already been reminded of their position in the new order by the requirement that they promulgate new laws at their Sunday Masses. But the first comprehensive attempt to define that position was the series of laws enacted in the spring and summer of 1790, the Civil Constitution (see de la Gorce 1909-1911: vol. I; Mathiez 1910; Latreille 1946-1950: vol. I).

The most important features of the laws were: 1) reorganization of the territorial divisions of the French church to correspond to the new civil divisions, 2) election of bishops and curés by the registered voters of the areas they were to serve, 3) fixed clerical salaries paid by the government, 4) great changes in the organization of church assemblies. The Constitution washed away the temporal power of the Pope in France, while cutting down the independence of the French ecclesiastical hierarchy. In effect, it made the Church a state agency, and the priests elected civil servants. . . .

Most of these changes, real of threatened, were just as imminent in many other parts of France as in the Mauges. The character of the local community in the Mauges made them particularly ominous there. The priest had dominated the *parish* and had held the strategic position in the internal operation of the *commune* as well. The new regime attacked his position in each. It limited his religious power by putting his salary in the hands of government officials with the power to discipline him for prolonged absence or other failings, by taking away his control over welfare activities and charities, by the very act of making him a governmental functionary.

It curtailed his political power by forbidding him to be mayor, municipal, or district officer, by transferring most of his administrative functions to the newly formed, increasingly bourgeois municipality, by effectively undermining the vestry, by centralizing and strengthening the new administrative system. It even attacked his economic power by wiping out the rents, tithes, and offerings he had formerly collected. In all regards, that great independence of both civil and ecclesiastical hierarchy which had been such a support to his power in the local community was threatened by the Revolutionary changes. His losses were the gains of his most ambitious rivals, the most anticlerical part of the population, the bourgeoisie. The Civil Constitution of the Clergy, in short, was a direct threat to the power of the parish priest; it was the greatest threat where that power was the greatest.

One legislative move in particular made it possible for resistance to the Civil Constitution to crystallize: the oath prescribed for the salaried clergy. The civic oath was standard practice for all public servants in the new France of 1790. It is not surprising that it was made part of the installation of the newly elected religious officials. But the lawmakers, growing impatient and fearful with the lack of enthusiasm (and worse) that greeted the Civil Constitution, decided that all bishops, curés, and vicars then in office would have to take the oath or lose their posts (see Godechot 1951: 228). They asked for a showdown, and got a schism.

The oath in question was quite simple: "I swear to be faithful to the nation, the law and the king, and support with all my power the constitution decreed by the national assembly and accepted by the king." The wording hardly seems menacing. The sentiment is far from feverish. But the oath required the clergy to put themselves on public record in support of the Revolutionary government, its reforms, and above all, the Civil Constitution itself. In southern Anjou it signified alignment with the Patriots and continued enthusiasm for their goals. The curé was asked, simultaneously and publicly, to ratify the reforms which were undermining his position in the community and to acknowledge the new-found eminence of his rivals.

The Civil Constitution was officially promulgated in Maine-et-Loire early in January, 1791. It had already been attacked by most of France's bishops, and was denounced roundly again by most of those of the West. By the time the papal bull of 13 April arrived, labeling the Civil Constitution "heretical and schismatic," the opposition was long established.

The announcement of the new laws brought commotion to the bocage. On 24 January, sixty men from St. Aubin-de-Baubigné invaded the offices of the District of Châtillon-sur-Sèvre to protest the impending loss of their curé (A.N. F⁷ 3690¹). At Maulèvrier, later in the month, three days of disorders began with the declaration by the crowd that they would not let the city officials ask the curé to take the oath (A.D. M-et-L 1 L 357). In Le May, the combination of raucous demonstrations and direct threats convinced several of the local officials that it would be prudent to resign at once (A.D. M-et-L 1 L 364). The letter from La Plaine already cited, signed on 6 February "at the end of the High Mass," gives an idea of the way the countrymen understood the situation:

> The municipal officers of the parish of La Plaine and all the other inhabitants of the parish have the honor to tell you that having learned that there was a decree requiring all curés and vicars of France to take an oath, under pain of losing their salary and being driven out of their curés to be replaced by others, not only our parish but all the neighboring ones have decided never to recognize any other curé or vicar but those who are now in our parishes or their legitimate successors, and that as for anyone who comes to us from elsewhere (who would doubtless have taken the oath) we will not allow him in our parishes (A.N. D xxix bis 21).

The issue is nicely simplified. There it is: The law condemns them to lose their curé and vicar and to receive an interloper. I cannot help suspecting that the villagers had just heard a sermon on the subject.

In many places, the new law could never be officially announced, since the old curé refused to read it to his congregation as he was supposed to, and demonstrators made it impossible for the Patriots of the commune to read it in public (see Walter 1953: 7 ff.). This, however, was nothing but a formality, since the contents of the law were widely known long before the official copies arrived.

Throughout southern Anjou, the priests had reached their decisions and had made them known by the end of January, 1791. From the beginning the Revolutionary administrations strove to convince the uncertain and staged ceremonious public initiations for those who came into the fold. All parties in the Mauges recognized that the oath aligned the priest with the Revolutionary party. So did the leaders of that party most of all (see Gruget 1902). It was the leaders of Val-Saumurois who were satisfied, then, and those of the Mauges who were disappointed, for the one place saw widespread acceptance of the oath, and other massive refusal. . . . In the Mauges, 8 percent of the clergy took the oath; in the Layon area, 35 percent; in Val and Saumurois, 53 percent. . . .

## The New Clergies

The application of the required oath in January, 1791, in effect created two clergies, the "Constitutional" and the "Refractory," those who took the oath and those who refused it. The Refractories had signified their resistance to the new religious order; they were to be replaced by Constitutionals as soon as possible. The Constitutionals had thrown in their lots with the Revolution; they kept their posts or received better ones. Most of them, indeed, had been its active supporters long before. Martineau, Constitutional curé of Les Gardes, was the son of a local Patriot leader; the same was true of Thubert, of Melay.

There was, of course, a distinct shortage of Constitutionals in the Mauges. Among the 110 Constitutional curés for whom I have been able to collect the relevant information, the percentages of *replacements* who came from a previous post in the same district were: Saumur, 86; Angers, 19; Vihiers, 40; St. Florent, 27; Cholet, 22; total, 37. The figure for Angers is phony, since it refers only to the small section of the district below the Loire. Otherwise, it is clear that the replacements in Val-Saumurois tended to be from the region, while in the

Mauges they were ordinarily outsiders. Add to this the fact that many more of the curés of Val-Saumurois, having taken the oath, simply stayed in place. Result: the reception of outsiders as state-imposed curés was almost entirely the problem of the Mauges. . . .

The first important uproar was at Maulèvrier.[3] The little city of Maulèvrier is near the border of Poitou, southeast of Cholet. . . . Nearby, the communities of La Tessoualle, Tilliers, and St. Aubin-de-Baubigné all had their own similar but smaller flare-ups early in 1791 (A.D. M-et-L 1 L 356-358). . . . In the face of this unrest and resistance, the departmental administrators had to perform four strenuous tasks: 1) recruitment of Constitutional clergy, 2) arrangement and administration of elections to vacated posts, 3) installation of the newly elected curés in their parishes, 4) support of those curés against the disaffected members of their parishes. Recruitment turned out to be almost entirely a matter of finding candidates outside the Mauges. Elections were made easier by the widespread abstention of all but the Patriots, due to scruples concerning the elections themselves and extensive rejection of the oath required of electors (A.D. M-et-L 1 L 364). But installation of the new curés was from the beginning a delicate and difficult operation. The Constitutional brought the new regime to the community, and did it by replacing the old curé. People were made inescapably aware of the conflict by their retiring curés. All had denounced the Civil Constitution and its attendant oath as intolerable, and all had accordingly denounced its supporters. Few, in fact, failed to label their replacements as heretics, schismatics, usurpers. The outgoing curé, Coulonnier, of Le May was only one of many who preached that the titles of the Constitutionals to their offices were invalid and their administration of the sacraments tainted (A.D. M-et-L 1 L 357). Young people were urged to marry before the Constitutional arrived, since his marriages would be worse than none at all. Preached against by his predecessor, his motives suspect, his allies already unpopular, his very coming a threat to his new community, the hapless Constitutional of the Mauges could hardly expect anything but trouble. The common labels for the two clergies in the Mauges reveal the flavor of popular feeling: *intrus* for the Constitutional and *bon prêtre* for the Refractory. It was the war of the Intruders and the Good Priests. . . .

To accompany verbal violence, there were threats of physical violence. . . . The long and short of it is that the countrymen of the Mauges gave the Constitutionals the full, time-honored treatment that rural communities reserve for unwelcome visitors. There was little the Constitutionals could do in reponse to the endless badgering they received. Some flooded the higher echelons of the government with detailed complaints and pleas for help; some wrote denunciations of the Refractories who were stirring up trouble in their parishes; some even called for the National Guard to "maintain order." But in general they were frustrated by the inability of the government, of even the Patriotic municipalities, to change the ways of the countrymen.

In all their attempts the new curés were handicapped by the fact that there were a multitude of Refractories in the Mauges, but very few Constitutionals. As a result, none had vicars to help them, and many remained surrounded by communities with unreplaced Refractories instead of friendly Constitutionals until late in 1791. The shortage was so great that the Department took the expedient of closing down a number of churches rapidly.

This redistribution of parishes stirred intense discontent. The standard procedure was to remove the sacred objects, take down the bells, and formally close the church, turning over custody of parishioners and sacred objects to a neighboring Constitutional. Each one of these moves struck at the local loyalties of the people of the Mauges, and each aroused an energetic protest. In La Fosse-de-Tigné, it took two months to get together a large enough force to overcome the crowds that were barring the removal of the bells and ornaments (A.D. M-et-L 1L 360) . . . .

## Refractory Religion

The Refractories themselves were displaced, but not idle. While the Constitutionals were intoning the Mass in empty churches, the Refractories were meeting large crowds. According to Chassin (1892: I, 183-184), the Bishop of La Rochelle had disseminated instructions for the continuation of the ministry by the Refractories after they were formally replaced; certainly many of them did carry it on. At first, parishioners simply went to a nearby church where the curé had not yet been replaced; either they went to the friendly priest's services or their curé held his own in the church. As the number of Constitutionals and the number of closed churches mounted, this became more difficult. .Then a number of Refractories took to saying Mass in closed and abandoned churches and in private chapels. Even this became more difficult as the Patriots became more vigilant and the Constitutionals more vociferous. Although the use of churches and chapels continued up to the counterrevolution, more and more services were held in private homes, barns, open fields, wherever the Patriots were unlikely to find them, as time went on. These services were not as regular or as formal as those of the parish church had been, but they were followed with more enthusiasm, often by great crowds. Clandestine Masses gave religious life in the Mauges a flavor of conspiracy. Most people attended at one time or another. Most, then, were reached by the message of the displaced priests. . . .

One kind of public religious manifestation continued to grow regardless of what Patriots did: the pilgrimage. Like the mission, it was a custom of the old regime adapted to new circumstances. For centuries, the faithful of the Mauges had filed ceremoniously to special chapels, wayside crosses, and sacred places on appropriate days. In 1791, the number of faithful and the number of appropriate days began to grow wildly. By the end of the year, crowds of thousands were reported as assembling almost nightly in the most popular locales (A.D. M-et-L 1 L 364, 1 L 367). . . .

Pilgrimages proliferated crazily after August, 1791. By the following April, according to an agitated local account, four to five thousand people were gathering regularly in Chanzeaux, ammunition was being distributed, and an armed guard for the Refractory was formed (A.D. M-et-L 1 L 365). One does not need to take the statistics literally to realize that these crowds, pilgrimages, and processions were beginning to take on the cast of rebellion.

These great movements did not take place without the

collaboration of the Refractories. Many of them continued to preach the illegitimacy of the claims of the Constitutionals, and the obligation of the faithful to have nothing to do with them. Some added to the profusion of anti-Constitutional tracts circulating in the Mauges by late in 1791. Besides, the Refractories were giving the example of direct resistance to the new order themselves.

Before they were replaced, it was the standard practice of the Refractories to frustrate all the efforts of the Constitutionals who had already been installed in neighboring churches. They refused to honor the banns of their ecclesiastical neighbors. They did not report baptizing children from the Constitutionals' parishes. They refused confession and absolution to those who would not promise to stay away from the new clergy. This program is not surprising, not inconsistent with the view that the Constitutionals were sinful interlopers.

The resistance of the Refractories, however, was on a wider front than religion alone. It was aimed at the position of the whole body of supporters of the new regime, which meant the bourgeois administrators of the new regime, and the handful of Patriots in the country community. The Refractory clergy were commonly accused of impeding the collection of local taxes. While still in office, they often refused to read new Revolutionary decrees. Many citizens left or refused public positions on their account, if not on their instigation. In general, the Refractories preached and practiced subversion.

The most important single act of defiance to the Revolutionary government was hiding out in the countryside. The law and the decisions of the Directory of Maine-et-Loire varied, but before long it was illegal for Refractories to stay in their own parishes. Yet many stayed, even when they had been ordered deported. The curé of Neuvy practiced his ministry openly until 1792, when he went into hiding until the counter-revolution began (Uzureau 1923). Throughout the Mauges, that story was repeated. In fact, Refractories from less congenial areas flooded into the Mauges. Large gatherings of priests were reported in Bouzillé, and the tiny chapel of Sainte Foy became a "cathedral" for Refractories in 1791 (A.D. M-et-L 1 L 211, 1 L 365; Uzureau 1946; Conin n.d.).

From the time the oath to support the Constitution was enforced, the clergy of the Mauges were in an unbending stance of public opposition. From the point of view of the Patriots, their attitude was intolerable, not to mention illegal. Despite the pleas of various communities to maintain the Refractories who had not been replaced, and some abortive attempts to put the whole body of Refractories in the same legal category as Protestant ministers (featuring beguiling appeals to "freedom of religion"), there was little hope on the one side and no intention on the other of legalizing their position. So the clergy remained, scorning the law, soon proscribed, but always active.

## Control of the Refractories

The attempts of the Revolutionary administrators to control the Refractories began with the imposition of the oath, early in 1791. Wherever refusals of the oath were concentrated in Maine-et-Loire, agitation was high. (Indeed, in all of Anjou, there was an impressive correlation among the incidence of refusals, the incidence of local political disturbances in 1791 and 1792, and the incidence of open participation in the counterrevolution in 1793; cf. the distribution of reports in A.D. M-et-L 1 L 364-368.) The spatial pattern of the counterrevolution was well set by the middle of 1791. Yet the Department had taken no direct steps to control the Refractories until May of that year. On the 13th, they sent out a pair of roving commissars— who were later to report the necessity of taking "prompt measures to forestall the immediate explosion threatening in the whole countryside"—to investigate the reasons for the troubles (A.D. M-et-L 1 L 357 bis). Before their invetigators had returned, the Department practically outlawed the Refractories by making it possible to transport any ecclesiastic to Angers for surveillance on the complaint of a few citizens. In announcing the move, they made it clear that the Refractories had become their enemies: "These traitors to the fatherland, whose ruin they seem to have sworn, are intimidating municipalities and forcing them to resign; they are suggesting to impressionable persons that they attack the administrators and not respect their property, or the property of their associates" (Uzureau 1918: 267). In rapid succession came an unauthorized raid on the Mulotins and the unauthorized arrest of a prominent Refractory of Cholet. From that point on, the number of priests restricted to Angers rose steadily. By August, the National Guards of Angers, Chalonnes, and Cholet were in constant action against Refractories and their supporters.

It was about this time (16 July, 1791) that the National Assembly grew sufficiently concerned about the anxious reports arriving from the West to send out two representatives, Gallois and Gensonné, to make an investigation. Although they did not enter the Mauges, they discovered the same conditions in the adjacent areas of Vendée and Deux-Sèvres that the investigators of Maine-et-Loire had found in southern Anjou—division, bitterness, violence, and potential rebellion (*Moniteur*, 10 Nov., 1791). Gallois and Gensonné made rather moderate recommendations. But many other reports, less calm and conciliatory, reached the assemblies in Paris, to warn them of the volcanic situation in the West. Goupilleau, in August, described events in the southern part of Loire-Inférieure as "civil war" (Chassin 1892: II, 27). The Department of Deux-Sèvres, in September, used the familiar term "coalition" for the actions of the Refractories and their allies (Chassin 1892: II, 37-38). Dumouriez, then stationed in the Vendée, frequently mentioned "insurrection" in his correspondence with the Minister of War (Chassin 1892: II, *passim*). Delaunay, taking some liberties with the text of a latter from the Directory of Maine-et-Loire, told the assembly of troubles so serious that "if the National Assembly does not take prompt and severe action, incalculable misfortunes will result" (*Moniteur*, 7 Nov., 1791).

Despite such warnings, however, the National Assembly was generally more delicate in its dealings with the Refractories than the Patriots of the West would have liked. In September, for example, the national amnesty of political prisoners returned the Refractories who had been impounded in Angers to their parishes, and to their work against the Revolution. The urban Patriots and district administrators of the Mauges continued to importune the Department for sterner measures. The Department, in turn, appealed continually to the National

Assembly, and in February, 1792—disregarding the royal veto—applied the law of 29 November, interning the Refractories and seizing their property. The priests responded no more enthusiastically to this attempt to control them than to the last, and the disturbances in the Mauges continued.

In June, 1792, the National Guard took the initiative in actually imprisoning the priests who had come to Angers. By this time most of the Refractories of the Mauges, hunted, were in hiding. It was not long until the deportation of all Refractories, long sought by the Department, became law. In September, boatloads of priests began moving down the Loire, heading for Spain, Holland, and the rest of Europe, while other vessels carried priestly cargoes from Sables d'Olonne.

The mention of deportation raises an interesting question: who was left when the full-fledged counterrevolution began? It is possible to derive minimum estimates of the extent of absence through detention or deportation from E. Queruau-Lamerie's catalog of the clergy of Maine-et-Loire (1899). For the beginning of 1793, the proportions of all clergy listed who were gone from southern Anjou were, in percentages: from St. Florent, 25.2; Cholet, 29.8; Vihiers, 37.2; Angers, 47.6; Saumur, 11.2; total, 25.1. A minimum of a quarter of the priests of southern Anjou (and probably not too many more than that) were gone at the beginning of 1793. There were certainly enough still present to keep on causing trouble. Very few of the law-abiding priests of the Saumurois had been interned or exiled. Yet it was not the most troublesome areas that had the most absentees. What it seemed to take was a combination: a considerable number of Refractories *plus* a vigorous and effective group of local Patriots. So the Districts of Angers and Vihiers, where the parties of Patriots and Aristocrats were more evenly matched than they were deep in the Mauges, were able to rid themselves of many more of their nonconformist priests than the Districts of Cholet and St. Florent could. The conclusion overlaps the conclusions of the earlier discussion of emigration: where their defenders were strong enough, the Refractories apparently did not flee.

## WRITINGS CITED

Archival sources in the text refer to dossiers of French departmental archives. The largest single group of documents analyzed came from the departmental archives of Maine-et-Loire in Angers, which are abbreviated "A.D. M-et-L." Sources from the Archives Nationales are abbreviated "A.N."

Chamard, François. *Les Origines et les responsabilités de l'insurrection vendéenne.* Paris, 1898.

Chassin, Ch.-L. *La Préparation de la guerre de Vendée.* 3 vols. Paris, 1892.

Conin, René. "Recherches historiques sur St. Lambert-du-Lattay, Beaulieu et Ste. Foy," unpub. ms, Archives of the Bishopric of Angers [n.d.].

Godechot, Jacques. *Les Institutions de la France sous la Révolution et l'empire.* Paris: Presses Universitaires de France, 1951.

Gruget, S. "Histoire de la constitution civile du clergé en Anjou," *Anjou historique* (F. Uzureau, ed.), II (1902), 151-161, 223-242, 337-353.

La Gorce, Pierre de. *Histoire religieuse de la Révolution française,* vols. I-III. Paris: Plon, 1909-1911.

Latreille, André. *L'Église catholique et la Révolution française,* 2 vols. Paris: Hachette, 1946-1950.

Lefebvre, Georges. *Études sur la Révolution française.* Paris: Presses Universitaires de France, 1954.

Mathiez, A. *La Révolution et l'église.* Paris: Colin, 1910.

Port, Célestin. *Dictionnaire historique, géographique et biographique de Maine-et-Loire,* 3 vols. Paris and Angers, 1878.

Port, Célestin. *La Vendée angevine,* 2 vols. Paris, 1888.

Sagnac, Philippe. *La Législation civile de la Révolution française.* Paris, 1898.

[Savary, J.-J.-M.]. "Un Officier supérieur des armées de la république," *Guerres des Vendéens et des Chouans contre la république française,* vol. I. Collection des mémoires relatifs à la Révolution française, no. XVIII. Paris, 1824.

Tilly, Charles. "Civil Constitution and Counter-Revolution in Southern Anjou," *French Historical Studies,* I (no. 2, 1959), 172-199.

Tilly, Charles. "The Social Background of the Rebellion of 1793 in Southern Anjou," unpub. diss. Harvard University, 1958.

Uzureau, F. "Le Canton de Nueil-sous-Passavant (1792-1801)," *Anjou historique,* XLVI (1946), 119-121.

_____ "Le Clergé de Neuvy-en-Mauges pendant la Révolution," *Anjou historique,* XXIII (1923), 228-233.

_____ "Pourquoi Beaupréau et Saint-Florent demandaient le tribunal du district (1790)," *Anjou historique,* XVIII (1918), 215-221.

_____ "Troubles à Maulèvrier (1791)," *Anjou historique,* XXIV (1924), 232-235.

Walter, Gérard. *La Guerre de Vendée.* Paris: Plon, 1953.

## NOTES

1. Much of the material in this chapter is drawn from Tilly 1958: ch. 7, and Tilly 1959.
2. For an intriguing historiographical question, the reader might consider how to sort out the evidence of a shift in sentiment among the clergy. He must somehow allow for the massive changes both in the system and in the personnel of provincial and local government in the second half of 1790, at precisely the time when the retreat of the clergy from the Revolution is supposed to have occurred. These changes meant that 1) a much more revolutionary administration than the Interim Commission, and one surely more sensitive to any suspicion of infidelity on the part of the clergy, stepped in; 2) a much more comprehensive and efficient governmental organization established sturdy lines of communication and representation from the newly elected communal officers right up to the National Assembly; it often meant the end of the curé's role as the principal reporter of local politics, and may have made it more difficult for those curés who were really not well disposed toward reform to substitute flowery phrases for revolutionary action; 3) the sheer volume of political reporting (as represented by the documents which survived to find a final resting place in the archives) swelled immensely; the contrast between series C (old regime) and series L (revolutionary regime) in the departmental archives shows this clearly. Any of these could help create an illusion of drastic change after the middle of 1790. Are the documents playing a joke on historians?
3. Sources: A.D. M-et-L II F 1, 1 L 357; Poet 1878: II, 619-623; Port 1888: I, 121-123; Uzureau 1924; Savary 1824: I, 32-33; Walter 1953: 8-9.

# 6.
# CHINESE XENOPHOBIA AND THE FOREIGN MISSIONARY

## Paul A. Cohen

The pages of this book have repeatedly been addressed to one or the other of two interrelated phenomena: first, the growing tide of Chinese antiforeignism after 1860 and, second, the progressive deterioration after this date of the Chinese government's position at all levels. Because both developments played a major part in bringing about the transformation of the traditional order in China, it is important that my concluding remarks characterize with as much precision as possible the role which the foreign missionary played in connection with them.

The fundamental causes of Chinese antiforeignism in the modern era may well have been in the nature of intangibles, such as resentment against the unwanted intrusion of the West as a whole; the natural tendency of any society which has been seriously disturbed by internal disorders to seek an external scapegoat which it can hold responsible for all its woes; and, last but not least, the strong tradition of Chinese ethnocentrism which, it will be remembered, had been vented against Indian Buddhism long before it was unleashed against European Christianity.

My concern, however, is less with the roots of Chinese anti-foreignism as such than with the fact of its spectacular growth in the latter half of the nineteenth century. Here, I would submit, the foreign missionary played a critical role. In part, this was a simple consequence of the missionary's immediate presence in the Chinese interior. He was the first foreigner to leave the treaty ports and venture into the interior in large numbers and, for a long time, virtually the only foreigner whose field of day-to-day operations extended over the length and breadth of the Chinese empire. For a large segment of the Chinese population in the nineteenth century, therefore, the missionary was the only concrete manifestation of the foreign intrusion and, as such, the only flesh-and-blood object against which opposition to this intrusion could be directed. If missionaries had not entered the interior in large numbers after 1860, it is all but certain that antiforeignism would still have been a prominent theme in the writings of China's intellectuals, as it had been to a lesser degree for centuries past. But it is highly unlikely that it would have become the widespread social phenomenon that it did until many years had gone by, and it would have been quite impossible for it to have been manifested in such a violent manner. In effect, then, however one chooses to view the underlying origins of nineteenth-century Chinese antiforeignism, the foreign missionary—by the mere fact of his presence in the interior—played a decisive part both in popularizing and in activating this force.

This conclusion is considerably strengthened when we recall the many ways in which the missionary of this era made his presence felt on the local Chinese scene. By indignantly waging battle against the notion that China possessed a monopoly of all civilization and, more particularly, by his attack on many facets of Chinese culture itself, the missionary directly undermined the cultural hegemony of the gentry class. Similarly, by virtue of his privileged position under the new treaties and the simple fact that he was literate, he posed an effective threat to the gentry's dominant position in the social sphere. The members of Chinese officialdom, to the extent that they shared the intellectual and emotional commitments of the gentry, were equally resentful of the missionary's onslaught against cherished Chinese values. But more directly angering to the official was the missionary's extraterritorial status in the interior and his deliberate and frequently tactless abuse of this status.

Lastly, the Chinese populace at large, despite the contemporary foreigner's sanguine view to the contrary, proved itself to be intensely antiforeign in numerous instances. For, although the people were not directly threatened by the missionary, in the sense that the gentry and official were, they had ample cause to take umbrage against him. The missionary's attack on such practices as ancestor worship and idolatry offended all Chinese, not merely the elite. Moreover, it was the hapless commoner who often had to foot the bill for the indemnities that the missionary demanded following antiforeign incidents. The ordinary Chinese, again, was irritated by the unscrupulousness that not a few of his fellows exhibited after becoming converts, and he was profoundly bewildered by the strange ways of the foreigner within his midst, providing fertile ground for the gentry propaganda which, in these pages, we have so often had occasion to examine. In sum, although it was the Chinese intellectual who undoubtedly furnished most of the inspiration and impetus for Chinese hostility to Christianity after 1860, there is ample evidence to indicate that this hostility was not the monopoly of any one class, but the common property of all.

The missionary then—partly by the mere fact of his presence in the Chinese interior and partly by the manner in which he made his presence felt there—clearly played a major role in encouraging the growth of Chinese antiforeignism after 1860. Moreover, to the extent that the progressive weakening and eventual breakdown of the Chinese government's political authority was a consequence of its inability to cope with this antiforeignism, the missionary must again be charged with a heavy share of the responsibility. It is essential that this last point be made absolutely clear. The collapse of Ch'ing political authority in the late nineteenth and early twentieth centuries was due not to any one factor alone but to a multiplicity of factors operating together. In this study I have been concerned with only one of these: Chinese xenophobia at the grassroots level and the total inability of the Chinese government to carry out the new treaties effectively in the face of this xenophobia.

At the local and provincial levels, as we have seen, the Chinese official was faced with a variety of equally unsatisfactory alternatives. If he chose to accommodate the foreign missionary, he enraged the sensibilities of the gentry, the populace, and the more xenophobic of his fellow officials, and thereby crippled his future effectiveness as an official. If he elected to oppose the foreign missionary, he aroused the anger of the foreigner and, if the matter was sufficiently grave, risked punishment by the throne. Confronted with this dilemma, many a Chinese official tried to circumvent it by doing nothing. But this, too, proved to be entirely unacceptable to the foreigner and a source of considerable embarrassment to the Chinese central government, in particular the Tsungli Yamen. The Yamen, in turn, by earnestly seeking to carry out the treaties after 1860, alienated the gentry and populace of the interior and progressively· weakened its position vis-à-vis large segments of the provincial bureaucracy. At the same time, however, because of its ultimate failure to carry out the treaties effectively, its standing in the eyes of the foreign powers steadily deteriorated as the years went by. At all levels of the Chinese bureaucracy, in short, the effort to implement the new treaties in the Chinese interior was a self-destructive one, corroding the authority of the provincial official if successful and damaging the position of the Tsungli Yamen if unsuccessful.

It remains only to determine the degree to which Sino-foreign friction in the interior after 1860 involved the foreign missionary, as opposed to other foreign forces on the local scene. During the decade of the sixties, the missionary was virtually the only representative of foreign influence in the Chinese interior. But, as the Ch'ing dynasty drew to a close, other foreigners, to an ever-increasing extent, made their way into the interior for either business or pleasure. Nevertheless, even at this point, the record indicates that friction involving the missionary was far more extensive than that involving any other type of foreigner. In the Tsungli Yamen (and after 1901 in the Wai-wu-pu) archives, the number of volumes dealing with missionary difficulties from 1860 to 1909—nine hundred and ten, *not* including the materials on the Boxer uprising—is more than double that for any other subject category in the sphere of Sino-foreign relations over a comparable span of time. Most of the other categories, moreover, have little to do with Sino-foreign relations in the Chinese interior, and the one that most clearly does—mining affairs in the provinces—is represented by only eighty-six volumes of materials, less than one tenth of the number concerning missionary difficulties.

This evidence, however indirect, lends strong support to the contention that, on the foreign side, the missionary remained the most prominent source of Sino-foreign friction in the Chinese interior right up to the end of the Ch'ing. And as this friction was a significant factor in the ultimate downfall of the dynasty, the part played by the missionary in bringing about this downfall cannot be disputed.

# 7.

# CHINESE STUDENTS IN JAPAN, 1900-1910

## R. F. Hackett

## Introduction

In the course of historical change regimes are sometimes led to take actions which sow the seeds of their own destruction. In the first decade of the present century China was engaged in a desperate attempt to contain the challenge of the West within an unaltered Chinese framework. This was to be accomplished by a selective adoption of such Western institutions as were fitted to revitalize and save the decaying regime.

Within traditional Chinese society, the student population formed a strategic segment of the governing class. Their education in the "new learning," therefore, was essential to the rejuvenation of China. It is an irony of history that the Manchu rulers who encouraged the education of thousands of Chinese in Japan unknowingly facilitated the creation of a new and powerful political force which was to aid in the undermining and ultimate breakdown of the traditional order. There developed a student movement in Japan which was no longer imbued with loyalty to the world of Chinese culture but animated instead by a spirit of modern nationalism. Returning to China, these students constituted a progressive force which found its natural place, not as a buttress of the old order, but as an

Reprinted with permission of the East Asian Research Center from *Papers on China*, Vol. 3, 1949. Copyright 1949 by R. F. Hackett.

added impetus to the revolutionary process which was tearing down the traditional political and social structure.

The purpose of this paper is to examine the circumstances surrounding the mass emigration of Chinese students to Japan in the first decade of the present century, and to analyze the factors which molded this group into a new force impelled by a common faith in nationalism.

## Historical Setting

The impact of Western civilization on China in the last half of the nineteenth century caused a fundamental dislocation in the traditional pattern of its society. Successive set-backs at the hands of Western powers made China conscious of her inferior and inadequate methods of dealing with the foreign threat. The leading scholars of the Manchu government recognized that the penalties of backwardness could be avoided only by buttressing their own society with the institutions which gave superiority to the aggressive "barbarians." The conviction that extreme measures were required to revitalize the authority of the government emerged in a vigorous movement for reform. The movement gained force, however, at a time when the ruling house, which had already spent its energy in vain attempts to stem the foreign penetration, lay debilitated from corruption and decadence.

The unsettling effect of the failure to contain the foreign incursion was climaxed by a humiliating military defeat at the hands of a new Japan in 1894. With this defeat, rude notice was served by one of the satellite and peripheral states which for China had formed the Confucian family of states that the concept of the Middle Kingdom no longer had any meaning. Japan's convincing demonstration of the advantages of assimilating Western institutions raised the movement for reform to a new level of importance in China. The pressure of imminent disaster aided the exponents of reform in persuading Emperor Kwang Hsü of the need for radical changes. Holding up the experience of Japan as a model, K'ang Yu-wei, the intellectual leader of the movement, succeeded in promoting a series of sweeping reform edicts in the summer of 1898.

While the duration of this period of reforms was limited

to one hundred days by a court coup d'etat, and its intentions side-tracked during the period of the Boxer Rebellion, the Empress Dowager, who held the reins of government, revived the movement in the first years of the present century. Indeed, she made a remarkable effort to carry out the ambitious reforms announced in 1898. No longer doubting the necessity for bold measures to rejuvenate the nation, and receiving the encouragement of Chang Chih-tung, Li Hung-chang, Yuan Shih-k'ai and other prominent statesmen, she issued edicts calling for military, administrative and educational reforms. Thus at the turn of the century China was engaged in a monumental effort to avoid impending disaster by legislative decrees designed to assimilate many of the political and social institutions of the West.

## Encouragement for Education Abroad

*Impetus from China*
Reform of the ancient Chinese educational system was fundamental to this process of assimilation. Yuan Shih-k'ai had declared that "the examples before us of the wealth and power of Japan and the countries of the West have their foundations in no other than their own schools."[1] The formulation of measures to reform education was attended by the statements of prominent officials who exhorted the student to acquire the "new learning." It was Chang Chih-tung's opinion that "travel abroad for one year is more profitable than study at home for five years. . . . One year's study in a foreign institution is better than three years in a Chinese."[2] Consequently decrees were issued encouraging the establishment of modern schools and the education of Chinese abroad.

A series of edicts relating to education abroad appeared in 1901. On August 18, viceroys and governors were commanded to select capable men and provide them with expenses for overseas training. When they attained proficiency they were to be admitted to special examinations for government appointments. This order was repeated in a second edict of September, 1901. In February, 1902, an edict was issued relating to the selection of Imperial Clansmen for study abroad. In July, 1905, an edict conferred degrees and official positions on students who had received their education in foreign countries.[3] These specific decrees provided a great stimulus to go abroad. And with the abolition of the old examination system in September, 1905, any remaining practical advantage in pursuing a classical Chinese education disappeared. Study abroad became the most desirable channel for entering the ruling bureaucracy. . . .

Thus we see that the mass migration of Chinese students abroad was fostered in China by a political and social climate favorable to the acquisition of Western learning. Intellectual stimulus for study in Japan was bolstered by specific government decrees and the compelling practical advantage of economy. In Japan, we have seen, a favorable response to this student movement was the result of newly-won prestige and a sincere desire for inter-cultural advancement, on the one hand, and of calculated political and economic advantages on the other. . . .

## Chinese Students in Japan

*Number of Students*
The edicts of 1901, discussed above, account for the steady rise in the figures in 1902; the adoption of the new educational system modelled on the Japanese system explains the continual increase in 1904 to an average of 100 new students a month. After the abolition of the examination system and the defeat of Russia the monthly increment rose to 500. In 1906 the figure nearly doubled. In the latter part of 1906, however, actions taken by the Chinese Government which will be discussed below caused a rapid falling off. The figures appearing in the *Japan Weekly Mail* are listed below, together with a few figures of the number of Chinese students going to the United States in the same years.

| 1902 | Feb. | 570 | |
|------|------|------|------|
| | Aug. | 600 | |
| | Sept. | 1,058 | |
| 1903 | No figures | | |
| 1904 | 1,200-1,400 | | |
| 1905 | July 1 | 2,641 | (106 in United States) |
| | July 15 | 3,000 | |
| | Dec. | 8,000 | |

| 1906 | Jan. | 7,000 | (300 in United States) |
|------|------|-------|------------------------|
|      | July | 10,000 | |
|      | Sept. | 13,000 | |
| 1907 | June | 8,000 | |
| 1908 | July | 4,896 | |
| 1909 | July | 5,174 | |
| 1910 | July | 4,600 | (650 in United States)[4] |

*Types of Students and Institutions*
One writer has grouped the students into three categories according to the nature of the education they pursued: first, those engaged in the "practical" studies of engineering, agriculture, commerce, manufacturing or medicine; second, those in the field of the social sciences (law, political science, education, history) and philosophy; third, those who pursued a military education. This last group was entirely government-supported.[5] In addition to these three main groups there were many in language schools (in 1909 there were 300 enrolled at the Seisoku English School)[6] and other miscellaneous institutions.

The mass of the Chinese students were concentrated within a living-radius of a mile and a half in the northwestern section of Tokyo.[7] Most of them were enrolled in a few schools established expressly for them, while the rest were widely scattered in many different institutions.

*Student Organization*
In the early years in Japan there was no formal organization among the students other than the association common to all Chinese abroad. The concentration of the vast majority of students in one section of Tokyo lent itself to the development of some sort of organization. In 1903 a Chinese Student Union was formed with 274 charter members[8] and with headquarters in a large foreign home in the Kanda district of Tokyo. Established originally for "exchanging knowledge and to promote a spirit of comeraderie (sic),"[9] in due course it became the social and political center of student life in Tokyo. Within two years the Union grew to a membership of 4,500, with paid secretaries and a well-organized central office.[10] It was equipped with a library, reading room, dining and reception

rooms. The Union held frequent meetings to exchange ideas on the important political questions of the day. Through constant intercourse the students became a well organized body permitting a harmony of action which gave the organization considerable influence and power. The influence of the Union was expressed in a *North China Herald* statement of March 16, 1906, which stated that "few organizations are better articulated and more effectively control their field than this one."

Subsidiary to the Student Union were provincial clubs for every province, each with its own club house.[11] These organizations also held frequent meetings and selected leaders to represent them on the Union Council.

The Student Union was financed by membership assessment (25 sen per month), benefactors, plus an annual contribution of 1200 yen from the Chinese Legation.[12] With this considerable treasury, the Union carried out varied functions. . . .

A less publicized activity of the Union was the printing of publications reflecting the ideas of the students relating to a wide variety of problems. One author claims that when there were fewer than 1000 Chinese students in Tokyo there were six monthly reviews of 200 pages each being published.[13] Most writers refer to four magazines which were printed by the Union and which regularly advanced "reform ideas and the doctrine of China for the Chinese."[14] In addition to these periodicals, provincial journals of various political shades were printed, with the Hunanese the most rabidly anti-Manchu.[15] As these publications were distributed in China by special agents, the influence of the student organizations was not limited to Japan but spread throughout their homeland.

## Influences Acting upon the Students

### Environmental Influences

The young Chinese travelling to Japan to study came in contact with a new and different environment. He usually found himself among many hundreds like himself, living in the cramped quarters of some boarding-house in the Kanda section of Tokyo. The food he received was generally poor and recreational facilities were entirely lacking. Yet the Japan of that day was a remarkable contrast with his native land. The city of Tokyo had made strides toward modernization which were nothing short of startling. While his living conditions were unsatisfactory, witnessing the advances of his new environment extended his vision. This was his real introduction to the possible accomplishments of Western learning. Modern transportation, modern communications, efficient postal service—these were before him, not only as constant reminders of Japan's progress, but as rude awakeners of the backwardness of his homeland. Removed from his own society, he could stand back and examine it intelligently and unemotionally. In this light the advantages and feasibility of an oriental nation's adopting Western institutions were plain to see.

In the midst of this new cultural setting the student was removed from the customs and other aspects of the system of social control which patterned his life in China. The restraints of his early environment, home and family (many of them were married) were greatly weakened. He enjoyed a freedom of thought and expression he had not known before. . . .

*Intellectual Influences*

More far-reaching than the influences of the new cultural environment were the new ideas to which the students were exposed. Chang Chih-tung had warned: "When abroad do not forget your own native country; when you see strange customs, do not forget the holy sages."[16] The students, however, showed an undeliberative readiness to accept radical ideas. A sudden and shallow introduction to the ideas which had molded the Western World created in them an intellectual restlessness. Japanese translations of Western works were available to acquaint them with new economic, social and political theories. For example, Spencer's *Evolution and Ethics* gained great popularity among the students. They became conscious of the social implications of Darwinism through the writings of Thomas Huxley, immediately applying the theory of the survival of the fittest to China's future. Revolutionary ideas and skepticism gained ground, and a deep distrust of the Confucian tradition developed.

Anti-dynastic feelings were stirred when they studied China's history and the details of the Manchu conquest. Japanese scholars who respected "the past history of China, advised time and again for the restoration of the government of China proper."[17] Count Okuma, a supporter of the cause of the Chinese reformers, delivered addresses to the Chinese students at Wasdea University in which he indicated that the purpose of their study must be directed toward the rise of China as a modern nation.[18] Reading Rousseau and Thomas Paine produced the belief that "blood must flow before any improvement can come."[19] An example of the effect of these convictions can be seen in the case of Liu Chen-yu, who, at a students' meeting on New Year's Day, 1902, made an impassioned speech calling for a revolution to overthrow the Manchu dynasty in order to save their nation. At the insistence of the Chinese Minister in Tokyo he was expelled from his university.[20]

Other sources were also present from which disquieting ideas were spread to the students. Some of the reformers and revolutionists, who had been expelled from China, had found a haven in Japan, and from that vantage point continued to turn out inflammatory literature. Through the pages of the *New Peoples' Review*, Liang Ch'i-ch'ao provided eager students with the main substance of their intellectual nourishment. The influence of this brilliant scholar, who Hu Shih pronounced "the most powerful writer of the age,"[21] was widespread among Chinese students both at home and in Japan. His translation of Western works from Japanese into Chinese also served to introduce many new ideas to these young men.

While Liang's writings, emphasizing the need for a constitutional monarchy, represented one political stream, the writings of Wang Ch'ing-wei, another brilliant and respected writer, emphasizing the need for the establishment of a republic, represented the other main stream. The *Min Pao (Peoples' Paper)*, the weekly publication of Sun Yat-sen's revolutionary organization, appeared in 1905, and through its pages Wang Ch'ing-wei, the editor, carried on a literary duel with Liang Ch'i-ch'ao. Advocating the establishment of a republic, he vigorously attacked the Manchu government and those who only sought reforms within the framework of its dynasty. Before its brief suppression in 1908, the *Peoples' Paper* reached a circulation of several thousands, one thousand copies being distributed in China.[22]

Through the pages of these journals the students in Japan were constantly stirred by radical ideas which kindled a new zeal and ambition, and which were earnestly discussed at their clubs. As Sun Yat-sen recounts in his memoirs, "all the arguments of the students of that day and all their thoughts, turned on revolutionary questions."[23] Argument and discussion in an atmosphere of relative freedom led to the shaping of new patterns of thought and belief.

*New Attitudes*

Removal of the restrictions of traditional patterns introduced an element of disorder and insecurity into the minds of the students. This produced a receptive attitude toward change and experimentation. The new effect of the environmental and intellectual influence to which this large group of students were subjected was the emergence of a new bond, a new sense of patriotism. Isolated by an unfriendly social environment, they developed a feeling of group-consciousness. The material environment made them acutely aware of the inferiority of their own culture. These sentiments combined to evoke a new sense of national pride. The new molding idea, however, was that their loyalty must no longer be focused upon the traditional Chinese culture, but upon China as a nation within a world where only the strong nations could survive. The object of fealty and devotion should no longer be China, viewed as a total cultural world in itself, but China viewed as a national unit in a world of competing national units. Alienated from their own cultural ethos by these radical ideas, the students focused their faith on a new China rather than on the old order. . . .

*Expressions of Nationalism*

More important, in historical perspective, than the frequent disorders arising from the attempts to supervise the Chinese students were the political demonstrations which arose from the growing feeling of nationalism among them. We have already reviewed the various influences which transformed this body of Chinese from sedate representatives of an ancient culture to militant enthusiasts for a strong, invigorated nation. It remains for us to examine the ways in which this growing sense of nationalism precipitated bold actions by the students in Japan.

Imbued with the new spirit, they successfully protested against the placing of Formosan Chinese in the Aborigines Village at the Osaka Exposition of 1902. At a later date the failure of the Japanese to include a Chinese flag in the decorations at the graduating exercises of a military academy caused the Chinese graduating students to refuse attendance even after the omission was corrected. Such actions as these, each inconsequential in itself, revealed the strength of the new nationalistic drive.

Located close to their homeland, the students never really lost touch with developments in China. A steady flow of news recounted conditions at home, which were vigorously discussed at their frequent club meetings. Discussion often led to arguments which precipitated action. For example, when the Kwangtung Viceroy Wang Chih-chun recommended using French troops to quell a local riot the students sent a telegram to Peking demanding his discharge as a traitor.

In April, 1903, when the Russians failed to execute the evacuation agreement made at the time of the Boxer Rebellion, the students in Tokyo organized a "Chinese Students' Army." Three hundred of them drilled under Japanese tutelage for three months, when they were requested to change their name and cease exercises. When by October of the same year the Russians still had not withdrawn, the students in Tokyo sent a message to Yuan Shih-k'ai demanding that a war be waged against Russia and volunteering to fight.[24]

Early in 1911 considerable excitement was created by Russo-Chinese developments. At a large gathering the students agreed that the Peking government was culpable in its dealings with Russia. Messages were sent to several provincial assemblies and an organization was formed to encourage a strong foreign policy. Twelve hundred students were selected to represent all the Chinese studying in Tokyo and these, in turn, selected ninety representatives—five from each province. The organization in Japan was to be known as the "Society of Self-Control" and its counterpart in China the "Popular Society." Pledged to arouse China and promote its progress through the press and books, the Society's prime purpose was "to educate the Chinese nation and create a fuller knowledge of the essentials of Occidental civilization as well as to foster a martial spirit without which no country can maintain its independence in modern times. . . ."[25]

## Revolutionary Activities

The demonstrative actions outlined above disclosed a feeling of impatience, a restlessness driven by a new growth of national consciousness. . . .

Sun Yat-sen and other radicals were equally aware of the possibility of winning a student following. Over a period of years Sun had maintained headquarters for his revolutionary activities in Yokohama. Liang Ch'i-ch'ao had organized a reform society in 1900 known as the *Pao Kuo Tang* (Association for the Protection of the Empire).[26] Through various changes in name the society's purpose remained the constitutionalizing of the monarchy. In the minds of the students, however, the competition between the reform and revolutionary schools of thought seemed resolved for many of them in favor of the latter. Extreme action was felt to be the only solution to China's problems. This was illustrated by an incident which occurred in July, 1907. Liang Ch'i-ch'ao organized a political group known as the *Cheng Wen She* (Political Culture Association), and at its first gathering the revolutionists in sympathy with Dr. Sun took complete control of the meeting and produced a speaker of their own.

Secret student organizations of different political shades existed but it was not until 1905 that the most radical of these were molded into a revolutionary weapon. Among the students in Japan, Sun's reputation had risen as a result of his early abortive attempts to inspire a revolution in China. Upon his return to Japan from Europe, where he had organized student groups in Brussels, Berlin and Paris,[27] a large welcoming committee met him. At a gathering soon after this event, Sun suggested that a revolutionary organization be formed embracing all the sympathetic elements among the students. Thus the *T'ung Meng Hui* (Together Sworn Society) was secretly organized in Japan in the autumn of 1905.

At the inaugural meeting some four hundred students, representing every province in China but Kansu, took the secret oath of the society.[28] The oath of membership included a pledge to overthrow the Manchu dynasty and establish a republic. These students constituted the most important element in the society. And although many of them were being educated at the expense of their own government, they were secretly plotting to overthorw it.[29] In large measure, this brazen attitude on the part of the students was made possible by the fact that both Liang Ch'i-ch'ao and Sun Yat-sen, who had been expelled from China, were receiving Japanese protection in exile.

The number of students joining the society rapidly increased to one thousand by the beginning of 1906. On returning to China they established party nuclei in important educational institutions, "which their prestige as 'returned students' enabled them to penetrate."[30] Those members who graduated from military schools spread revolutionary ideas in the Chinese armies when they returned, "a factor of supreme importance in the later stages of the Revolution."[31] It is interesting to note that a leading historian of these revolutionary activities writes that many of these students "were not consistent revolutionaries, they were mere nationalists."[32]

The students contributed monthly dues, which for those supported by the government amounted to $3 per month, or about 10% of their income.[33] Private students, being less well off, were asked to contribute less. One of the centers for these revolutionary activities was the Students Union, where they often heard rousing speeches. In October, 1906, Judge Paul Linebarger, a zealous American supporter of Sun Yat-sen, addressed a large gathering of students working for the revolutionary cause at the Student Union. In his address Judge Linebarger claimed that China would throw off the yoke of the Manchus just as America threw off the yoke of England. He told the students that on their manner of support would depend the eventual success of Sun. . . .

### Role of the "Returned Student"
By 1910 the number of students in Japan had levelled off

near the 5,000 mark. Many thousands had returned to China
to take their places in their own society. As they returned
to their homes they disseminated the new ideas they had learned
and they were stirred to unite the country in an effort to
hasten the acquisition of the blessings of Western civilization.
As Timothy Richard, a leading American educator in China,
put it, "the sons of the Chinese nobility and ruling classes are
being educated in Japan by the thousands and return home
fired by her example and emulous to repeat it."[34]

Many of the students returned to occupy influential positions
in the government. Many of them became members of the
provincial assemblies. In Szechwan, for example, a large percentage of the provincial assemblymen were returned students
and "no other assembly in China was more free in its criticisms
of the imperial authorities."[35] They occupied one-third of the
seats in the first national parliament.

Many of the military graduates from China flocked to join
Yuan Shih-k'ai's new army and comprised a large percentage
of its officer staff. Perhaps the most important result, however,
was in the field of education. Large numbers of returned students became teachers and administrators in the new educational system. The Bureau of Education was dominated by
them. Others established private schools of their own and
directed them with exemplary efficiency. Others entered the
field of journalism and precipitated the phenomenal growth
of the press in China. In their writings, thousands of Japanese
terms were adopted into Chinese, and new sentence construc-
tions and the paragraph forms were introduced.

The new social ideas spread by these men were of great
importance. The new ideas they infused into the minds of
all classes helped to remove the prejudice against railways and
other modern conveniences. They were energetic in the drive
against opium and footbinding, and favored the emancipation
of women.[36] They advocated the same freedom that they had
enjoyed abroad.

In a number of localities they organized secret societies.[37] Some
led local uprisings. As disturbers of the Chinese scene they
had been prominent ever "since 1903, when the Empress
Dowager had one of them, Shen Chin, beaten to death."[38] They

had nominated themselves as "prophets of a new dispensation for China."[39] They desired a political regeneration, a bursting of the shackles hampering China's progress. In so far as there was any common policy it was in the direction of a "China for the Chinese" doctrine. Their policy was based on a militant nationalism which contained the germ of anti-foreignism. They agitated for a strong united nation which could take a foremost position in the world.

Thus we find the effect of wide-scale education abroad was to create within the Chinese ruling classes a group not content to witness moderate measures for a political rebirth. The returned students represented a groundswell of discontent, and formed the hard determined core in the movement for sweeping progress. Is it surprising, then, that the returned students from Japan formed the vanguard in the Revolution of 1911? Indeed, it was "largely started, fostered, planned and engineered"[40] by them.

## NOTES

1. F. G. Wang, *Japanese Influence on Education Reform in China, 1895-1911*, p. 48.
2. Chang Chih-tung, *China's Only Hope*, p. 91.
3. F. G. Wang, p. 48-50.
4. Figures for students in U.S. from T.C. Wang, *The Youth Movement in China*, p. 67.
5. V. K. Ting, "Chinese Students," *Westminster Review*, January, 1908.
6. *Japan Weekly Chronicle* (hereafter *J.W.C.*), July 10, 1909.
7. D. S. Lyon, *Chinese Students in Japan*, p. 3.
8. Willard Straight, "Chinese Students in Japan," *Nation*, August 31, 1905.
9. W. W. Yen, "Chinese Students in Japan," *East of Asia*, June, 1905, p. 195.
10. H. F. MacNair, *The Chinese Abroad*, p. 246.
11. H. S. Chang, "Chinese Students in Japan," *The Chinese Student's Monthly*, April, 1918, p. 325.
12. Straight, p. 180.
13. Ting, p. 52.

14. *J.W.C.*, November 23, 1905.
15. *Ibid.* loc. cit.
16. Chang Chih-tung, p. 25.
17. Y.S. Tsao, "The Relation of the Returned Students to the Chinese Revolution," *Recent Developments in China*, p. 171.
18. *Okuma Ko Hachi Ju Go Nen Shi Hensan Kai (Collected Papers of the Life of Marquis Okuma)* Tokyo, 1926, Vol. II, (hereafter cited as *Okuma Ko*), pp. 561-562.
19. M. Cameron, *The Reform Movement in China*, p. 183.
20. Sun Yat-sen, *Memoirs of a Chinese Revolutionary*, p. 200.
21. Quoted by L. Sharman, *Sun Yat-sen*, p. 74.
22. T'ang Leang-li, *The Inner History of the Chinese Revolution*, p. 53.
23. Sun Yat-sen, p. 200.
24. These examples are cited by Straight, *Nation*, April 31, 1915.
25. *Japan Weekly Mail*, March 4, 1911.
26. T'ang, p. 41.
27. Sun Yat-sen, p. 202.
28. T'ang Leang-li, *Wang Ch'ing-wei: A Political Biography*, p. 29.
29. H. B. Restarick, *Sun Yat-sen: Liberator of China*, p. 95.
30. T'ang, p. 29.
31. *Ibid.*, p. 29.
32. T'ang, *Inner History of the Chinese Revolution*, p. 52.
33. T'ang, *Wang Ch'ing-wei*, p. 36.
34. T. Richard, "China and the West," *Living Age*, March 10, 1906.
35. Frederick McCormick, "Japan, America and the Chinese Revolution," *Japan and Japanese-American Relations* (Blakeslee ed.), p. 340.
36. Ting, *Westminster Review*, January, 1908.
37. Restarick, p. 70.
38. McCormick, p. 339.
39. T. F. Millard, *The New Far East*, p. 264.
40. H. S. Chang, *The Chinese Students' Monthly*, April, 1918.

# 8.

# CONTEMPORARY STUDENT REBELLIONS — INTELLECTUAL REBELLION AND GENERATIONAL CONFLICT

## S. N. Eisenstadt

### I

Student rebellions and adolescent violence are not new in the history of human society. Student violence has been reported already in the middle ages while student rebellions and movements—especially as parts of wider social and national movements—have been an integral part of the history of modern societies.

Similarly, various types of adolescent rebellions or deviance, rooted to no small degree in generational discontinuity or conflict, can be found throughout the history of human society.[1]

In some cases these two phenomena—youth deviance or violence and student rebellions—have tended to converge and some element of intergeneration and conflict has probably been present in many student movements.[2]

Most of such features which could have been discerned in the types of youth rebellion or student movements throughout history and modern history in particular, can also be found in many of the contemporary expressions of youth rebellion and student radicalism.

But beyond these features, contemporary student movements evince also some new ones. Of these, two are perhaps most

Reprinted with permission of the author and publisher from *Acta Sociologica*, Vol. 14 No. 3, 1971. Copyright 1971 by S. N. Eisenstadt.

outstanding. There is, first, as Edward Shils has noted, that probably for the first time in history at least some parts of these movements tend to become entirely dissociated from broader social or national movements, from the adult world, and do not tend to accept any adult models or association—thus stressing intergenerational discontinuity and conflict to an unprecedented extent.[3]

Second, many of these movements tend also to combine their political activities with violence and destructive orientation which go much beyond the anarchist or bohemian traditions of youth or artistic, intellectual subcultures and with a very far-reaching general and widespread alienation from the existing social order. Although these *new* specific characteristics are certainly not the only ones to be found in the contemporary youth scene, and they certainly do not obliterate many older types of youth cultures, youth rebellion and student protest— yet they are indeed among the most salient new features on this scene.

Many explanations of these new features have been offered and it would not be possible to repeat or summarize them all here.

Rather, we would like to propose that part, at least, of the explanation of these new features of youth rebellion and student protest lies in the convergence and mutual reinforcement of the two major sets of conditions or processes, namely, of widespread intellectual antinomianism on the one hand, and of generational discontinuity and conflict, and of their simultaneous extension to the central zones of a society and to very wide groups and strata alike.

## II

Intellectual antinomianism is not something new in the history of mankind. It constitutes an extreme manifestation of the tensions and ambivalence between intellectuals and authority which to a large extent are given in all human societies. These tensions and ambivalence are rooted in two distinct yet strongly interconnected bases.

One is the close relation between the activities and orientations of intellectuals and those of the authorities and holders of power in the formation and crystallization of the specific cultural and social contours of the charismatic orientations and symbols of any society or civilization and of its tradition and centers.

The second is the close relations between some at least of the skills and technical knowledge of some groups of intellectuals and the organizational exigencies of the exercise of power and authority in any society. . . .[4]

Political authorities need the basic legitimation and support which can be provided mostly by intellectuals, by religious or secular intellectual élites. The intellectuals and intellectual organizations tend to need the protection and help of the political institutions for the establishment and maintenance of their own organizations and positions.

Hence the continuous tensions and ambivalence on the symbolic and structural levels alike, between the intellectuals and the holders of power or authority, focuses around the respective nature, scope, and relative autonomy of participation of the intellectuals and the political powers in the socio-political and cultural orders and is rooted in their continuous mutual interdependence.

Political authorities may naturally attempt to control entirely the activities of the intellectuals and to claim for themselves the sole right to represent the major religious and cultural symbols of the society, and they also expected the intellectual organizations to assure a certain level of political activity and involvement in central political activities which their respective regime may need.

Against this the intellectual élites would often attempt to be able to become the sole or major representatives of the pure social and cultural orders, to usurp central political offices and to remove their organizations from the political control and influence of the rulers.[5]

### III

The potentially "antinomian" tendencies of intellectuals become especially articulated in so far as the tensions between them and political authorities tend to converge with some of the major themes of protest, rebellion and heterodoxy. Such themes have been continuously recurring in the history of human societies and civilizations and have been largely rooted in the tensions inherent in any process of institutionalization of social life, in general, and of authority in particular.

Among these themes is first, the tension between the very complexity and fragmentation of human relations inherent in any institutional division of labour, as against the possibilities of some total unconditionality of participation in the basic social and cultural order.

Parallel to this are also the tensions inherent in the temporal dimension of human and social condition, in the tensions between the deferment of gratification in the present as against the possibility of their attainment in the future.

Hence many movements of protest tend to emphasize the suspension or negation of the structural and organizational division of labour in general, and to emphasize the ideal of "communitas" of direct, unmediated participation in the social and cultural orders.

They tend also to emphasize, together with such participation, the suspension of the tensions between "productivity" and "distribution" and tend to merge these two together through a basic commitment to the unconditional participation in the community.

Similarly, many such movements contain a strong emphasis on the suspension of the differences between various time-dimensions—between past, present and future—and of the relation between such dimensions to patterns of gratification and allocation of rewards. . . .

## IV

But perhaps the most important change related to these developments from the point of view of our discussion was in the social organization of the educational sphere. In most pre-modern societies the process of education was usually divided into several rather compartmentalized aspects. The central educational institutions were oriented mainly toward the education of an elite and upper strata, and to the upholding and development of the central cultural tradition in its varied manifestations.

The local educational institutions, which were usually only loosely connected with the central ones, were oriented chiefly to the maintenance of some general, diffuse and rather passive identification of the various strata with the overall symbols of society, without, however, permitting them any closer participation in the central political and cultural activities, and of provision of some technical know-how which would be appropriate to their position in society. Between the two were several educational institutions which served as either channels of restricted "sponsored" mobility into the central spheres of society, or of some specific vocational preparation.

On the whole, the educational system in these societies was geared to the maintenance and perpetuation of a given, relatively unchanging cultural tradition, and did not serve either as a channel of widespread occupational and social mobility, or of overall active participation of the broader strata in the cultural and political order and of their respective center. The type of education given to different classes was greatly, although not entirely, determined by their social-economic position and not vice-versa.

This began to change with the onset of modernity. Education started to deal with problems of forging new national communities and their common symbols, access to which tended to become more widely spread among different strata. At the same time, it began to serve increasingly as a channel of more general occupational and allegedly achievement-based selection. Moreover, the system of education tended to become more centralized and unified, thus assuring its permeation into wider strata of the society.

## V

This societal unification of the education system, when combined with the continuous developments of the structural and symbolical aspects of modernity, gave rise to a series of social and cultural contradictions and discontinuities which have become, on the one hand, extremely widespread throughout the society, while, on the other, they tended to become more and more focused around its very central symbols.

Most of these contradictions and discontinuities tended to

focus around the tension between the premises of plenitude and full participation inherent in the symbolism of modernity and the various actual structural limitations on the realization of these premises which tended to develop with the spread of modernity.

These problems and tendencies have developed in all the social spheres, and in the literature special emphasis was given to the occupational and economic sphere.

Thus it was often emphasized that the most important such developments in the economic fields were the bureaucratization of most types of economic markets and the growth of bureaucratization, specialization and professionalization in the occupational structure, increasing the close interrelationship between attainment and occupational placement.

These developments gave rise to problems and discontinuities in areas such as those of social mobility, educational selection and above all in the special service occupations which organized in bureaucratic settings the selection to which was based on meritocratic criteria.

But beyond these developments in the occupational and economic field, parallel processes developed also in the cultural field, and it is on these that we would like to focus our analysis here.

Perhaps the most important single overall development in this field—which, in a great variety of ways, has been common to many different countries—has been the transfer of emphasis from the creation of and participation in the future-oriented collective value, to the growing institutionalization of such values.

This has been very closely related with a very important shift in the whole patterns of protest in modern societies. Here, as in so many other cases, when many of the initial charismatic orientations and goals have indeed become—through the attainment of political independence, broadening of the scope of political participation, revolutionary changes of regimes or the development of welfare state policies and the like— at least partially institutionalized, they give rise to new processes of change, to new series of problems and tensions, and to new foci of protest.

It is important to emphasize that the same has been true of youth movements and activities, when the goals and values toward whose realization these movements aim become institutionalized through the acceptance as part of the structure of their societies. This has indeed happened in most modern societies. Thus, in Russia youth movements became fully institutionalized through the organization of the Komsomol. In many European countries the institutionalizing of youth groups, agencies, and ideologies came through association with political parties, or through acceptance as part of the educational system. In the United States, many (such as the Boy Scouts) have become an accepted part of community life and, to some extent, a symbol of differential social status. In many Asian and African countries, organized youth movements have become part of the official educational organizations.

All these changes have also been associated with a marked decline of ideology in the traditional nineteenth and early twentieth century sense, and a general flattening of traditional political-ideological interest. This decline, in turn, has been connected with the growth of the feeling of spiritual or cultural shallowness in the new social and economic benefits accruing from the welfare state or from the "consumers society."

This tendency is intensified by the fact that in many such countries, be they the New States of Asia and Africa or Russian post-revolutionary or European welfare states, the new generation of youth and students face not only reactionary parents but also successful revolutionaries who have become part of a new "establishment," creating a new collective reality which youth has to face, a reality that evinces all the characteristics of a bureaucratized establishment, but at the same time presents itself as the embodiment of revolutionary collective and spiritual values.

This tendency was also reinforced by the weakening of the ideological dimension of the Cold War and by the consequent loss of the negative images and symbols.

# VI

Within this general framework of developments of the cultural sphere several special developments or processes stand out. One such development is what may be called the breakdown of continuity of historical consciousness or awareness.

It is not only that the new generations have not experienced such events as the depression or the two World Wars which were crucial in the formation of their parents. What is more significant is that, probably partly due to the very process of the institutionalization of the collective goals of their parents on the one hand and the growing affluence on the other, the parent generation failed to transmit to the new generation the significance of the meaning of these historical events.

The very emphasis on the new goals has increased a tendency to stress the novelty of the world created by the parents— a tendency taken up and reinforced by the younger generations.

Another cultural process—closely related to the preceding one, and especially prominent in Western societies in general and in America in particular—has been the reversal of the hitherto existing relation between the definition of different age-spans and the possibilities of social and cultural creativity.

Unlike in the—even not so distant—past, youth became more and more seen not only as preparation for the possibilities of independent and creative participation in social and cultural life, but as the very embodiment of permissive, often unstructured-creativity—to be faced later on with the constraints of a relatively highly organized, constrictive, meritocratic and bureaucratic environment.

It was probably not the constraints as such—which in themselves certainly were probably not greater than those in most societies—but rather the discrepancy between the permissive premises of family and educational life and the realities of adult life which tended to create the feeling of frustration and disappointment. Moreover, these feelings were often shared by many members of the parent generation and reinforced by its guilt-feeling about the incomplete realization—because of their very institutionalization—of the goals of their own youth and of the movements in which they participated. . . .

# VII

It is highly significant, from the point of view of our analysis, that this type of protest is not borne only by small closed intellectual groups but by widespread circles of novices and aspirants to intellectual status, who constitute—given the spread of the modern educational system and the parallel effects of the spread of media of mass-communication—a very large part of the educated public on the one hand, while on the other hand, for the same structural reasons they impinge on the centers of intellectual creativity and cultural transmission and become integral, even if transient, parts thereof.

It is indeed owing to these processes that these institutions in general and universities in particular have become the loci in which the convergence of intergenerational conflict with potential intellectual protest and antinomianism has taken place.

It is this also which explains why the University is chosen as one of the focal symbols and objects of such total attack against the existing order.

It is not that the various bureaucratic or meritocratic features are necessarily much more developed in the University than in organizations and institutions, but rather in the social and cultural orders they tend to become more salient and articulated. The University is being here perceived as the major locus of the possibility of such participation, and as the very place in which the quest for such creativity could be institutionalized. In this way the University has tended to become the major focus of legitimation of modern social order and the attack on it indicates not only dissatisfaction with its own internal arrangements or even with the fact that it serves also as one mechanism of occupational and meritocratic selection. The choice of the University as the object of such attack rather emphasizes the denial that the existing order can realize these basic premises of modernity: to establish and maintain an order which could do justice to the claims to creativity and participation in the broader social order, and to overcome the various contradictions which have developed within it from the point of view of these claims.

It is, of course, very significant that this denial is also often shared and emphasized by many of the faculty itself which evinces here some of the guilt feelings alluded to above, of the parent generation in general and of the intellectuals among them in particular.

It is perhaps in the attack on the University that the new dimension of protest—the negation of the premises of modernity, the emphasis on the meaninglessness of the existing centers and the symbols of collective identity, become articulated in the most extreme—although certainly not necessarily representative —way.

It is also here that basic themes of youth rebellion become very strongly connected with those of intellectual antinomism. It is here that the rebellion against authority, hierarchy and organizational framework, directed by the dreams of plentitude and of permissive unstructured creativity, tends to become particularly prominent, especially as the University serves also as the institutional meeting point between the educational and the central cultural spheres of the society.

Perhaps the most significant fact about these movements against the University is that they develop throughout the world in marco-societal situations which are structurally basically different—in the centers of highly developed modern, as well as in those of developing and underdeveloped ones—but which are at the same time perceived by those participating in them as symbolically similar.

Those participating in them tend to develop rather similar attitudes toward the symbolic aspects, toward the premises and promises of modernity and the similar *perceptions* of being placed in situations of relative deprivation with regard to these premises and promises of modernity.

The fact that the bases of such deprivation or discontinuity differ greatly—that for instance, in the underdeveloped countries they are mostly those between traditional and modern sectors, in the Communist regimes between an authoritarian regime and those who want to extend the realism of liberty, and in the highly industrialized societies mostly between the sons of affluence and the structural-organizational aspects of their affluent society—does not necessarily abate their symbolic affinity which cuts across different historical and social situations (in a sense this symbolic affinity is reinforced by such broad structural variety) connected with the similarity in the place of the University in the spread of the vision of modernity.

It is in the attack on the University and from within the

University that these new extreme postures of rebellions and protest—due to the convergence of generational conflict and intellectual antinomism—tend to become especially prominent.

Needless to say, these are indeed only extreme postures and they certainly do not constitute the whole picture of contemporary youth or the intellectual scene.

Their relative importance and strength, both for social organization and in the life-spans of individuals may greatly vary, and it is indeed one of the tasks of social research—a task which indeed is being more and more discharged[6]—to attempt to identify some of the specific conditions which tend to give rise in the modern setting, to these, as against other manifestations of youth rebellion and intellectual protest.

But whatever the specific conditions which give rise in the contemporary scene to these, as against other types of youth rebellions, the very novelty of this phenomena can at least partially be explained in terms of the conditions leading to the convergence of intergenerational conflict and intellectual antinomianism.

# VIII

We now come to the problem of the possible impact of all these developments on the format of modern society.

It is, of course, difficult to predict the long-range impact of these new types of protest in general, and of youth and student rebellion in particular, on the structure of modern social, political, and cultural orders. Some may see them as the harbingers of an entirely new civilization, of the same order as the various sects which developed at the end of the Roman Empire, and which ushered in the Christian era. But even if one made no such extreme prediction, there can be no doubt that these developments will have several important repercussions on the structure of modern societies.

Perhaps the most important thing is to recognize both the continuous ubiquity as well as the changeability of the conditions giving rise in modern and modernizing societies to continuously changing and new types of youth rebellion protest, organizations and activities.

Second, it should not be forgotten that especially in industrial societies active age-groups or youth rebels are only a minority in their respective age-spans—minorities which tend to crystallize in the rather specific conditions outlined above.

Thus it seems quite true that despite the great upsurge of continuous youth rebellions, it is doubtful whether youth in modern, industrial societies will develop into a continuous organized political force capable of continuous organized political activities within the established political frameworks. It is only in very exceptional circumstances of the early closure of a new political system and the consequent lack of availability of adequate openings that the political struggle will become couched—as it tends to be in some African States—entirely in terms of "generational groups." But even there with regard to any specific generation it will be a passing—although continuously recurring—phenomenon.

Similarly, it will probably be only in relatively few cases, like in some rapidly urbanizing and industrializing countries like parts of Latin America, or in Italy, where there may develop conditions not dissimilar to those of the early European industrializing societies—that parts at least of these movements may become allied with some of the existing leftist parties.

Thus, given their orientations they will on the whole find it rather difficult to find continuous allies or to ally themselves to continuously organized political parties—although they may indeed perhaps be swallowed by some new movements which will then obliterate their own distinctiveness—as happened within the right and left wing authoritarian movements of the past.

Rather their impact on existing political frameworks will be mostly manifest by shifting the focus of political issues, influencing the selected candidates and the pattern of their activities, influencing public opinion and often changing its climate.

Beyond this they may probably also exacerbate the cleavages and polarization within these systems and possibly give rise to various extreme reactions.

## IX

But whatever the direct impact of these movements on the

working of existing political systems, organizations and groups, some other long-range repercussions of theirs may indeed be— even if tentatively—discerned.

One such impact will be the development of new foci of continuous protest which will add, in both organizational and symbolical terms, to the available reservoir of models and of traditions of protest in modern societies. It indicates a very important shift in the foci of protests in modern societies. As already indicated above, the major shift here is from greater participation in national political centers or attempts to influence socio-economic policies towards new directions. The most important of these seem to be first, attempts to strip these centers of their charismatic legitimacy—and perhaps of any legitimacy at all; second, continuous search for new loci of meaningful participation beyond these existing centers, and concomitant attempts to create new centers which would be independent of existing ones; third, attempts to couch the patterns of participation in these centers not so much in socio-political or economic terms, but in symbols of primordial relations or of direct social participation.

Truly enough, in a sense, these new foci of protest go back to anarchist and romantic traditions in which protest orientation was not focused around participation in the political center or was at least ambivalent to it. But as these movements of protest do arise from the very process of institutionalization of the former goals which assumed some congruency between the charismatic social, political and cultural centers, and their economic activities, they may already denote new dimensions of change in modern societies.

It seems that the more extreme of these movements, and especially those of the students, will constitute continuous reservoirs of new types of revolutionary activity—a revolutionary activity which will be fed and reinforced by the continuous spread of modernity throughout the world and by the problem and aspiration it raises.

Most of these movements and ideologies will be leftist oriented —thus continuing the predominant leftist orientation of most modern student movements, but the degree of their organizational proximity to leftist, socialist parties will greatly vary—and on the whole will probably be rather ambivalent and discontinuous.

However, given their great predilection against any "establishment" centers and organizations as their basic ideological and antinomian orientations, most fully seen, as has been mentioned above, in their revolt against the University, and the transitory nature of their members, it will be only in some of the exceptional conditions that these revolutionary groups and activities will develop into full fledged organized, continuous, political organizations or parties, working within the existing political frameworks.

They will, however, constitute nuclei of new international enclaves of various political and cultural subcultures with a highly mobile and changing population cutting across national and state boundaries and providing rather continuous "irritants" to the existing frameworks.

## NOTES

1. See on this in greater detail: S. N. Eisenstadt. *From Generation to Generation* (New York: The Free Press, 1956 and 1962).
2. See on this: K. Feuer, *The Conflict of Generations* (New York: Basic Books, 1969).
3. See Edward Shils, "Dreams of Plentitude, Nightmares and Scarcity," in S. M. Lipset and F. B. Altbach (eds.), *Students in Revolt* (Boston: Houghton Mifflin Co., 1969), pp. 1-35.
4. See, for instance, Edward Shils, "Intellectuals," *Encyclopedia of the Social Sciences*, New York, 1968; K. Mannheim, *Ideology and Utopia*, (London, 1933), and *Man and Society in an Age of Reconstruction*, (London, 1934); and the selections in G. B. de Hussar (ed.), *The Intellectuals. A Controversial Portrait* (New York, 1960).
5. For analysis on one such historical case see S. N. Eisenstadt, *The Political Systems of Empires* (New York: The Free Press, 1964 and 1969) esp. ch. VIII. Also: S. N. Eisenstadt, "Religious Organization and Political Process in Centralized Empires," *The Journal of Asian Studies*, Vol. XXI, May, 1962, pp. 74-94.
6. See, for instance, among many others: P. Abrams, "Rites de Passage: The Conflict of Generations in Industrial Society," *Journal of Contemporary History*, Vol. 5 (1970) No. 1, pp. 175-180. Also: M. Brewster Smith, Norma Haan and Jeanne Block, "Social-Psychological Aspects of Student Activism," *Youth and Society* Vol. 1 (1970) No. 3, pp. 261-289.

## 9

## SELECTIONS FROM
## *THE COMMUNIST MANIFESTO*

### Marx and Engels

The history of all hitherto existing society is the history of
class struggles. Freeman and slave, patrician and plebeian, lord
and serf, guild-master and journeyman, in a word, oppressor
and oppressed, stood in constant opposition to one another,
carried on an uninterrupted, now hidden, now open fight,
a fight that each time ended either in a revolutionary reconstitution of society at large, or in the common ruin of the
contending classes.

In the earlier epochs of history, we find almost everywhere
a complicated arrangement of society into various orders, a
manifold gradation of social rank. In ancient Rome we have
patricians, knights, plebeians, slaves; in the Middle Ages, feudal
lords, vassals, guild-masters, journeymen, apprentices, serfs; in
almost all of these classes, again, subordinate gradations.

The modern bourgeois society that has sprouted from the
ruins of feudal society has not done away with class antagonisms. It has but established new classes, new conditions of
oppression, new forms of struggle in place of the old ones.

Our epoch, the epoch of the bourgeoisie, possesses, however,
this distinctive feature; it has simplified the class antagonisms.
Society as a whole is more and more splitting up into two

great hostile camps, into two great classes directly facing each other: Bourgeoisie and Proletariat.

From the serfs of the Middle Ages sprang the chartered burghers of the earliest towns. From these burgesses the first elements of the bourgeoisie were developed.

The discovery of America, the rounding of the Cape, opened up fresh ground for the rising bourgeoisie. The East-Indian and Chinese markets, the colonization of America, trade with the colonies, the increase in the means of exchange and in commodities generally, gave to commerce, to navigation, to industry, an impulse never before known, and thereby, to the revolutionary element in the tottering feudal society, a rapid development.

The feudal system of industry, in which industrial production was monopolized by closed guilds, now no longer sufficed for the growing wants of the new markets. The manufacturing system took its place. The guild-masters were pushed on one side by the manufacturing middle-class; division of labor between the different corporate guilds vanished in the face of division of labor in each single workshop. Meantime the markets kept ever growing, the demand, ever rising. Even manufacture no longer sufficed. Thereupon steam and machinery revolutionized industrial production. The place of manufacture was now taken by the giant, modern industry, the place of the industrial middle-class, by industrial millionaires, the leaders of whole industrial armies, the modern bourgeois.

Modern industry has established the world-market, for which the discovery of America paved the way. This market has given an immense development to commerce, to navigation, to communication by land. This development has, in its turn, reacted on the extension of industry; and in proportion as industry, commerce, navigation, railways extended, in the same proportion the bourgeoisie developed, increased its capital, and pushed into the background every class handed down from the Middle Ages. We see, therefore, how the modern bourgeoisie is itself the product of a long course of development, of a series of revolutions in the modes of production and of exchange.

Each step in the development of the bourgeoisie was accompanied by a corresponding political advance of that class. An oppressed class under the sway of the feudal nobility, it became an armed and self-governing association in the mediaeval commune; here independent urban republic (as in Italy and Germany), there taxable "third estate" of the monarchy (as in France); afterwards, in the period of manufacture proper, serving either the semi-feudal or the absolute monarchy as a counterpoise against the nobility, and, in fact, cornerstone of the great monarchies in general, the bourgeoisie has at last, since the establishment of Modern Industry and of the world-market, conquered for itself, in the modern representative State, exclusive political sway. The executive of the modern State is but a committee for managing the common affairs of the whole bourgeoisie. . . .

The bourgeoisie keeps more and more doing away with the scattered state of the population, of the means of production, and of property. It has agglomerated population, centralized means of production, and has concentrated property in a few hands. The necessary consequence of this was political centralization. Independent, or but loosely connected provinces, with separate interests, laws, systems of taxation, and governments, became lumped together in one nation, with one government, one code of laws, one national class-interest, one frontier, and one customs tariff.

The bourgeoisie, during its rule of scarce one hundred years, has created more massive and more colossal productive forces than have all preceding generations together. Subjection of Nature's forces to man, machinery, application of chemistry to industry and agriculture, steam-navigation, railways, electric telegraphs, clearing of whole continents for cultivation, canalization of rivers, whole populations conjured out of the ground. What earlier century had even a presentiment that such productive forces slumbered in the lap of social labor?

We see then: the means of production and of exchange on whose foundation the bourgeoisie built itself up were generated in feudal society. At a certain stage in the development of these means of production and of exchange, the conditions under which feudal society produced and exchanged, the feudal organization of agriculture and manufacturing industry, in one word, the feudal relations of property became no longer compatible with the already developed productive forces; they became so many fetters. They had to burst asunder; they were burst asunder.

Into their places stepped free competition, accompanied by a social and political constitution adapted to it, and by the economical and political sway of the bourgeois class.

A similar movement is going on before our own eyes. Modern bourgeois society with its relations of production, of exchange and of property, a society that has conjured up such gigantic means of production and of exchange, is like the sorcerer, who is no longer able to control the powers of the nether world whom he has called up by his spells. For many a decade past the history of industry and commerce is but the history of the revolt of modern productive forces against modern conditions of production, against the property relations that are the conditions for the existence of the bourgeoisie and of its rule. It is enough to mention the commercial crises that by their periodical return put on its trial, each time more threateningly, the existence of the entire bourgeois society. In these crises a great part not only of the existing products but also of the previously created productive forces are periodically destroyed. In these crises there breaks out an epidemic that, in all earlier epochs, would have seemed an absurdity, the epidemic of overproduction. Society suddenly finds itself put back into a state of momentary barbarism; it appears as if a famine, a universal war of devastation had cut off the supply of every means of subsistence; industry and commerce seem to be destroyed; and why? Because there is too much civilization, too much commerce. The productive forces at the disposal of society no longer tend to further the development of the conditions of bourgeois property; on the contrary, they have become too powerful for these conditions, by which they are fettered, and so soon as they overcome these fetters, they bring disorder into the whole of bourgeois society, endanger the existence of bourgeois property. The conditions of bourgeois society are too narrow to comprise the wealth created by them. And how does the bourgeoisie get over these crises? On the one hand by enforced destruction of a mass of productive forces;

on the other, by the conquest of new markets, and by the more thorough exploitation of the old ones. That is to say, by paving the way for more extensive and more destructive crises, and by diminishing the means whereby crises are prevented.

The weapons with which the bourgeoisie felled feudalism to the ground are now turned against the bourgeoisie itself.

But not only has the bourgeoisie forged the weapons that bring death to itself; it has also called into existence the men who are to wield those weapons, the modern working-class, the proletarians.

In proportion as the bourgeoisie, i.e., capital, is developed, in the same proportion is the proletariat, the modern working-class, developed, a class of laborers, who live only so long as they find work, and who find work only so long as their labor increases capital. These laborers, who must sell themselves piecemeal, are a commodity, like every other article of commerce, and are consequently exposed to all the vicissitudes of competition, to all the fluctuations of the market.

Owing to the extensive use of machinery and to division of labor, the work of the proletarians has lost all individual character, and, consequently, all charm for the workman. He becomes an appendage of the machine, and it is only the most simple, most monotonous, and most easily acquired knack that is required of him. Hence, the cost of production of a workman is restricted, almost entirely, to the means of subsistence that he requires for his maintenance, and for the propagation of his race. But the price of a commodity, and also of labor, is equal to its cost of production. In proportion, therefore, as the repulsiveness of the work increases, the wage decreases. Nay more, in proportion as the use of machinery and division of labor increases, in the same proportion the burden of toil also increases, whether by prolongation of the working hours, by increase of the work enacted in a given time, or by increased speed of the machinery, etc.

Modern industry has converted the little workshop of the patriarchal master into the great factory of the industrial capitalist. Masses of laborers, crowded into the factory, are organized like soldiers. As privates of the industrial army they are placed under the command of a perfect hierarchy of officers and sergeants. Not only are they the slaves of the bourgeois class, and of the bourgeois State, they are daily and hourly enslaved by the machine, by the overlooker, and, above all, by the individual bourgeois manufacturer himself. The more openly this despotism proclaims gain to be its end and aim, the more petty, the more hateful and the more embittering it is.

The less the skill and exertion or strength implied in manual labor, in other words, the more modern industry becomes developed, the more is the labor of men superseded by that of women. Differences of age and sex have no longer any distinctive social validity for the working class. All are instruments of labor, more or less expensive to use, according to their age and sex.

No sooner is the exploitation of the laborer by the manufacturer, so far at an end, that he receives his wages in cash, than he is set upon by the other portions of the bourgeoisie, the landlord, the shopkeeper, the pawnbroker, etc.

The lower strata of the Middle class, the small tradespeople, shopkeepers, and retired tradesmen generally, the handicraftsmen and peasants, all these sink gradually into the proletariat, partly because their diminutive capital does not suffice for the scale on which Modern Industry is carried on, and is swamped in the competition with the large capitalists, partly because their specialized skill is rendered worthless by new methods of production. Thus the proletariat is recruited from all classes of the population.

The proletariat goes through various stages of development. With its birth begins its struggle with the bourgeoisie. At first the contest is carried on by individual laborers, then by the workpeople of a factory, then by the operatives of one trade, in one locality, against the individual bourgeois who directly exploits them. They direct their attacks not against the bourgeois conditions of production, but against the instruments of production themselves; they destroy imported wares that compete with their labor, they smash to pieces machinery, they set factories ablaze, they seek to restore by force the vanished status of the workman of the Middle Ages.

At this stage the laborers still form an incoherent mass scattered over the whole country, and broken up by their mutual competition. If anywhere they unite to form more compact bodies, this is not yet the consequence of their own active union, but of the union of the bourgeoisie, which class, in order to attain its own political ends, is compelled to set the whole proletariat in motion, and is moreover yet, for a time, able to do so. At this stage, therefore, the proletarians do not fight their enemies, but the enemies of their enemies, the remnants of absolute monarchy, the landowners, the non-industrial bourgeois, the petty bourgeoisie. Thus the whole historical movement is concentrated in the hands of the bourgeoisie; every victory so obtained is a victory for the bourgeoisie.

But with the development of industry the proletariat not only increases in number, it becomes concentrated in greater masses, its strength grows, and it feels that strength more. The various interests and conditions of life within the ranks of the proletariat are more and more equalized, in proportion as machinery obliterates all distinctions of labor, and nearly everywhere reduces wages to the same low level. The growing competition among the bourgeois, and the resulting commercial crises, make the wages of the workers ever more fluctuating. The unceasing improvement of machinery, ever more rapidly developing, makes their livelihood more and more precarious; the collisions between individual workmen and individual bourgeois take more and more the character of collisions between two classes. Thereupon the workers begin to form combinations (Trades' Unions) against the bourgeois; they club together in order to keep up the rate of wages; they found permanent associations in order to make provision beforehand for these occasional revolts. Here and there the contest breaks out into riots.

Now and then the workers are victorious, but only for a time. The real fruit of their battles lies, not in the immediate result, but in the ever expanding union of the workers. This union is helped on by the improved means of communication that are created by modern industry, and that place the workers of different localities in contact with one another. It was just this contact that was needed to centralize the numerous local struggles, all of the same character, into one national struggle between classes. But every class struggle is a political struggle. And that union, to attain which the burghers of the Middle Ages, with their miserable highways, required centuries, the modern proletarians, thanks to railways, achieve in a few years.

This organization of the proletarians into a class, and consequently into a political party, is continually being upset again by the competition between the workers themselves. But it ever rises up again, stronger, firmer, mightier. It compels legislative recognition of particular interests of the workers by taking advantage of the divisions among the bourgeoisie itself. Thus the ten-hour bill in England was carried.

Altogether collisions between the classes of the old society further, in many ways, the course of development of the proletariat. The bourgeoisie finds itself involved in a constant battle. At first with the aristocracy; later on with those portions of the bourgeoisie itself, whose interests have become antagonistic to the progress of industry; at all times, with the bourgeoisie of foreign countries. In all these battles it sees itself compelled to appeal to the proletariat, to ask for its help, and thus to drag it into the political arena. The bourgeoisie itself, therefore, supplies the proletariat with its own elements of political and general education, in other words, it furnishes the proletariat with weapons for fighting the bourgeoisie.

Further, as we have already seen, entire sections of the ruling classes are, by the advance of industry, precipitated into the proletariat, or are at least threatened in their conditions of existence. These also supply the proletariat with fresh elements of enlightenment and progress.

Finally, in times when the class-struggle nears the decisive hour, the process of dissolution going on within the ruling class, in fact, within the whole range of old society, assumes such a violent, glaring character, that a small section of the ruling class cuts itself adrift, and joins the revolutionary class, the class that holds the future in its hands. Just as, therefore, at an earlier period, a section of the nobility went over to the bourgeoisie, so now a portion of the bourgeoisie goes over to the proletariat, and in particular, a portion of the bourgeois ideologists, who have raised themselves to the level of comprehending theoretically the historical movements as a whole. . . .

Though not in substance, yet in form, the struggle of the proletariat with the bourgeoisie is at first a national struggle. The proletariat of each country must first of all settle matters with its bourgeoisie. In depicting the most general phases of the development of the proletariat, we traced the more or less veiled civil war, raging within existing society, up to the point where that war breaks out into open revolution, and where the violent overthrow of the bourgeoisie, lays the foundation for the sway of the proletariat. . . .

The development of Modern Industry therefore cuts from under its feet the very foundation on which the bourgeoisie produces and appropriates products. What the bourgeoisie therefore produces, above all, are its own grave-diggers. Its fall and the victory of the proletariat are equally inevitable.

# 10.

# ON PEASANT REBELLIONS

Eric R. Wolf

Six major social and political upheavals, fought with peasant support, have shaken the world of the twentieth century: the Mexican revolution of 1910, the Russian revolutions of 1905 and 1917, the Chinese revolution which metamorphosed through various phases from 1921 onwards, the Vietnamese revolution which has its roots in the Second World War, the Algerian rebellion of 1954 and the Cuban revolution of 1958. All of these were to some extent based on the participation of rural populations. It is to the analysis of this participation that the present article directs its attention.

Romantics to the contrary, it is not easy for a peasantry to engage in sustained rebellion. Peasants are especially handicapped in passing from passive recognition of wrongs to political participation as a means for setting them right. First, a peasant's work is more often done alone, on his own land, than in conjunction with his fellows. Moreover, all peasants are to some extent competitors, for available resources within the community as for sources of credit from without. Secondly, the tyranny of work weighs heavily upon peasants: their life is geared to an annual routine and to planning for the year to come. Momentary alterations of routine threaten their ability to take up the

Reprinted with permission of Unesco from the *International Social Science Journal*, Vol. 21 No. 2, 1969. Copyright 1969 by E. R. Wolf.

routine later. Thirdly, control of land enables them, more often than not, to retreat into subsistence production should adverse conditions affect their market crop. Fourthly, ties of extended kinship and mutual aid within the community may cushion the shocks of dislocation. Fifthly, peasants' interests—especially among poor peasants—often cross-cut class alignments. Rich and poor peasants may be kinfolk, or a peasant may be at one and the same time owner, renter, share-cropper, labourer for his neighbours and seasonal hand on a near-by plantation. Each different involvement aligns him differently with his fellows and with the outside world. Finally, past exclusion of the peasant from participation in decision-making beyond the bamboo hedge of his village deprives him all too often of the knowledge needed to articulate his interests with appropriate forms of action. Hence peasants are often merely passive spectators of political struggles or long for the sudden advent of a millennium, without specifying for themselves and their neighbours the many rungs on the staircase to heaven.

If it is true that peasants are slow to rise, then peasant participation in the great rebellions of the twentieth century must obey some special factors which exacerbated the peasant condition. We will not understand that condition unless we keep in mind constantly that it has suffered greatly under the impact of three great crises: the demographic crisis, the ecological crisis and the crisis in power and authority. The demographic crisis is most easily depicted in bare figures, though its root causes remain ill understood. It may well be that its ultimate causes lie less in the reduction of mortality through spreading medical care, than in the diffusion of American food crops throughout the world which provided an existential minimum for numerous agricultural populations. Yet the bare numbers suffice to indicate the seriousness of the demographic problem. Mexico had a population of 5.8 million at the beginning of the nineteenth century; in 1910— at the outbreak of the revolution—it had 16.5 million. European Russia had a population of 20 million in 1725; at the turn of the twentieth century it had 87 million. China numbered 265 million in 1775, 430 million in 1850 and close to 600 million at the time of the revolution. Viet-Nam is estimated to have sustained a population of between 6 and 14 million in 1820; it had 30.5 million inhabitants in 1962. Algeria had an indigenous population of 10.5 million in 1963, representing a fourfold increase since the beginnings of French occupation in the first part of the nineteenth century. Cuba had 550,000 inhabitants in 1800; by 1953 it had 5.8 million. Population increases alone and by themselves would have placed a serious strain on inherited cultural arrangements.

The ecological crisis is in part related to the sheer increase in numbers; yet it is also in an important measure independent of it. Population increases of the magnitude just mentioned coincided with a period in history in which land and other resources were increasingly converted into commodities—in the capitalist sense of that word. As commodities they were subjected to the demands of a market which bore only a very indirect relation to the needs of the rural populations subjected to it. Where, in the past, market behaviour had been largely subsidiary to the existential problems of subsistence, now existence and its problems became subsidiary to the market. The alienation of peasant resources proceeded directly through outright seizure or through coercive purchase, as in Mexico, Algeria and Cuba; or it took the form—especially in China and Viet-Nam—of stepped-up capitalization of rent which resulted in the transfer of resources from those unable to keep up to those able to pay. In addition, capitalist mobilization of resources was reinforced through the pressure of taxation, of demands for redemption payments and through the increased needs for industrially produced commodities on the part of the peasantry itself. All together, however, these various pressures disrupted the precarious ecological balance of peasant society. Where the peasant had required a certain combination of resources to effect an adequate living, the separate and differential mobilization of these resources broke that ecological nexus. This is perhaps best seen in Russia where successive land reforms threatened continued peasant access to pasture, forest and ploughland. Yet it is equally evident in cases where commercialization threatened peasant access to communal lands (Algeria, Mexico, Viet-Nam), to unclaimed land (Cuba, Mexico), to public granaries (Algeria, China), or where it threatened the balance between pastoral and settled populations (Algeria). At the same time as commercialization disrupted rural life, moreover, it also created new and unsettled ecological niches in industry. Disruptive change in the rural area went hand in hand with the opening up of incipient but uncertain opportunities for numerous ex-industrial peasants. Many of these retained formal ties with their home villages (Algeria, China, Russia); others migrated between country and industry in continuous turnover (especially Viet-Nam). Increased instability in the rural area was thus accompanied by a still unstable commitment to industrial work.

Finally, both the demographic and the ecological crisis converged in the crisis of authority. The development of the market produced a rapid circulation of the *élite*, in which the manipulators of the new 'free-floating resources'—labour bosses, merchants, industrial *entrepreneurs*—challenged the inherited power of the controllers of fixed social resources, the tribal chief, the mandarin, the landed nobleman.[1] Undisputed and stable claims thus yielded to unstable and disputed claims. This rivalry between primarily political and primarily economic power-holders contained its own dialectic. The imposition of the market mechanism entailed a diminution of social responsibilities for the affected population: the economic *entrepreneur* did not concern himself with the social cost of his activities; the traditional power-holder was often too limited in his power to offer assistance or subject to co-optation by his successful rivals. The advent of the market thus not merely produced a crisis in peasant ecology; it deranged the numerous middle-level ties between centre and hinterland, between the urban and the rural sectors. Commercialization disrupted the hinterland; at the very same time it also lessened the ability of power-holders to perceive and predict changes in the rural area. The result was an ever-widening gap between the rulers and the ruled. That such a course is not inevitable is perhaps demonstrated by Barrington Moore,[2] who showed how traditional feudal forms were utilized in both Germany and Japan to prevent the formation of such a gap in power and communication during the crucial period of transition to a commercial and industrial order. Where this was not accomplished —precisely where an administrative militarized feudalism was absent—the continued widening of the power gap invited the formation of a counter-*élite* which could challenge both a disruptive leadership based on the operation of the market and the impotent heirs of traditional power, while forging a new consensus through communication with the peasantry. Such a counter-*élite* is most frequently made up of members of provincial *élites*, relegated to the margins of commercial mobilization and political office; of officials or professionals who stand midway between the rural area and the centre and are caught in the contradictions between the two; and of intellectuals who have access to a system of symbols which can guide the interaction between leadership and rural area.

Sustained mobilization of the peasantry is, however, no easy task. Such an effort will not find its allies in a rural mass which is completely subject to the imperious demands of necessity. Peasants cannot rebel successfully in a situation of complete impotence; the powerless are easy victims. Therefore only a peasantry in possession of some tactical control over its own resources can provide a secure basis for on-going political leverage. Power, as Richard Adams[3] has said, refers ultimately 'to an actual physical control that one party may have with respect to another. The reason that most relationships are not reduced to physical struggles is that parties to them can make rational decisions based on their estimates of tactical power and other factors. Power is usually exercised, therefore, through the common recognition by two parties of the tactical control each has, and through rational decision by one to do what the other wants. Each estimates his own tactical control, compares it to the other, and decides he may or may not be superior'.

The poor peasant or the landless labourer who depends on a landlord for the largest part of his livelihood, or the totality of it, has no tactical power: he is completely within the power domain of his employer, without sufficient resources of his own to serve him usefully in the power struggle. Poor peasants, and landless labourers, therefore, are unlikely to pursue the course of rebellion, unless they are able to rely on some external power to challenge the power which constrains them. Such external power is represented in the Mexican case by the action of the Constitutionalist army in Yucatan, which liberated the peons from debt bondage 'from above'; by the collapse of the Russian army in 1917 and the reflux of the peasant soldiery, arms in hand, into the villages; by the creation of the Chinese Red Army as an instrument designed to break up landlord power in the villages. Where such external power is present the poor peasant and landless labourer have latitude of movement; where it is absent, they are under near-complete constraint. The rich peasant, in turn, is unlikely to embark on the course of rebellion. As employer of the labour of others, as money-lender, as notable co-opted by the State machine, he exercises local power in alliance with external power-holders. His power domain with the village is derivative; it depends on the maintenance of the domains of these power-holders outside the village. Only when an external force, such as the Chinese Red Army, proves capable of destroying these other superior power domains, will the rich peasant lend his support to an uprising.

There are only two components of the peasantry which possess sufficient internal leverage to enter into sustained rebellion. These are (a) a landowning 'middle peasantry' or (b) a peasantry located in a peripheral area outside the domains of landlord control. Middle peasantry refers to a peasant population which has secure access to land of its own and cultivates it with family labour. Where these middle-peasant holdings lie within the power domain of a superior, possession of their own resources provides their holders with the minimal tactical freedom required to challenge their overlord. The same, however, holds for a peasantry, poor or 'middle', whose settlements are only under marginal control from the outside. Here landholdings may be insufficient for the support of the peasant household; but subsidiary activities such as casual labour, smuggling, live-stock raising—not under the direct constraint of an external power domain—supplement land in sufficient quantity to grant the peasantry some latitude of movement. We mark the existence of such a tactically mobile peasantry: in the villages of Morelos in Mexico; in the communes of the central agricultural regions of Russia; in the northern bastion established by the Chinese Communists after the Long March; as a basis for rebellion in Vietnam; among the *fellaheen* of Algeria; and among the squatters of Oriente Province in Cuba.

Yet this recruitment of a 'tactically mobile peasantry' among the middle peasants and the 'free' peasants of peripheral areas poses a curious paradox. This is also the peasantry in whom anthropologists and rural sociologists have tended to see the main bearers of peasant tradition. If our account is correct, then —strange to say—it is precisely this culturally conservative stratum which is the most instrumental in dynamiting the peasant social order. This paradox dissolves, however, when we consider that it is also the middle peasant who is relatively the most vulnerable to economic changes wrought by commercialism, while his social relations remain encased within the traditional design. His is a balancing act in which his equilibrium is continuously threatened by population growth; by the encroachment of rival landlords; by the loss of rights to grazing, forest and water: by falling prices and unfavourable conditions of the market: by interest payments and foreclosures. Moreover, it is precisely this stratum which most depends on traditional social relations of kin and mutual aid between neighbours; middle peasants suffer most when these are abrogated, just as they are least able to withstand the depredations of tax collectors or landlords.

Finally—and this is again paradoxical—middle peasants are also the most exposed to influences from the developing proletariat. The poor peasant or landless labourer, in going to the city or the factory, also usually cuts his tie with the land. The middle peasant, however, stays on the land and sends his children to work in town; he is caught in a situation in which one part of the family retains a footing in agriculture, while the other undergoes 'the training of the cities'.[4] This makes the middle peasant a transmitter also of urban unrest and political ideas. The point bears elaboration. It is probably not so much the growth of an industrial proletariat as such which produces revolutionary activity, as the development of an industrial work force still closely geared to life in the villages.

Thus it is the very attempt of the middle and free peasant to remain traditional which makes him revolutionary.

If we now follow through the hypothesis that it is middle peasants and poor but 'free' peasants, not constrained by any power domain, who constitute the pivotal groupings for peasant uprisings, then it follows that any factor which serves to increase the latitude granted by that tactical mobility reinforces their revolutionary potential. One of these factors is peripheral location with regard to the centre of State control. In fact, frontier areas quite often show a tendency to rebel against the central authorities, regardless of whether they are inhabited by peasants or not. South China has constituted a hearth of rebellion within the Chinese State, partly because it was first a frontier area in the southward march of the Han people, and later because it provided the main zone of contact between Western and Chinese civilization. The Mexican north has similarly been a zone of dissidence from the centre in Mexico City, partly because its economy was based on mining and cattle-raising rather than maize agriculture, partly because it was open to influences from the United States to the north. In the Chinese south it was dissident gentry with a peasant following which frequently made trouble for the centre; in the Mexican north it was provincial business men, ranchers and cowboys. Yet where there exists a poor peasantry located in such a peripheral area beyond the normal control of the central power, the tactical mobility of such a peasantry is 'doubled' by its location. This has been the case with Morelos, in Mexico; Nghe An province in Vietnam; Kabylia in Algeria; and Oriente in Cuba. The tactical effectiveness of such areas is 'tripled' if they also contain defensible mountainous redoubts: this has been true of Morelos, Kabylia and Oriente. The effect is 'quadrupled' where the population of these redoubts differs ethnically or linguistically from the surrounding population. Thus we find that the villagers of Morelos were Nahuatl-speakers, the inhabitants of Kabylia Berber-speakers. Oriente province showed no linguistic differences from the Spanish spoken in Cuba, but it did contain a significant Afro-Cuban element. Ethnic distinctions enhance the solidarity of the rebels; possession of a special linguistic code provides for an autonomous system of communication.

It is important, however, to recognize that separation from the State or the surrounding populace need not only be physical or cultural. The Russian and the Mexican cases both demonstrate that it is possible to develop a solid enclave population of peasantry through State reliance on a combination of communal autonomy with the provision of community services to the State. The organization of the peasantry into self-administering communes with stipulated responsibilities to State and landlords created in both cases veritable fortresses of peasant tradition within the body of the country itself. Held fast by the surrounding structure, they acted as sizzling pressure-cookers of unrest which, at the moment of explosion, vented their force outward to secure more living-space for their customary corporate way of life. Thus we can add a further multiplier effect to the others just cited. The presence of any one of these will raise the peasant potential for rebellion.

But what of the transition from peasant rebellion to revolution, from a movement aimed at the redress of wrongs, to the attempted overthrow of society itself? Marxists in general have long argued that peasants without outside leadership cannot make a revolution; and our case material would bear them out. Where the peasantry has successfully rebelled against the established order —under its own banner and with its own leaders—it was sometimes able to reshape the social structure of the country-side closer to its heart's desires; but it did not lay hold of the State, of the cities which house the centres of control, of the strategic non-agricultural resources of the society. Zapata stayed in his Morelos; the 'folk migration' of Pancho Villa simply receded after the defeat at Torreon; The Ukrainian rebel Nestor Makhno stopped short of the cities; and the Russian peasants of the Central Agricultural Region simply burrowed more deeply into their local communes. Thus a peasant rebellion which takes place in a complex society already caught up in commercialization and industrialization tends to be self-limiting, and hence anachronistic.

The peasant Utopia is the free village, untrammelled by tax collectors, labour recruiters, large landowners, officials. Ruled over, but never ruling, peasants also lack any acquaintance with the operation of the State as a complex machinery, experiencing it only as a 'cold monster'. Against this hostile force, they had learned, even their traditional power-holders provided but a weak shield, though they were on occasion willing to defend them if it proved to their own interest. Thus, for peasants, the State is a negative quantity, an evil, to be replaced in short shrift by their own 'home-made' social order. That order, they believe, can run without the State; hence peasants in rebellion are natural anarchists.

Often this political perspective is reinforced still further by a wider ideological vision. The peasant's experience tends to be dualistic, in that he is caught between his understanding of how the world ought properly to be ordered and the realities of a mundane existence, beset by disorder. Against this disorder, the peasant has always set his dreams of deliverance, the vision of a *mahdi* who would deliver the world from tyranny, of a Son of Heaven who would truly embody the mandate of Heaven, of a 'white' Tsar as against the 'black' Tsar of the disordered present.[5] Under conditions of modern dislocation, the disordered present is all too frequently experienced as world order reversed, and hence evil. The dualism of the past easily fuses with the dualism of the present. The true order is yet to come, whether through miraculous intervention, through rebellion, or both. Peasant anarchism and an apocalyptic vision of the world, together, provide the ideological fuel that drives the rebellious peasantry.

The peasant rebellions of the twentieth century are no longer simple responses to local problems, if indeed they ever were. They are but the parochial reactions to major social dislocations, set in motion by overwhelming societal change. The spread of the market has torn men up by their roots, and shaken them loose from the social relationships into which they were born. Industrialization and expanded communication have given rise to new social clusters, as yet unsure of their own social positions and interests, but forced by the very imbalance of their lives to seek a new adjustment. Traditional political authority has eroded or collapsed; new contenders for power are seeking new constituencies for entry into the vacant political arena. Thus when the peasant protagonist lights the torch of rebellion, the edifice of society is already smouldering and ready to take fire. When the battle is over, the structure will not be the same.

No cultural system—no complex of economy, society, polity and ideology—is ever static; all of its component parts are in constant change. Yet as long as these changes remain within tolerable limits, the over-all system persists. If they begin to exceed these limits, however, or if other components are suddenly introduced from outside, the system will be thrown out of kilter. The parts of the system are rendered inconsistent with each other; the system grows incoherent. Men in such a situation are caught painfully between various old solutions to problems which have suddenly shifted shape and meaning, and new solutions to problems they often cannot comprehend. Since incoherence rarely appears all at once, in all parts of the system, they may for some time follow now one alternative, now another and contradictory one; but in the end a breach, a major disjuncture will make its appearance somewhere in the system.[6] A peasant uprising under such circumstances, for any of the reasons we have sketched, can—without conscious intent—bring the entire society to the state of collapse.

## NOTES

1. S. N. Eisenstadt, *Modernization: Protest and Change*, Englewood Cliffs, Prentice-Hall, 1966.
2. Barrington Moore, Jr., *Social Origin of Dictatorship and Democracy*, Boston, Beacon Press, 1966.
3. Richard N. Adams, 'Power and Power Domains', *Americana Latina*, Year 9, 1966, p. 3-21.
4. Germaine Tillion, *France and Algeria: Complementary Enemies*, p. 120-1, New York, Knopf, 1961.
5. Emanuel Sarkisyanz, *Russland und der Messianismus des Orients: Sendungsbewusstsein und politischer Chiliasmus des Ostens*, Tubingen, J. C. B. Mohr, 1955.
6. Godfrey and Monica Wilson, *The Analysis of Social Change*, Cambridge, Cambridge University Press, 1945.

# PART IV

# Mobilization of Resources in Revolutionary Struggle

# 1.
# THE MESSAGE OF THE
# HUNGARIAN REVOLUTION

## Michael Polanyi

In February 1956, Krushchev denounced the insane regime of Stalin at the Twentieth Party Congress. Four months later, in June 1956, the repercussions of this act led to an open rebellion of the Hungarian writers at the meetings of the Petöfi Circle in Budapest. This was the actual beginning of the Hungarian Revolution, which broke out violently in October of the same year.

It has often been mentioned, but never realized in its full importance, that the rebellion of the Petöfi Circle was an uprising of Communist Party members. There were many among them who had won high honors and great financial benefits from the government. They had been, until shortly before, its genuine and passionate supporters.

The Petöfi Circle, where this first rebellion broke out, was an official organ of the Party, presided over by trusted representatives of the ruling clique. But in June 1956 other Party members, forming the bulk of the audience, overcame the platform. They demanded a reversal of the position assigned to human thought in the Marxist-Leninist scheme. Marxism-Leninism taught that public consciousness is a superstructure of the underlying relations of production; public thought under socialism, therefore, must be an instrument of the Party controlling Socialist production.

The meetings rejected this doctrine. They affirmed that truth

Reprinted with permission of the University of Chicago Press from *Knowing and Being*, by Michael Polanyi. Copyright 1969 by Michael Polanyi.

must be recognized as an independent power in public life. The press must be set free to tell the truth. The murderous trials based on faked charges were to be publicly condemned and their perpetrators punished; the rule of law must be restored. And, above all, the arts corrupted by subservience to the Party must be set free to rouse the imagination and to tell the truth. It was this outbreak that created the center of opposition which later overthrew the Communist government of Hungary. . . .

What did we think, what do we think today, of this change of mind among many of the most devoted Hungarian Stalinists? Do we realize that this was a wholesale return to the ideals of nineteenth-century liberalism? In the Hungarian Revolution of 1956 its fighters were clearly going back to the ideals of 1848, to Liberty, Equality, Fraternity. After the French Revolution the ideas of liberty had filtered through the whole of Europe, and in 1848 these ideas aroused a chain of insurgences. Starting from Paris, rebellions swept through the German states and through Austria into Hungary. The Hungarian revolutionaries of 1956 revived these same ideas; they believed that the ideals of truth, justice and liberty were valid, and they were resolved to fight and conquer in their names. . . .

I think that to understand this rebellion we must see it as part of a major historical progression, composed of three stages to be seen jointly. The first was the defection of leading intellectuals of the West, abandoning 'the God that failed'. Some turned away during the trials of 1937-38, others after the Stalin-Hitler pact of 1939, others still later. But by the end of the Second World War there was an ardent band of former Communists desperately warning against the Soviets, whose philosophy made them impervious to our values.

The next decisive change occurred in Soviet Russia itself on the day Stalin died. The first act of his successors was to release the thirteen doctors of the Kremlin who had recently been sentenced to death on their own false confessions of murderous attempts against Stalin and other members of the government. This action had a shattering effect on the Party. If Party-truth was to be refuted by mere bourgeois objectivism, then Stalin's whole fictitious universe would presently dissolve.

The alarm was justified. After the further revelations of the Twentieth Party Congress, it became clear that the new masters of the Kremlin had acted as they did because they felt that their position would be safer if they had more truth on their side and less against them. They sacrificed the most powerful weapon of terror for this end—the weapon of faked trials; no such trial was held in the Soviet empire after the Jewish doctors were set free. A radical change of the foundations had begun.

The third major step in the growth of the power to vindicate the truth—and the values resting on the right to tell the truth —was the rebellion of Hungarian writers. We can see this now as part of the historical process which had started with the numerous defections from Communism among Western intellectuals about fifteen years earlier.

The rebellion of the Petöfi Circle was a change of mind by dedicated Communists forming an intellectual *avant-garde*. Though undertaken against the still ruling Stalinism, it spread under the very eyes of the secret police, until one day it brought the workers out into the streets and won over the army to its support. The government was overthrown. And, though a few days later the Russians moved in with new tanks, they did not restore the Stalinists to power. Since October 23, 1956, ideas had never ceased to circulate freely in Hungary. You cannot fully print them, but you can spread them effectively by word of mouth.

When seen in this context these events might appear self-explanatory. They would indeed be so if the truth of the Enlightenment appeared self-evident today. But though these truths still dominate our public statements and largely dominate also the day-to-day judgments of men, they are, for the most part, ignored by social scientists. Most academic experts will refuse to recognize today that the mere thirst for truth and justice has caused the revolts now transforming the Soviet countries. They are not Marxists, but their views are akin to Marxism in claiming that the scientific explantation of history must be based on more tangible forces than the fact that people change their minds. . . .

Returning once more to Hungary, look at a case in which 'the smashing of the glasses' happened, long before its official enforcement by the Party and even before any public manifestations by the Hungarian intellectuals. It happened to the Hungarian Communist writer Paloczi-Horvath, while imprisoned at the orders of Rakosi, as described in his book *The Undefeated*. Since his arrest in September 1949, Paloczi had suffered incessant cruelties, inflicted on him to make him confess to false charges; yet he had never wavered in his Communist faith. Then suddenly, after two years in prison, in a matter of a few days, he changed his mind and rejected the Party. His sufferings in prison continued unchanged, but from this moment he felt free, even happy—a new person. . . .

Remember that the whole person is involved in trusting a particular comprehensive outlook. Any criticism of it is angrily rejected. To question it is felt to be an attack on an existential assurance protected by the dread of mental disintegration. We have many testimonies by Communists that their minds clung to Marxism-Leninism for fear of being cast into the darkness of a meaningless, purposeless universe. Paloczi-Horvath himself describes how, after his abandonment of the Communist faith, he at first felt lost, incapable of coherent thought. It was only after a few days that he began to experience a new way of making sense, which he felt to be a more honest, decenter way of thinking, bringing him a happiness that transcended his sufferings in prison.

Gimes confirms this emotional value of a comprehensive framework. Looking back on his time as a devoted member of the Party when he believed that advantage to the revolution was the criterion of truth and of all other human values, he feels horrified by the mental corruption caused by this doctrine. The scornful rejection of objectivity as a bourgeois delusion and fraud, which he had previously accepted as an intellectual triumph, now appears to him as an abysmal loss, the loss of the capacity to see any truth at all.

We have many descriptions also of conversions in the opposite direction. Thousands of leading intellectuals have joined the Communist Party because they found in Marxism an interpretation of history and a guide to action far superior to the outlook predominant since the French Revolution among progressive circles in the West. In 1917, when President Wilson was confronted by Lenin on the world scene, these people laughed Wilson's language to scorn and dedicated themselves instead to Lenin's doctrine, which they felt to be intellectually and morally superior.

We may take it, then, as an established fact that during the past half century radical changes of mind have taken place, which were motivated each time by passionate affirmations of value. . . .

Remember now the contemptuous rejection by the science of social behavior of such questions as "What is a good society?" Such inquiries, belonging to traditional political science, were derided as "social theology." But what the revolution in Hungary —and the whole movement of thought of which it formed a part —declared was a doctrine of political science in the traditional sense of the term. The movement condemned a society in which thought—the thought of science, morality, art, justice, religion— is not recognized as an autonomous power. It rejected life in such a society as corrupt, suffocating and stupid. This was clearly to raise, and to answer up to a point, the question "What is a good society?" It was to establish a doctrine of political science.

Actually the current transformation of thought in the Soviet countries had added to political science new and remarkable insights. We have seen that this social transformation was achieved by a smashing of spectacles. Its typical utterances, such as those I have quoted, manifest the deep emotional upheaval caused by recognizing once more that truth, justice, and morality have an intrinsic reality; and this is the decisive fact. Paloczi-Horvath remained in prison, but his conversion made him free; and that symbolizes the character of this whole immense political movement. It was not started by demands for institutional reform, and it went on without materially changing the institutional framework of the countries it transformed.

# 2.

# COUNTERREVOLUTIONARY AMERICA

## Robert L. Heilbroner

Is the United States fundamentally opposed to economic development? The question is outrageous. Did we not coin the phrase, "the revolution of rising expectations"? Have we not supported the cause of development more generously than any nation on earth, spent our intellectual energy on the problems of development, offered our expertise freely to the backward nations of the world? How can it possibly be suggested that the United States might be opposed to economic development?

The answer is that we are not at all opposed to what we conceive economic development to be. The process depicted by the "revolution of rising expectations" is a deeply attractive one. It conjures up the image of a peasant in some primitive land, leaning on his crude plow and looking to the horizon, where he sees dimly, but for the *first time* (and that is what is so revolutionary about it), the vision of a better life. From this electrifying vision comes the necessary catalysis to change an old and stagnant way of life. The pace of work quickens. Innovations, formerly feared and resisted, are now eagerly accepted. The obstacles are admittedly very great—whence the need for foreign assistance— but under the impetus of new hopes the economic mechanism begins to turn faster, to gain traction against the environment. Slowly, but surely, the Great Ascent begins.

Reprinted with permission of the author and publisher from *Commentary*, Vol. 43 No. 4, 1967. Copyright 1967 by Robert L. Heilbroner.

There is much that is admirable about this well-intentioned popular view of "the revolution of rising expectations." Unfortunately, there is more that is delusive about it. For the buoyant appeal of its rhetoric conceals or passes in silence over by far the larger part of the spectrum of realities of the development process. One of these is the certainty that the revolutionary aspect of development will not be limited to the realm of ideas, but will vent its fury on institutions, social classes, and innocent men and women. Another is the great likelihood that the ideas needed to guide the revolution will not only be affirmative and reasonable, but also destructive and fanatic. A third is the realization that revolutionary efforts cannot be made, and certainly cannot be sustained, by voluntary effort alone, but require an iron hand, in the spheres both of economic direction and political control. And the fourth and most difficult of these realities to face is the probability that the political force most likely to succeed in carrying through the gigantic historical transformation of development is some form of extreme national collectivism or Communism.

In a word, what our rhetoric fails to bring to our attention is the likelihood that development will require policies and programs repugnant to our "way of life," that it will bring to the fore governments hostile to our international objectives, and that its regnant ideology will bitterly oppose capitalism as a system of world economic power. If that is the case, we would have to think twice before denying that the United States was fundamentally opposed to economic development.

But is it the case? Must development lead in directions that go counter to the present American political philosophy? Let me try to indicate, albeit much too briefly and summarily, the reasons that lead me to answer that question as I do.

I begin with the cardinal point, often noted but still insufficiently appreciated, that the process called "economic development" is not primarily economic at all. We think of development as a campaign of production to be fought with budgets and monetary policies and measured with indices of output and income. But the development process is much wider and deeper than can be indicated by such statistics. To be sure, in the end what is hoped for is a tremendous rise in output. But this will not come to pass until a series of tasks, at once cruder and more delicate, simpler and infinitely more difficult, has been commenced and carried along a certain distance.

In most of the new nations of Africa, these tasks consist in establishing the very underpinnings of nationhood itself—in determining national borders, establishing national languages, arousing a basic national (as distinguished from tribal) self-consciousness. Before these steps have been taken, the African states will remain no more than names insecurely affixed to the map, not social entities capable of undertaking an enormous collective venture in economic change. In Asia, nationhood is generally much further advanced than in Africa, but here the main impediment to development is the miasma of apathy and fatalism, superstition and distrust that vitiates every attempt to improve hopelessly inefficient modes of work and patterns of resource use: while India starves, a quarter of the world's cow population devours Indian crops, exempt either from effective employment or slaughter because of sacred taboos. In still other areas, mainly Latin America, the principal handicap to development is not an absence of national identity or the presence of suffocating cultures (although the latter certainly plays its part), but the cramping and crippling inhibitions of obsolete social institutions and reactionary social classes. Where landholding rather than industrial activity is still the basis for social and economic power, and where land is held essentially in fiefdoms rather than as productive real estate, it is not surprising that so much of society retains a medieval cast.

Thus, development is much more than a matter of encouraging economis growth within a given social structure. It is rather the *modernization* of that structure, a process of ideational, social, economic, and political change that requires the remaking of society in its most intimate as well as its most public attributes.[1] When we speak of the revolutionary nature of economic development, it is this kind of deeply penetrative change that we mean—change that reorganizes "normal" ways of thought, established patterns of family life, and structures of village authority as well as class and caste privilege.

What is so egregiously lacking in the great majority of the societies that are now attempting to make the Great Ascent is precisely this pervasive modernization. The trouble with India and Pakistan, with Brazil and Ecuador, with the Philippines and Ethiopia, is not merely that economic growth lags, or proceeds at some pitiable pace. This is only a symptom of deeper-lying ills. The trouble is that the social physiology of these nations remains so depressingly unchanged despite the flurry of economic planning on top. The all-encompassing ignorance and poverty of the rural regions, the unbridgeable gulf between the peasant and the urban elites, the resistive conservatism of the village elders, the unyielding traditionalism of family life—all these remain obdurately, maddeningly, disastrously unchanged. In the cities, a few modern buildings, sometimes brilliantly executed, give a deceptive patina of modernity, but once one journeys into the immense countryside, the terrible stasis overwhelms all.

To this vast landscape of apathy and ignorance one must now make an exception of the very greatest importance. It is the fact that a very few nations, all of them Communist, have succeeded in reaching into the lives and stirring the minds of precisely that body of the peasantry which constitutes the insuperable problem elsewhere. In our concentration on the politics, the betrayals, the successes and failures of the Russian, Chinese, and Cuban revolutions, we forget that their central motivation has been just such a war à l'outrance against the arch-enemy of backwardness— not alone the backwardness of outmoded social superstructures but even more critically that of private inertia and traditionalism.

That the present is irreversibly and unqualifiedly freed from the dead hand of the past is, I think, beyond argument in the case of Russia. By this I do not only mean that Russia has made enormous economic strides. I refer rather to the gradual emancipation of its people from the "idiocy of rural life," their gradual entrance upon the stage of contemporary existence. This is not to hide in the smallest degree the continuing backwardness of the Russian countryside where now almost fifty—and formerly perhaps eighty—per cent of the population lives. But even at its worst I do not think that life could now be described in the despairing terms that run through the Russian literature of our grandfathers' time. Here is Chekhov:

During the summer and the winter there had been hours and days when it seemed as if these people [the peasants] lived worse than cattle, and it was terrible to be with them. They were coarse, dishonest, dirty, and drunken; they did not live at peace with one another but quarreled continually, because they feared, suspected, and despised one another. . . . Crushing labor that made the whole body ache at night, cruel winters, scanty crops, overcrowding, and no help, and nowhere to look for help.

It is less certain that the vise of the past has been loosened in China or Cuba. It may well be that Cuba has suffered a considerable economic decline, in part due to absurd planning, in part to our refusal to buy her main crop. The economic record of China is nearly as inscrutable as its political turmoil, and we may not know for many years whether the Chinese peasant is today better or worse off than before the revolution. Yet what strikes me as significant in both countries is something else. In Cuba it is the educational effort that, according to the New York *Times,* has constituted a major effort of the Castro regime. In China it is the unmistakable evidence—and here I lean not alone on the sympathetic account of Edgar Snow but on the most horrified descriptions of the rampages of the Red Guards—that the younger generation is no longer fettered by the traditional view of things. The very fact that the Red Guards now revile their elders, an unthinkable defiance of age-old Chinese custom, is testimony of how deeply change has penetrated into the texture of Chinese life.

It is this herculean effort to reach and rally the great anonymous mass of the population that is *the* great accomplishment of Communism—even though it is an accomplishment that is still only partially accomplished. For if the areas of the world afflicted with the self-perpetuating disease of backwardness are ever to rid themselves of its debilitating effects, I think it is likely to be not merely because antiquated social structures have been dismantled (although this is an essential precondition), but because some shock treatment like that of Communism has been administered to them.

By way of contrast to this all-out effort, however short it may have fallen of its goal, we must place the timidity of the effort to bring modernization to the peoples of the non-Communist world.

Here again I do not merely speak of lagging rates of growth. I refer to the fact that illiteracy in the non-Communist countries of Asia and Central America is increasing (by some 200 million in the last decade) because it has been "impossible" to mount an educational effort that will keep pace with population growth. I refer to the absence of substantial land reform in Latin America, despite how many years of promises. I refer to the indifference or incompetence or corruption of governing elites: the incredible sheiks with their oildoms; the vague, well-meaning leaders of India unable to break the caste system, kill the cows, control the birthrate, reach the villages, house or employ the labor rotting on the streets; the cynical governments of South America, not one of which, according to Lleras Camargo, former president of Colombia, has ever prosecuted a single politician or industrialist for evasion of taxes. And not least, I refer to the fact that every movement that arises to correct these conditions is instantly identified as "Communist" and put down with every means at hand, while the United States clucks or nods approval.

To be sure, even in the most petrified societies, the modernization process is at work. If there were time, the solvent acids of the 20th century would work their way on the ideas and institutions of the most inert or resistant countries. But what lacks in the 20th century is time. The multitudes of the underdeveloped world have only in the past two decades been summoned to their reveille. The one thing that is certain about the revolution of rising expectations is that it is only in its inception, and that its pressures for justice and action will steadily mount as the voice of the 20th century penetrates to villages and slums where it is still almost inaudible. It is not surprising that Princeton historian C. E. Black, surveying this labile world, estimates that we must anticipate "ten to fifteen revolutions a year for the foreseeable future in the less developed societies."

In itself, this prospect of mounting political restiveness enjoins the speediest possible time schedule for development. But this political urgency is many times compounded by that of the population problem. Like an immense river in flood, the number of human beings rises each year to wash away the levees of the preceding year's labors and to pose future requirements of monstrous proportions. To provide shelter for the three billion human beings who will arrive on earth in the next forty years will require as many dwellings as have been constructed since recorded history began. To feed them will take double the world's present output of food. To cope with the mass exodus from the overcrowded countryside will necessitate cities of grotesque size—Calcutta, now a cesspool of three to five millions, threatens us by the year 2000 with a prospective population of from thirty to sixty millions.

These horrific figures spell one importunate message: haste. That is the *mene mene, tekel upharsin* written on the walls of government planning offices around the world. Even if the miracle of the loop is realized—the new contraceptive device that promises the first real breakthrough in population control— we must set ourselves for at least another generation of rampant increase.

But how to achieve haste? How to convince the silent and disbelieving men, how to break through the distrustful glances of women in black shawls, how to overcome the overt hostility of landlords, the opposition of the Church, the petty bickerings of military cliques, the black-marketeering of commercial dealers? I suspect there is only one way. The conditions of backwardness must be attacked with the passion, the ruthlessness, and the messianic fury of a jehad, a Holy War. Only a campaign of an intensity and singlemindedness that must approach the ludicrous and the unbearable offers the chance to ride roughshod over the resistance of the rich and the poor alike and to open the way for the forcible implantation of those modern attitudes and techniques without which there will be no escape from the misery of underdevelopment.

I need hardly add that the cost of this modernization process has been and will be horrendous. If Communism is the great modernizer, it is certainly not a benign agent of change. Stalin may well have exceeded Hitler as a mass executioner. Free inquiry in China has been supplanted by dogma and catechism; even in Russia nothing like freedom of criticism or of personal expression is allowed. Furthermore, the economic cost of industrialization in both countries has been at least as severe as that imposed by primitive capitalism.

Yet one must count the gains as well as the losses. Hundreds of millions who would have been confined to the narrow cells of changeless lives have been liberated from prisons they did not even know existed. Class structures that elevated the flighty or irresponsible have been supplanted by others that have promoted the ambitious and the dedicated. Economic systems that give rise to luxury and poverty have given way to systems that provide a rough distributional justice. Above all, the prospect of a new future has been opened. It is this that lifts the current ordeal in China above the level of pure horror. The number of human beings in that country who have perished over the past centuries from hunger or neglect, is beyond computation. The present revolution may add its dreadful incrdment to this number. But it also holds out the hope that China may finally have been galvanized into social, political, and economic attitudes that for the first time make its modernization a possibility.

Two questions must be answered when we dare to risk so favorable a verdict on Communism as a modernizing agency. The first is whether the result is worth the cost, whether the possible—by no means assured—escape from underdevelopment is worth the lives that will be squandered to achieve it.

I do not know how one measures the moral price of historical victories or how one can ever decide that a diffuse gain is worth a sharp and particular loss. I only know that the way in which we ordinarily keep the books of history is wrong. No one is now toting up the balance of the wretches who starve in India, or the peasants of Northeastern Brazil who live in the swamps on carbs, or the undernourished and permanently stunted children of Hong Kong or Honduras. Their sufferings go unrecorded, and are not present to counterbalance the scales when the furies of revolution strike down their victims. Barrington Moore has made a nice calculation that bears on this problem. Taking as the weight in one pan the 35,000 to 40,000 persons who lost their lives— mainly for no fault of theirs—as a result of the Terror during the French Revolution, he asks what would have been the death rate from preventable starvation and injustice under the *ancien regime* to balance the scales. "Offhand," he writes, "it seems unlikely that this would be very much below the proportion of

.0010 which [the] figure of 40,000 yields when set against an estimated population of 24 million."[2]

Is it unjust to charge the *ancien regime* in Russia with ten million preventable deaths? I think it not unreasonable. To charge the authorities in pre-revolutionary China with equally vast and preventable degradations? Theodore White, writing in 1946, had this to say: . . . "some scholars think that China is perhaps the only country in the world where the people eat less, live more bitterly, and are clothed worse than they were five hundred years ago."[3]

I do not recommend such a calculus of corpses—indeed, I am aware of the license it gives to the unscrupulous—but I raise it to show the onesidedness of our protestations against the brutality and violence of revolutions. In this regard, it is chastening to recall the multitudes who have been killed or mutilated by the Church which is now the first to protest against the excesses of Communism.

But there is an even more terrible second question to be asked. It is clear beyond doubt, however awkward it may be for our moralizing propensities, that historians excuse horror that succeeds; and that we write our comfortable books of moral philosophy, seated atop a mound of victims—slaves, serfs, laboring men and women, heretics, dissenters—who were crushed in the course of preparing the way for our triumphal entry into existence. But at least we are here to vindicate the carnage. What if we were not? What if the revolutions grind flesh and blood and produce nothing, if the end of the convulsion is not exhilaration but exhaustion, not triumph but defeat?

Before this possibility—which has been realized more than once in history—one stands mute. Mute, but not paralyzed. For there is the necessity of calculating what is likely to happen in the absence of the revolution whose prospective excesses hold us back. Here one must weigh what has been done to remedy underdevelopment—and what has not been done—in the past twenty years; how much time there remains before the population flood enforces its own ultimate solution; what is the likelihood of bringing modernization without the frenzied assault that Communism seems most capable of mounting. As I make this mental calculation I arrive at an answer which is even more painful than that of revolution. I see the alternative as the continuation, without substantial relief—and indeed with a substantial chance of deterioration—of the misery and meanness of life as it is now lived in the sinkhole of the world's backward regions.

I have put the case for the necessity of revolution as strongly as possible, but I must now widen the options beyond the stark alternatives I have posed. To begin with, there are areas of the world where the immediate tasks are so far-reaching that little more can be expected for some decades than the primary missions of nation    identification and unification. Most of the new African states fall into this category. These states may suffer capitalist, Communist, Fascist, or other kinds of regimes during the remainder of this century, but whatever the nominal ideology in the saddle, the job at hand will be that of military and political nation-making.

There is another group of nations, less easy to identify, but much more important in the scale of events, where my analysis also does not apply. These are countries where the pressures of population growth seem sufficiently mild, or the existing political and social framework sufficiently adaptable, to allow for the hope of considerable progress without resort to violence. Greece, Turkey, Chile, Argentina, Mexico may be representatives of nations in this precarious but enviable situation. Some of them, incidentally, have already had revolutions of modernizing intent —fortunately for them in a day when the United States was not so frightened or so powerful as to be able to repress them.

In other words, the great arena of desperation to which the revolutionizing impetus of Communism seems most applicable is primarily the crowded land masses and archipelagoes of Southeast Asia and the impoverished areas of Central and South America. But even here, there is the possibility that the task of modernization may be undertaken by non-Communist elites. There is always the example of indigenous, independent leaders who rise up out of nowhere to overturn the established framework and to galvanize the masses—a Gandhi, a Marti, a pre-1958 Castro. Or there is that fertile ground for the breeding of national leaders—the army, as witness Ataturk or Nasser, among many.[4]

Thus there is certainly no inherent necessity that the revolutions of modernization be led by Communists. But it is well to bear two thoughts in mind when we consider the likely course of non-Communist revolutionary sweeps. The first is the nature of the mobilizing appeal of any successful revolutionary elite. Is it the austere banner of saving and investment that waves over the heads of the shouting marchers in Jakarta and Bombay, Cairo and Havana? It most certainly is not. The banner of economic development is that of nationalism, with its promise of personal immortality and collective majesty. It seems beyond question that a feverish nationalism will charge the atmosphere of any nation, Communist or not, that tries to make the Great Ascent— and as a result we must expect the symptoms of nationalism along with the disease: exaggerated xenophobia, a thin-skinned national sensitivity, a search for enemies as well as a glorification of the state.

These symptoms, which we have already seen in every quarter of the globe, make it impossible to expect easy and amicable relations between the developing states and the colossi of the developed world. No conceivable response on the part of America or Europe or, for that matter, Russia, will be able to play up to the vanities or salve the irritations of the emerging nations, much less satisfy their demands for help. Thus, we must anticipate an anti-American, or anti-Western, possibly even anti-white animus from any nation in the throes of modernization, even if it is not parroting Communist dogma.

Then there is a second caution as to the prospects for non-Communist revolutions. This is the question of what ideas and policies will guide their revolutionary efforts. Revolutions, especially if their whole orientation is to the future, require philosophy equally as much as force. It is here, of course, that Communism finds its special strength. The vocabulary in which it speaks—a vocabulary of class domination, of domestic and international exploitation—is rich in meaning to the backward nations. The view of history it espouses provides the support of historical inevitability to the fallible efforts of struggling leaders. Not least, the very dogmatic certitude and ritualistic repetition that stick in the craw of the Western observer offer the psychological assurances on which an unquestioning faith can be maintained.

If a non-Communist elite is to persevere in tasks that will prove Sisyphean in difficulty, it will also have to offer a philosophical interpretation of its role as convincing and elevating, and a diagnosis of social and economic requirements as sharp and simplistic, as that of Communism. Further, its will to succeed at whatever cost must be as firm as that of the Marxists. It is not impossible that such a philosophy can be developed, more or less independent of formal Marxian conceptions. It is likely, however, to resemble the creed of Communism far more than that of the West. Political liberty, economic freedom, and constitutional law may be the great achievements and the great issues of the most advanced nations, but to the least developed lands they are only dim abstractions, or worse, rationalizations behind which the great powers play their imperialist tricks or protect the privileges of their monied classes.

Thus, even if for many reasons we should prefer the advent of non-Communist modernizing elites, we must realize that they too will present the United States with programs and policies antipathetic to much that America "believes in" and hostile to America as a world power. The leadership needed to mount a jehad against backwardness—and it is my main premise that only a Holy War will begin modernization in our time—will be forced to expound a philosophy that approves authoritarian and collectivist measures at home and that utilizes as the target for its national resentment abroad the towering villains of the world, of which the United States is now Number One.

All this confronts American policymakers and public opinion with a dilemma of a totally unforeseen kind. On the one hand we are eager to assist in the rescue of the great majority of mankind from conditions that we recognize as dreadful and ultimately dangerous. On the other hand, we seem to be committed, especially in the underdeveloped areas, to a policy of defeating Communism wherever it is within our military capacity to do so, and of repressing movements that might become Communist if they were allowed to follow their internal dynamics. Thus, we have on the one side the record of Point Four, the Peace Corps, and foreign aid generally; and on the other, Guatemala, Cuba, the Dominican Republic, and now Vietnam.

That these two policies might be in any way mutually incompatible, that economic development might contain revolutionary implications infinitely more far-reaching than those we have so blandly endorsed in the name of rising expectations, that Communism or a radical national collectivism might be the only vehicles for modernization in many key areas of the world— these are dilemmas we have never faced. Now I suggest that we do face them, and that we begin to examine in a serious way ideas that have hitherto been considered blasphemous, if not near-traitorous.

Suppose that most of Southeast Asia and much of Latin America were to go Communist, or to become controlled by revolutionary governments that espoused collectivist ideologies and vented extreme anti-American sentiments. Would this constitute a mortal threat to the United States?

I think it fair to claim that the purely *military* danger posed by such an eventuality would be slight. Given the present and prospective capabilities of the backward world, the addition of hundreds of millions of citizens to the potential armies of Communism would mean nothing when there was no way of deploying them against us. The prospect of an invasion by Communist hordes—the specter that frightened Europe after World War II with some (although retrospectively, not too much) realism—would be no more than a phantasm when applied to Asia or South America or Africa.

More important, the nuclear or conventional military power of Communism would not be materially increased by the armaments capacities of these areas for many years. By way of indication, the total consumption of energy of all kinds (in terms of coal equivalent) for Afghanistan, Bolivia, Brazil, Burma, Ceylon, Colombia, Costa Rica, Dominican Republic, Ecuador, El Salvador, Ethiopia, Guatemala, Haiti, Honduras, India, Indonesia, Iran, Iraq, Korea, Lebanon, Nicaragua, Pakistan, Paraguay, Peru, Philippines, U.A.R., Uruguay, and Venezuela is less than that annually consumed by West Germany alone. The total steel output of these countries is one-tenth of U.S. annual production. Thus, even the total communization of the backward world would not effectively alter the present balance of military strength in the world.

However small the military threat, it is undeniably true that a Communist or radical collectivist engulfment of these countries would cost us the loss of billions of dollars of capital invested there. Of our roughly $50 billions in overseas investment, some $10 billions are in mining, oil, utility, and manufacturing facilities in Latin America, some $4 billions in Asia including the Near East, and about $2 billions in Africa. To lose these assets would deal a heavy blow to a number of large corporations, particularly in oil, and would cost the nation as a whole the loss of some $3 to $4 billions a year in earnings from those areas.

A Marxist might conclude that the economic interests of a capitalist nation would find such a prospective loss insupportable, and that it would be "forced" to go to war. I do not think this is a warranted assumption, although it is undoubtedly a risk. Against a Gross National Product that is approaching ¾ of a trillion dollars and with total corporate assets over $1.3 trillions, the loss of even the whole $16 billions in the vulnerable areas should be manageable economically. Whether such a takeover could be resisted politically—that is, whether the red flag of Communism could be successfully waved by the corporate interests—is another question. I do not myself believe that the corporate elite is particularly war-minded—not nearly so much so as the military or the congressional—or that corporate seizures would be a suitable issue for purposes of drumming up interventionist sentiment.

By these remarks I do not wish airily to dismiss the dangers of a Communist avalanche in the backward nations. There would be dangers, not least those of an American hysteria. Rather, I want only to assert that the threats of a military or economic kind would not be insuperable, as they might well be if Europe were to succumb to a hostile regime.

But is that not the very point?, it will be asked. Would not a Communist success in a few backward nations lead to successes in others, and thus by degrees engulf the entire world, until the United States and perhaps Europe were fortresses besieged on a hostile planet?

I think the answer to this fear is twofold. First, as many beside myself have argued, it is now clear that Communism, far from constituting a single unified movement with a common aim and dovetailing interests, is a movement in which similarities of economic and political structure and ideology are more than outweighed by divergencies of national interest and character. Two bloody wars have demonstrated that in the case of capitalism, structural similarities between nations do not prevent mortal combat. As with capitalism, so with Communism. Russian Communists have already been engaged in skirmishes with Polish and Hungarian Communists, have nearly come to blows with Yugoslavia, and now stand poised at the threshhold of open fighting with China. Only in the mind of the *Daily News* (and perhaps still the State Department) does it seem possible, in the face of this spectacle, to refer to the unified machinations of "international Communism" or the "Sino-Soviet bloc."

The realities, I believe, point in a very different direction. A world in which Communist governments were engaged in the enormous task of trying to modernize the worst areas of Asia, Latin America, and Africa would be a world in which sharp differences of national interest were certain to arise within these continental areas. The outlook would be for frictions and conflicts to develop among Communist nations with equal frequency as they developed between those nations and their non-Communist neighbors. A long period of jockeying for power and command over resources, rather than anything like a unified sharing of power and resources, seems unavoidable in the developing continents. This would not preclude a continuous barrage of anti-American propaganda, but it would certainly impede a movement to exert a coordinated Communist influence over these areas.

Second, it seems essential to distinguish among the causes of dangerous national and international behavior those that can be traced to the tenets of Communism and those that must be located elsewhere. "Do not talk to me about Communism and capitalism," said a Hungarian economist with whom I had lunch this winter. "Talk to me about rich nations and poor ones."

I think it *is* wealth and poverty, and not Communism or capitalism, that establishes much of the tone and tension of international relations. For that reason I would expect Communism in the backward nations (or national collectivism, if that emerges in the place of Communism) to be strident, belligerent, and insecure. If these regimes fail—as they may—their rhetoric may become hysterical and their behavior uncontrolled, although of small consequence. But if they succeed, which I believe they can, many of these traits should recede. Russia, Yugoslavia, or Poland are simply not to be compared, either by way of internal pronouncement or external behavior, with China, or, on a smaller scale, Cuba. Modernization brings, among other things, a waning of the stereotypes, commandments, and flagellations so characteristic of (and so necessary to) a nation engaged in the effort ot alter itself from top to bottom. The idiom of ceaseless revolution becomes less relevant—even faintly embarrassing—to a nation that begins to be pleased with itself. Then, too, it seems reasonable to suppose that the vituperative quality of Communist invective would show some signs of abating were the United States to modify its own dogmatic attitude and to forego its own wearisome clichés about the nature of Communism.

I doubt there are many who will find these arguments wholly reassuring. They are not. It would be folly to imagine that the next generation or two, when Communism or national collectivism in the underdeveloped areas passes through its jehad stage, will be a time of international safety. But as always in these matters, it is only by a comparison with the alternatives that one can choose the preferable course. The prospect that I have offered as a plausible scenario of the future must be placed against that which results from a pursuit of our present course. And here I see two dangers of even greater magnitude: (1) the prospect of many more Vietnams, as radical movements assert themselves in other areas of the world; and (2) a continuation of the present inability of the most impoverished areas to modernize, with the prospect of an eventual human catastrophe on an unimaginable scale.

Nevertheless, there *is* a threat in the specter of a Communist or near-Communist supremacy in the underdeveloped world. It is that the rise of Communism would signal the end of capitalism as the dominant world order, and would force the acknowledgement that America no longer constituted the model on which the future of world civilization would be mainly based. In this way, as I have written before, the existence of Communism frightens American capitalism as the rise of Protestantism frightened the Catholic Church, or the French Revolution the English aristocracy.

It is, I think, the fear of losing our place in the sun, of finding ourselves at bay, that motivates a great deal of the anti-Communism on which so much of American foreign policy seems to be founded. In this regard I note that the nations of Europe, most of them profoundly more conservative than America in their social and economic dispositions, have made their peace with Communism far more intelligently and easily than we, and I conclude that this is in no small part due to their admission that they are no longer the leaders of the world.

The great question in our own nation is whether we can accept a similar scaling-down of our position in history. This would entail many profound changes in outlook and policy. It would mean the recognition that Communism, which may indeed represent a retrogressive movement in the West, where it should continue to be resisted with full energies, may nonetheless represent a progressive movement in the backward areas, where its advent may be the only chance these areas have of escaping misery. Collaterally, it means the recognition that "our side" has neither the political will, nor the ideological wish, nor the stomach for directing those changes that the backward world must make if it is ever to cease being backward. It would undoubtedly entail a more isolationist policy for the United States *vis-à-vis* the developing continents, and a greater willingness to permit revolutions there to work their way without our interference. It would mean in our daily political life the admission that the ideological battle of capitalism and Communism had passed its point of usefulness or relevance, and that religious diatribe must give way to the pragmatic dialogue of the age of science and technology.

I do not know how to estimate the chances of affecting such deepseated changes in the American outlook. It may be that the pull of vested interests, the inertia of bureaucracy, plus a certain lurking fundamentalism that regards Communism as an evil which admits of no discussion—the anti-christ—will maintain America on its present course, with consequences that I find frightening to contemplate. But I believe that our attitudes are not hopelessly frozen. I detect, both above and below, signs that our present view of Communism is no longer wholly tenable and that it must be replaced with a new assessment if we are to remain maneuverable in action and cogent in discourse.

Two actions may help speed along this long overdue modernization of our own thought. The first is a continuation of the gradual thawing and convergence of American and Russian views and interests—rapprochement that is proceeding slowly and hesitantly, but with a discernible momentum. Here the initiative must come from Russia as well as from ourselves.

The other action is for us alone to take. It is the public airing of the consequences of our blind anti-Communism for the underdeveloped world. It must be said aloud that our present policy prefers the absence of development to the chance for Communism —which is to say, that we prefer hunger and want and the existing inadequate assaults against the causes of hunger and want to any regime that declares its hostility to capitalism. There are strong American currents of humanitarianism that can be directed as a counterforce to this profoundly anti-humanitarian view. But for this counterforce to become mobilized it will be necessary to put fearlessly the outrageous question with which I began: is the United States fundamentally opposed to economic development?

## NOTES

1. See C. E. Black, *The Dynamics of Modernization.*
2. *Social Origins of Dictatorship and Democracy,* p. 104.
3. *Thunder Out of China,* p. 32.

4. What are the chances for modernizing revolutions of the Right, such as those of the Meiji Restoration or of Germany under Bismarck? I think they are small. The changes to be wrought in the areas of greatest backwardness are much more socially subversive than those of the 19th century, and the timespan allotted to the revolutionists is much smaller. Bourgeois revolutions are not apt to go far enough, particularly in changing property ownership. Still, one could imagine such revolutions with armed support and no doubt Fascistic ideologies. I doubt that they would be any less of a threat than revolutions of the Left.

3.

# THE RISE AND ROLE OF
# CHARISMATIC LEADERS

## Ann Ruth Willner and Dorothy Willner

The term "charismatic leader" has recently attained widespread and almost debased[1] currency. In the past, it was occasionally applied to Gandhi, Lenin, Hitler, and Roosevelt. Now nearly every leader with marked popular appeal, especially those of new states, is indiscriminately tagged as charismatic. In the absence of clear-cut specifications of traits of personality or behavior shared by the many and apparently diverse men[2] to whom charisma has been attributed and of any inventory of the common characteristics of the publics who have been susceptible to charismatic appeal, it is not surprising that scholars should question the meaning and utility of the concept of charismatic leadership.[3]

To avoid such indiscriminate and therefore meaningless use of the term, we should know what is or should be included in the category of charismatic leadership to distinguish it from other forms of leadership. Such knowledge might help us recognize whether the phenomenon—as distinct from the term—has really been particularly frequent in recent years. If it has, it is important to understand how and when charismatic leadership appears and what it can or cannot contribute to political change.

Max Weber adapted the term *charisma*[4] from the vocabulary of early Christianity to denote one of three types of authority in

Reprinted with permission of the authors and publisher from *The Annals of the American Academy of Political Science*, Vol. 358, 1965. Copyright 1965 by A. R. Willner and Dorothy Willner.

his now classic classification of authority on the basis of claims to legitimacy. He distinguished among (1) traditional authority, whose claim is based on "an established belief in the sanctity of immemorial traditions," (2) rational or legal authority, grounded on the belief in the legality of rules and in the right of those holding authoritative positions by virtue of those rules to issue commands, and (3) charismatic or personal authority, resting on "devotion to the specific sanctity, heroism, or exemplary character of an individual person, and of the normative pattern or order revealed by him."[5]

Of these types—and it must be emphasized that they are "ideal types" or abstractions—charismatic authority, according to Weber, differs from the other two in being unstable, even if recurrent, and tending to be transformed into one of the other two types.[6] While elements of charismatic authority may be present in all forms of leadership,[7] the predominantly charismatic leader is distinguished from other leaders by his capacity to inspire and sustain loyalty and devotion to him personally, apart from his office or status. He is regarded as possessing supernatural or extraordinary powers given to few to have. Whether in military prowess, religious zeal, therapeutic skill, heroism, or in some other dimension, he looms "larger than life." He is imbued with a sense of mission, felt as divinely inspired, which he communicates to his followers. He lives not as other men. Nor does he lead in expected ways by recognized rules. He breaks precedents and creates new ones and so is revolutionary. He seems to flourish in times of disturbance and distress.[8]

The somewhat misleading search for the source of charisma in the personalities of such leaders may have resulted from misreading of Weber's frequently cited definition of charisma as "a certain quality of an individual personality by which he *is set apart* from ordinary men and *treated as endowed* with supernatural, superhuman, or at least specifically exceptional powers or qualities."[9] For, as the words deliberately italicized here suggest and Weber repeatedly emphasized, it is not so much what the leader is but how he is regarded by those subject to his authority that is decisive for the validity of charisma. His charisma resides in the perceptions of the people he leads.

There are those who deny that the term can be properly applied to leaders whose "call" neither comes from God nor can be considered divinely inspired in the specifically religious sense. On the grounds that one ought not to class together the works of a Luther and a Hitler, they deplore Weber's extension of an originally Christian concept to include leaders who are seized with and communicate a darkly secular fervor.[10] As individuals, we can commend the motives of those who wish to distinguish on moral or esthetic grounds between men whose mission leads to Heaven and men whose mission leads to Hell. But as social scientists we must recognize that the empirical or earthly manifestation of inspired and inspiring leadership is one and the same whether in the service of good or evil.

We therefore can redefine charisma—without departing from Weber's intrinsic intention—as a leader's capacity to elicit from a following deference, devotion, and awe toward himself as the source of authority. A leader who can have this effect upon a group is charismatic for *that* group. An analysis of *how* leaders achieve such an effect, of the means by which and the conditions under which this kind of loyalty is generated and maintained, might give us a better intellectual grasp of charismatic leadership.

It may be that systematic comparison of political leaders who have been regarded by their peoples as superhumanly inspired and inspiring would reveal certain traits common to all of them. Further systematic comparison of the societies where and the conditions under which such leaders have come to the fore might eventually take the concept of charismatic leadership out of the realm of speculation into that of empirically based social science. The lack of such systematic research since Weber familiarized us with the concept is somewhat surprising. In its absence we can offer no firmly based findings. We hope the following reflections may be relevant to such an investigation.

First we consider the conditions that appear to have been conducive to the rise of charismatic leadership in new states. Then we attempt to explain how the charismatic leader emerges and gains recognition. Finally, we try to assess the functions and significance of charismatic leadership for the kinds of changes which are customarily called "development."

## New States and the Emergence of Charismatic Leadership

Weber gave little attention to the conditions under which charismatic leadership can emerge, merely mentioning times of psychic, physical, economic, ethical, religious, or political distress.[11] Since he defined this phenomenon as abnormal and intermittent —indeed he considered that the pure form of charismatic authority existed only at the time of origin[12]—he was more interested in its routinization. We attempt to expand Weber's treatment, and perhaps depart from it in some respects, by concentrating on what might be termed the other pole of the developmental continuum.

Charismatic leadership seems to flourish today particularly in the newer states that were formerly under colonial rule. Their very attainment of independence generally signified that the old order had broken down and the supports that sustained it had disappeared or were rapidly being weakened. We might more correctly distinguish two "old" orders in postcolonial countries: (1) the precolonial traditional system, many of whose elements survived during colonial rule and (2) the colonial system, a close approximation of Weber's rational-legal type, which was superimposed upon but did not completely efface the traditional system. Particularly under the "indirect rule" type of colonial regime, much of traditional belief and observance, political as well as socioeconomic, existed beneath the order imported from and imposed by the metropolitan country and in the more rural areas side-by-side with it.

The basis of traditional authority, however, was eroded by colonialism and indigenous nationalism, and the basis of legal authority was undermined by indigenous nationalism. Traditional authority, whether exercised through kingship and dominant caste, chieftainship and special lineage, or whichever of the many and varied institutions found in the many traditional societies, had been part of and based upon indigenous patterns of social organization, land tenure, economic activity, and other elements of a relatively integrated social system. Traditional social systems tended to disintegrate or be transformed under the impact of institutions imposed by the colonial power. Concomitantly, traditional prescriptions and procedures for the selection of rulers, for the control of conflict and the settlement of disputes, and for the maintenance of what had been considered appropriate relations between rulers and ruled were modified and in varying degrees displaced by colonial systems of authority. Even where colonial administrations supported or tolerated some maintenance of traditional authority, this was restricted to traditional contexts.

The attitude that traditional authority systems were inadequate to cope with the urban and industrial institutions introduced into colonies by Europeans was transmitted to and absorbed by the native elites educated in accordance with European standards and values and recruited into the colonial bureaucracies and business organizations. Nationalist intellectuals among the native elites also came to deprecate their own traditions, seeing them as weaknesses which had made colonialism possible and which were used by their colonial rulers to keep them in subjection.

We consider the typical colonial order to have been a fair approximation of the Weberian ideal type of legal-rational authority. For an administrative bureaucracy formulated and applied a system of rules, in accordance with what it considered rational criteria, relatively free from the constraints and controls of domestic political pressures. Problems ultimately arose, as they frequently do, when such rules are imposed upon people who cannot either participate in their making, or accept the norms on which they are based, or successfully resist or modify their application.

In retrospect, it is clear why one of the major difficulties faced by leaders of successful national independence movements as they sought to establish their own governmental systems was the lack of respect for impersonal legal authority based on rational norms. For in successfully having discredited the colonial rulers and their works, they also unwittingly discredited the rule of law introduced by the colonial powers. However, the certainty of the traditional order had already been shattered during the colonial period. Thus there were no longer clear-cut and generally acceptable norms for the legitimacy of authority and the mode of its exercise. Their absence created the need for leadership that could serve as a bridge between the discredited past and the uncertain future.

A climate of uncertainty and unpredictability is therefore a breeding ground for the emergence of charismatic leadership.

## Sources and Validation of Charisma

Having indicated the conditions propitious for the emergence of charismatic leadership, we now describe how it comes into existence and what sustains it. To suggest, as we have, that when other bases for authority are discredited, charismatic leadership can arise by default is to state merely the necessary but not the sufficient conditions for its emergence. We need to know what the charismatic leader does to assert and impose his authority over those he presumes to lead and how he does it. Since his charisma has been defined as validated through the perceptions of a following, we are concerned with the process by which this validation occurs. We also wish to understand how some leaders, rather than others, can gain this validation.

The process, broadly stated, is one of interaction between the leader and his followers. In the course of this interaction the leader transmits, and the followers accept, his presentation of himself as their predestined leader, his definitions of their world as it is and as it ought to be, and his conviction of his mission and their duty to reshape it. In actuality, the process is more complicated, involving several groups of followers and several stages of validation. There is the small group of the "elect" or "disciples," the initial elite whom the leader first inspires or who throw up from among themselves one who can inspire others. There is the public at large which, in turn, can be divided into those of predominantly traditional orientation and those oriented toward a newer order. In the societies with which we are concerned, further divisions may exist along ethnic, tribal, religious, regional, and linguistic lines. The point to be made is that the nationally significant charismatic leader can command the loyalty of all or most of these groups.

To understand how he can do so, it seems advisable to distinguish two levels on which his appeal is communicated and responded to. The first level is that of special grievance and special interest of each group; its significance is probably greatest during the stage in which the charismatic leader mobilizes the population in opposition to a prevailing order and in assertion of the possibility of a new order. In the situations of transition with which we deal, this stage is that of opposition to the rule of a colonial power.

Changes during the colonial period resulted in losses and uncertainties for many groups in the colonized population. Traditional agrarian land rights were interfered with, and unfamiliar forms of taxation were imposed on peasants. The monetary gains of those pushed or pulled out of their traditional agricultural, pastoral, or handicrafts occupations to become plantation and industrial workers may have been more than offset by the problems of adapting to unfamiliar environments. Traditional merchants and traders often lost out to the competition of imported manufactures. Traditional ruling groups may have given outward obedience to colonial overlords who allowed them to retain their titles and some vestiges of their past powers, but often resented their loss of real power. Those who gained from the new opportunities generated by the colonial system—and there were many—chafed at the limits placed upon their continued advancement. Native embryonic capitalists could not easily compete on equal terms with European businesses backed by the facilities of the metropolitan country. Native officials of the governmental and business bureaucracies often felt themselves unfairly excluded from the high-level posts. The intellectuals, especially those who were trained at European universities, became bitter at the disparity between the expectations aroused by their education and the blocks that appeared in the way of maximizing this education. For all of these groups, the colonial system was or could be made to appear the case of their grievance.

While the attraction exercised by the charismatic leader can, in part, be attributed to his ability to focus and channel diverse grievances and interests in a common appeal, unifying a segmented population in pursuit of a common goal, this explanation is insufficient to account for the acceptance of a given leader. Nor does it tell us how a leader maintains charisma in the conditions of uncertainty and fractionalization following the attainment of the goal of independence.

To turn to a deeper level, we suggest that the charisma of a leader is bound up with and, indeed, may even depend upon his becoming assimilated, in the thought and feelings of a populace, to its sacred figures, divine beings, or heroes. Their actions and the context of these actions, recounted in myth, express the fundamental values of a culture, including its basic categories for organizing experience and trying to resolve basic cultural and human dilemmas.

Of the overlapping and conflicting theories of myth to be found in the recent anthropological literature, all seem to agree in regarding myths as tales referring to events that took place in the past, usually a legendary past. However, as Lévi-Strauss points out, "what gives the myth an operational value is that the specific pattern [i.e., combination of elements] is timeless; it explains the present and the past as well as the future." Immediately following this statement is the comparison, significant for our purposes, "between myth and what appears to have largely replaced it in modern societies, namely politics." The comparison is really no more than a statement that the French Revolution, while a non-reversible sequence of past happenings, also constitutes for the French politician and his followers "a timeless pattern which can be detected in the contemporary French social structure and which provides a clue for its interpretation, a lead from which to infer future developments."[13]

We wish to suggest that recent events in a people's politics, particularly those marking a major transition or extraordinary occurrence in public life, can become endowed with the quality of myth if they fit or can be fitted into the pattern of a traditional myth or body of myths. Furthermore, insofar as myths can be regarded as charters for action, validating ritual and moral acts,[14] or, indeed, any culturally prescribed behavior, the assimilation of a historical event to the pattern of traditional myth or of a given individual to a mythic figure endows the event or individual with the aura or sanction of the myth itself.

The charismatic leader, we suggest, is able to communicate to his followers a sense of continuity between himself and his mission and their legendary heroes and their missions. Since "a myth remains the same as long as it felt as such,"[15] he and his claims are legitimated by his ability to draw on himself the mantle of myth. How a particular leader does this can be considered his strategy of "cultural management,"[16] in part conscious and deliberate, in part probably unconscious and intuitive.

The particular strategies of individual charismatic leaders are a subject for empirical investigation.[17] Elements of such strategies might be broken down into such categories as: rhetoric employed in speeches, including rhythm; [18] use of simile and metaphor and allusions[18] to myth and history; use of gesture and movement; employment of ritual and ceremony; manner of dealing with felt doubt and opposition; and mode of handling crises. While this list can be refined and extended, it suggests some of the categories in terms of which the charismatic appeal of leaders can be analyzed.

It should be stressed that the elements of behavior indicated by such categories vary from culture to culture. This, of course, would be true of the behavior of any leader, charismatic or not, who seeks to mobilize popular support. Specific to the charismatic leader, according to our theory, is the role of myth in validating his authority. His appeal, therefore, can best be understood by reference to the body of myth in a given culture that his strategy taps and manipulates, and the actions and values associated with and sanctioned by these myths.[19] In brief, the charismatic leader is charismatic because, in the breakdown of other means of legitimizing authority, he is able to evoke and associate with himself the sacred symbols of his culture.

It follows that the charismatic appeal of a leader is, by definition, limited to those who share the traditions of a given culture, that is, to those who understand and respond to the symbols expressed in the myths a charismatic leader evokes.[20] It further follows that the attributes of the charismatic leader will vary from society to society.[21] Concomitantly, within any society, the charismatic appeal of competing leaders will depend on their relative strength in evoking myths with the broadest common appeal, and in maintaining the association of themselves and their actions with mythical figures and their actions.

We do not, however, suggest or wish to imply that a charismatic leader either achieves power or retains it on the basis of charisma alone. Charismatic appeal provides the source of and legitimates his authority. Other supports may be needed and are frequently employed to gain and maintain power, especially when charismatic appeal begins to decline.[22]

## NOTES

1. When a recent book groups together as "charismatic statesmen" Sukarno, Abdul Rahman, Macapagal, Diem, Sihanouk, Captain Kong Le, General Ne Win and the King of Thailand, one wonders whether every leader who achieves any sort of prominence in Southeast Asia is automatically charismatic or whether Southeast Asia simply boasts a perpetually charismatic climate. See Willard A. Hanna, *Eight Nation Makers: Southeast Asia's Charismatic Statesmen* (New York: American Universities Field Staff, 1964).
2. Peron, Nehru, Ben Gurion, Nkrumah, Magasaysay, Churchill, DeGaulle, Sukarno, Castro, Touré, Lumumba, Eisenhower, Kenyatta, Kennedy, and Khrushchev are just a few of the political leaders who have been called charismatic in recent years.
3. See K. J. Ratnam, "Charisma and Political Leadership," *Political Studies*, Vol. XII, No. 3 (October 1964), pp. 341-354 for one of the more cogent critiques of contemporary uses of the concept.
4. The term is of Greek origin, meaning "gift," and was originally identified as a "gift of grace" or a divinely inspired calling to service, office or leadership.
5. Max Weber, *The Theory of Social and Economic Organization*, ed. by Talcott Parsons (New York: Oxford University Press, 1947), p. 328.
6. This notion of transformation or "routinization" has led to criticism that Weber uses the concept of charisma ambiguously, that is, on the one hand as a characteristic of certain classes of people in certain situations, on the other as a more general quality that can be transmitted to and identified with institutions such as the family and the office; see *Ibid.*, p. 75 and Carl J. Friedrich, "Political Leadership and the Problem of Charismatic Power," *The Journal of Politics*, 23 (February 1961), p. 13. Such criticism overlooks the possibility that *during the course of* charismatic leadership, a transfer can be effected of aspects of the belief induced by the leader toward another object, especially if designated by him.
7. Authority is here defined as the sanctioned basis for the exercise of a leadership role, whereas leadership refers to the individual seen as capable of exercising the role for the situation in which direction is called for.

8. Weber, *op. cit.*, pp. 358-362; also H. H. Gerth and C. Wright Mills, *From Max Weber: Essays in Sociology* (New York: Oxford University Press, 1946), pp. 245-250.
9. Weber, *op. cit.*, p. 358.
10. For a striking example of this point of view, see Friedrich, *op. cit.*, pp. 14-16, 19.
11. Gerth and Mills, *op. cit.*, p. 245.
12. Weber, *op. cit.*, p. 364.
13. Claude Lévi-Strauss, "The Structural Study of Myth," *The Journal of American Folklore,* Vol. 68 (October-December 1955), p. 430.
14. Bronislaw Malinowski, "Myth in Primitive Psychology," *Magic, Science and Religion* (Boston: Beacon Press, 1948), pp. 96-108.
15. Lévi-Strauss, *op. cit.*, p. 435.
16. See Lloyd A. Fallers, "Ideology and Culture in Uganda Nationalism," *American Anthropology,* Vol. 63 (August 1961), pp.677-678 and McKim Marriott, "Cultural Policy in New States," in *Old Society and New States* (New York, 1963), p. 29.
17. We deliberately refrain from giving concrete examples of strategies here; for, as is suggested below, to make meaningful the illustration of even a single strategy of a single leader would require an elaboration of the myths and values of his culture which lack of space prohibits.
18. For example, it might be worth examining the frequency of Biblical allusions in the speeches of FDR, such as the reference in his first inaugural address to driving the money-changers out of the temple, and the extent to which his rhetoric paralleled the cadences of the St. James Bible. Similarly, it would be interesting to compare the rhythmic patterns of the speeches of Nkrumah and other African leaders with the predominant drum and dance rhythms of their societies.
19. See Malinowski, *op. cit.*
20. We cannot here examine the means by which the binding force of mythology is maintained and transmitted, although obviously involved are the socialization and educational practices obtaining in a society.
21. Precisely because of this cultural variation, criticisms by Ratnam, *op. cit.*, and others of the concept of charismatic leadership on the basis that clear statements of the personality qualities of charismatic leaders do not exist are neither relevant nor tenable.
22. As David Apter points out in *Ghana in Transition* (New York: Atheneum, 1963), pp. 328-29, charisma can decline in favor of secular authority or, as he found in Ghana, as a result of conflict with traditional authority.

# 4.

# CRYSTALLIZATION: THE ACTIVE NUCLEUS

## Kurt Lang and Gladys E. Lang

In society, as in nature, process and structure are aspects of the same set of events. As the individual repeats and repeats some activity, it congeals into habit; emergencies are "coded" until what was crisis becomes routine. Group routines congeal into group norms and group ritual. So, too, when the spontaneous and nonroutine forms of interaction result in some kind of equilibrium, elements of social structure are at once discernible. Any collective alienation from the existing social structure contains—potentially, at any rate—the seeds of new organization. For instance, panic reflects the unrest out of which emerge crowds as well as stable action groups. Mass conversion may form the basis for social movements.

*Crystallization* thus designates the process by which alienation from the social order finds expression in an elementary form of organization. Fluid forms of interaction become routinized, and fugitive patterns of behavior are transformed—we say they "crystallize"—into cohesive units with a sense of solidarity and with a more or less definite structure.

The resulting collectivity constitutes a *sectarian association*. The adjective *sectarian* signifies that such an association exists as a secondary phenomenon, which develops as a result of cleavage

Reprinted with permission of the Thomas Y. Crowell Co. from *Collective Dynamics*, by Kurt Lang and Gladys E. Lang. Copyright 1961 by the Thomas Y. Crowell Co.

from an already existing social order. Its members have turned away from the world. The *esprit de corps* that sets off the microcosm from the larger world is often based on hostility. . . .

The crucial fact about the sectarian association is that it is cemented as a result of conflict with the "outsiders." All who are not specifically included are thus excluded from the sectarian cells, which seek to subvert the superiority of the outside world. "The sectarians are forced to segregate themselves by a consciousness of unlikeness between themselves and their oppressors and are drawn together by a sense of mental and moral kinship."[1] The associations they form are outside the pale of society, and the sectarian consciously moves on a different plane of understanding from the rest of the population. If anything, he avoids being drawn into communication with them.

The sectarian nucleus is a form of organization because the sectarians who set themselves against constituted authority do so consciously and deliberately, and not merely under the impact of a momentary emotional impulse as they do in the crowd. In a manner of speaking, the sectarians consider themselves the elect. But initially they lack common interest, a concept of the group in its entirety, recognized roles, etc., which characterize groups generally. What unity they have derives from generalized dissatisfaction and unrest, which in the nucleus crystallize into antagonism. For unlike the crowd, the sectarian nucleus endures. Its initial psychological unity paves the way for a more permanent, usually highly disciplined, structured organization with positive goals.

### Sectarianism and Social Structure

Sectarian nuclei that develop a code subversive of official mores do not form by accident or whim. On the contrary, the sectarian's advocacy of counter mores reflects the unfocused quest by some segments of society for a group code responsive to their particular needs. Persons in social positions where they feel effectively shut off from legitimate expression of their needs show an inclination to achieve recognition in sectarian associations.

#### The lower classes

The persons at the bottom of the pit, the impoverished, the

proletariat probably come first to mind. There is, indeed, a relationship between position in the class structure and membership in small and exclusive religious sects. Christianity was about three hundred years old before it developed a significant following among the socially well-to-do. Later it was the poor—whose social and psychological needs were neglected by the conventional religion of the day—who joined the original Protestant sects that split away from the established Church. The Anabaptists, who revolted and sought later to found the kingdom of God in Muenster, had their firmest base among the poor peasants. John Wesley, the original Methodist preacher, stimulated the greatest emotional response among the outcasts of Newgate and Kingsbridge....

Using an attitude questionnaire, Dynes found that most of the American Protestants in Ohio who by their attitudes indicated acceptance of a "sect-type" religious organization had a low socioeconomic status rather than a high one. These differences remained significant even among persons with similar denominational affiliations....

*The young*
Not all sectarian groups recommend quietism, however. Nor are the moral communities based on the "holy" way of life the only sectarian solutions available to the lower strata. The moral community built around the "tough" way of life represents an entirely different kind of negativism, one that is entirely secular. Being deliberately "ornery" or simulating the tough way of life is a subcultural trait prevalent among boys' gangs in deteriorated urban areas. The delinquent way of life has recently been described as a solution to the "status problem" of these youths.[2] Lack of recognition of the lower-class youth by controlling agencies—the school, for example—which personify a middle-class moral code is countered by violent rejection of this code.

The tendency of boys to segregate themselves into exclusive groups is not confined, however, to deteriorated neighborhoods of the city. This is an age-graded phenomenon, peculiar neither to lower-class youth, nor to urban and congested neighborhoods, nor to a society that aggravates the status problem by placing a high premium on social mobility.

*Frontiers and sectarian associations*

Sectarian associations—whether sects, gangs, bands, etc.—are also "frontier" phenomena: they are most likely to form among people who push on against a hostile environment, whether geographic or moral. The American West not only sheltered gangs of marauders who warred against established authorities in the legendary style of Jesse James; it was also the locus of several great religious revivals, which reflected its political and economic cleavage with the comfortably settled East. . . . The frontiersman found the respectable religion of the East too tame. He demanded a voluntaristic church in harmony with his democratic and self-reliant way of life.

There is in every metropolitan city what Robert E. Park used to refer to as the *moral frontier*. Here persons from diverse cultural heritages come together. To the immigrant from another milieu such an environment is definitely hostile; he usually enters at the lowest rung of the social ladder and bears the scorn of his self-appointed betters. Most important, he is often forced to adapt to new modes of life without much prior preparation. The organizations among in-migrants are in part a protection against these surroundings. Some religious sects simply defend the migrants against the necessity of making a thoroughgoing readjustment. In-migrants to the North from the rural South have often joined typical secessionist "churches." Other groups, like the infamous Mafia, engage in violent and criminal activities.

*Marginality*

In minority group status lies still another impetus for sectarian associations. This need not always take the form of a return to old cultural traditions. The members of minorities, intent on gaining recognition, may swell the ranks of criminal, political, and esthetic sects. They are naturals for separatist groups, whether on a national, ethnic, or racial basis, as long as their antipathy toward a society that has thwarted their innermost aspirations finds support there. The basis of delinquent gangs and religious sects is often ethnic. Both tend to make use of the same feelings but channel them differently.

*Marginality*—the lack of full acceptance of persons who move on the margins of several groups—is not confined to minority group status. The "alienated" intellectual, trained to use symbols, often lacks the audience he craves for his product and thus seeks sectarian solutions. Some have joined in secret societies—like the Freemasons of the eighteenth and nineteenth centuries, which had strong religious as well as political overtones. Esthetic and religious sects also abound, and there have been many artistic "secessions." A recent example is the "beat" who joins with others in the desire for "genuine" experience. The cult of the "beat generation" seeks no converts. Instead the "beats" cultivate a special kind of experience inaccessible to "squares" with their deliberate bohemianism. . . .

When the attention of such cells turns toward politics, they become the catalysts of revolution. Discontented intellectuals formed the Bolsheviks, the purest of all cells, and beer-hall pamphleteers unable to find employment commensurate with their education developed the ideological hodgepodge that justified Hitler's policies. The various political, literary, intellectual, and even mystical sects both express and contribute to the ferment in society.

*Summary*

Psychologically, then, the majority of sectarians appear to be misfits or outcasts. Frustrated and disappointed in their expectations, they seek fulfillment in some more genuine experience or in devotion to some holy cause. These misfits do not, however, form a social category. But when controlling institutions—family, school, church, government, etc.—fail to function adequately with regard to large segments of the population, they are likely to be experienced as meaningless and, at their worst, as unjust. They become the target of warfare, or some higher power is "called on" to destroy them. Hence, one should expect the tendencies toward sectarian formations to be more pronounced during periods of unrest. Sectarian groups stem from the same— or very similar—objective conditions as the crowds of which they often form the active nuclei.

Those who are most prone to seek sectarian solutions in opposition to conventional modes are: (1) the socially inferior classes who are deprived of their "just" share of social values; (2) the preadolescents and adolescents whose developing adult interests go unrecognized in conventional groups; (3) minority groups and other "marginals" who are not fully accepted; and (4) the rootless intelligentsia frustrated in legitimate employment of their "creative" aspirations. Their readiness for such solutions is further aggravated by an oppressive system of social relationships that stifles the direct expression of deviant tendencies. Thus, despotic regimes, rigid class structure, and extreme conventionality would seem to promote sectarianism.

## Varieties of Active Nuclei

Since the sectarian association arises as an effort by some part of a community to integrate itself anew, its protest against the institutional order rarely encounters support from officialdom. But the radical break on the part of the sectarian takes many forms. These may crystallize in two generally opposite directions. One culminates in the formation of a *gang*; the other in the *sect*, taken in its more narrow religious meaning. Between these two extremes are many mixed forms.

1. By comparison with those of the religious sect, the interests of the gang are not only worldly but concerned with the here and now. The gang has no futuristic illusions and, in fact, often avoids concern with anything but the immediate present; whereas some apocalyptic hope, some promise of redemption, appears an indispensable characteristic of every sect—political as well as religious—although the image of this world is still a potent force.

2. The protest of the religious sect is against prevailing institutions as corruptions of a divine order. The sectarian code seeks to substitute positive rigor where laxness and compromise are the custom. By contrast, the practices of the typical gang are primarily a reversal of order. Instead of rigor, the gang aims to overthrow restraint and substitute license. While the member of the religious sect feels himself superior to secular institutions, the gang follower aspires to remain outside of them. . . .

Whether a gang or a sect will emerge as the predominant form of elementary organization depends on a number of factors, such as the temperaments of the leaders and the following they attract. Furthermore, during periods following decisive political defeat, when there is little hope of either influencing or escaping from one's "fate," protest is apt to be diverted into mysticism and quietism. This occurred in 1908 in Russia after what appeared to the revolutionaries an inexorable setback to an attempt to overthrow the czars. In the Depression decade the down-trodden and homeless poor in the United States turned in large numbers to the Pentecostal churches, while the more active and less enervated embraced Marxism, the Townsend Plan, Technocracy, etc. If, on the other hand, the controlling authorities appear subject to influence or merely ineffective, more active forms of protest are encouraged. The disasters suffered by German cities as a result of Allied bombings thus encouraged marauding by delinquent gangs and bands of foreign laborers. At all times gangs have thrived in the confusion of crowds or in the shelter of "open" spaces. Finally, a passive-resistance movement, a rather unique form of protest in that it combines active political warfare with moral perfectionism and otherworldly holiness usually emerges when it seems that open resistance cannot succeed.

## Gangs

There are many different sectarian associations of the gang variety. Not only groups of delinquent boys but also professional criminals banded together in larceny, bands of marauders, politically active seditious cells, etc., can all be considered as types of gang in active war against the social order. . . .

The emphasis of the political cell is on both mysticism and action. One finds the same linkage in the philosophies of Louis Blanqui, mid-nineteenth-century terrorist and mystic, and of the anarchists. The romanticism of the Russian terrorists—political gangs who had a humanitarian ideology and subscribed to a doctrine of direct action—is legion. In their demand for complete dedication to a revolutionary cause, even the "scientific" Bolsheviks exhibited some mysticism; they were altogether too preoccupied with scholastic doctrinal disputes about many impractical and irrelevant issues. The gang type of conflict association shades into the religious sect and into the conspiratorial group.

## The religious sect

The term "sect" has been applied broadly to include every kind of secessionist tendency, be it with regard to religious, political, scholastic, or esthetic matters. In its popular connotation, a *sect* designates, first, a small group and, second, a transgression of the limits within which all organizational, ideological, or cultural disputes are expected to stay. . . .

The sect has many characteristics that set it off from established religious groups, which are part of the social order. Two of these are essential: the sect is an association that (1) insists on original experience, a charism, as a criterion for admission and thereby (2) substitutes its own internal fellowship, based on an experience open only to the select, for formal religious authority. These characteristics account for the many other specific ones that differentiate the religious sect from the religious denomination. They also distinguish the sect from other types of religious protest: for example, a monastic order finds a place within the framework of the Church; or, again, many secessionist groups acquire, with or without political aid, the legitimate credentials of a dissenting church (as did the Anglican and Lutheran churches) or of a recognized denomination (for instance, religious groups in a pluralistic society).

The sect "gathers a select group and places it in sharp opposition to the world," wrote Troeltsch.[3] Hence the sect, like the gang, has some of the marks of a conflict group. Its survival in a hostile world is greatly facilitated by its rigorous demands on morality. Because of its size, the sect is often powerless. It usually lacks men of influence among its following. In the intensity of devotion on the part of its members and in its doctrinal purity, the sect does however seem able to offset partially what it lacks in worldly resources. The opposition from the social milieu fosters *esprit de corps* and heightens the morale of its members.

But the type of conflict in which the sect engages is very different from that of the gang. The strength of the sect, Faris suggests, lies in the fact that its conflict is with a "world" that is a subjective image. Since the members are so certain of ultimate success, it is possible for the sect to survive great disasters.[4] While the avowed attitude of sectarians to the world may range from toleration and indifference to active hostility, the sect's opposition to existing institutions is masked by apocalyptic and messianic hopes. Prophecies of doom and redemption offer ultimate salvation only for the select. The sectarian, regardless of his explicit avowals, has to some extent turned away from the world. "The sects substitute religious status for social status."[5] They are differentiated according to the varying states of grace. . . .

## The secret society

To protect their association and to cement unity among the membership, many a sectarian group takes on some characteristics of a secret society with an elaborate ritual from which non-members are barred; the neophyte qualifies only after a period of trial and gradual initiation. Unlike the sectarian association, out of which it arises, the secret society is hardly the result of spontaneous interaction. On the contrary, its structure is largely a matter of conscious design, in which nothing is left to chance. The common possession of a secret in itself binds the members together in a pledge of nonbetrayal. In the way the secret represents a unity against outsiders, the secret society has much in common with the other types of sectarian nucleus.

The pledge of silence effectively protects the association from external influence: sometimes by concealing its very existence, as in a revolutionary conspiracy or a criminal band; sometimes by merely preventing the diffusion of knowledge to outsiders about its membership and practices, as in certain fraternal associations. The shared secrets, from which outsiders are excluded, inevitably strengthen internal bonds, because everyone must have explicit confidence in the psychological capacity and honor of those sworn to secrecy.

The protest that differentiates gang from sect is a substantive distinction, but the category of secret society is a formal one. Thus, secrecy has a role in the development of a religious sect, where admission is also made contingent on passing a series of "tests." Access to the secret always marks the initiates as an elite, from which those not yet proved worthy are excluded. In this exclusiveness one observes the foundation of an aristocratic principle. Because secrecy is able to reinforce the superiority of the religiously elect, the natural inclination of the isolated sect is to move in the direction of the secret society.

Gangs also tend to become secret societies. Naturally gangs of assassins, like the Thugs or the Mafia, have employed secrecy to avoid detection, while secret codes and hiding places fascinate even the most innocent of boys' gangs. . . .

Because of its secrecy, the clandestine association enjoys a measure of license. It can transgress normal conventions. In this respect it matters little whether the association harbors a political conspiracy or rebels against the law by engaging in collective crimes. Secret orgies or unorthodox forms of worship (the infamous black mass) may also be substantive motives. Or the association may usurp for itself the right to take the law into its own hands —for example, the twelfth-century Vendicosi, the German Vehmgericht (resurrected in modern form by nationalists following the German surrender after World War I), or the Ku Klux Klan. The essence of the secret society is at least a partial autonomy from the social order from which it segregates itself.

But this autonomy, as Simmel cautions, may easily lead to anarchy. Therefore, the coercive, seemingly senseless, and highly conventionalized practices of the secret society have a definite function: to answer the need for some normative order. . . . The cells of social movements, especially under despotic regimes, thus germinate in the shelter of secrecy.

*The mechanisms of elementary association*
The variety of forms in which alienation from the social order finds elementary expression, the variety of forms which provide shelter in which new norms mature should not obscure their underlying similarities. The following propositions outlining the natural history by which these nuclei come into being summarize the general pattern and need to be modified in relation to the specific forms that they take.

1. Sectarian associations form at the fringes of the social order in response to needs unrecognized by established organizations.

2. The subjective origins of the sectarian association lie in the spontaneous interaction among persons drawn together by some vague disaffection.

3. The opposition that the divergent nucleus excites from its environment solidifies the loose affinities into an association with a group consciousness. Its solidarity, morale, esprit de corps, its conventional practices, and the rudiments of its ideology are promoted by the clash with hostile forces.

4. During its early phases, the internal structure evolves as the direct response to each individual's participation in the common activity.

5. The sectarian association, because of its opposition to the larger society, demands more complete commitment and greater devotion than more segmented organizations. There are few areas in which discretion vis-à-vis fellow members is to be allowed.

6. Two courses appear to be open to the sectarian association that would preserve its integrity in the face of opposition: conventionalization as a clandestine sect or underground organization—a secret society; or accommodation to the dominant society so that it may operate openly as part of it. The readiness with which the sectarian association is able to gain acceptance seems to determine which of the two courses it follows.

## Significance of the Alienated Nucleus

The sectarian association would hardly be considered more than an incidental rubric under collective dynamics were it not for the fact that it marks the transition from elementary and unorganized social patterns into the more organized ones. Thus, the significance of such a group goes beyond the activities of its participants; it constitutes more than a whimsical aberration or a temporary pathology. Not only is it symptomatic of general disaffection but the sectarian association forms the fundament for efforts at general social reconstruction. In this respect its significance is threefold: (1) it offers the psychological support requisite for permanence by which doctrines, cultish fads, and other practices in violation of norms are sustained; (2) ideologies and doctrines, in the shelter of the group, are nurtured to the point at which they can be openly presented; and (3) through agitation and proselytizing the message is ultimately carried to a larger following which constitutes a social movement.

### Psychological validation

The "group psychological support" that participants render to one another in their counternorm behavior constitutes one of the most important facets of the sectarian's psychology. An association usually develops around a key individual, such as an especially daring delinquent, a person endowed with charisma, or a glamorous Hollywood idol. His personal qualities spark behavior among a following. To the extent that the sectarian group monopolizes the loyalties of its following, it lowers self-consciousness in terms of the norms of the larger world by means of a group code, which provides insurance against conventional values and worldly possessions. The group climate is thus conducive to the free expression of unconventional behavior In contrast to the transitory redefinition of behavior in the crowd, the influence of the sectarian association appears to operate to some degree even if other members are not physically together.

One encounters this mutual insurance time and again. A band of criminals bears the guilt evoked by their antisocial acts more easily when they have a model who acts free of guilt. Marie Hossenlopp in her study of juvenile thieves gives an excellent description of how they mutually reinforced one another's behavior.[6] For some members of these gangs, participation under a boy much more antisocial than they constitutes a regression toward a form of infantile activity and sociability; in other words, they revert to the irresponsibility of infancy. In the more highly organized gang, such "guilt insurance" comes from the delinquent code that protects them against identification with individuals who threaten the basic allegiance to the sectarian principles. The Youth Board Worker must be accepted by the "group" as no "threat" before he can hope to make contact with the boys. And "the only good cop is a dead one," so nobody makes friends with a cop—even his brother.

*Maturation of ideology*

To the degree that the sectarian association evolves some more or less stable group code, there is an insistence on purity and full commitment. This, in turn, facilitates the development of an ideology and a strategy for action, which may ultimately reach full fruition in a larger social movement. Thus, the delinquent gang is often the training ground for initiation into the codes and techniques of professional crime. The Essene, pledged to a code of absolute love for his fellow sectarians, prepared the way for the ultimate victory of Christianity.

The role of the "ideologically pure" sectarian nucleus has sometimes been ignored, at other times exaggerated. Wesley used small prayer groups in which mutual confessors kept watch on each other. Lenin in 1902, during the split among Russian Social Democrats, insisted on complete ideological purity. Each revolutionary was to be a professional and subject to the strict supervision of the party. Persons like Martov and Plekhanov (known as Lenin's teacher), who held "heretical" views, were expelled. While it would be an exaggeration to say that the subsequent revolutions occurred according to blueprint, the general ideology, rationale, and thought patterns were nevertheless developed in these nuclei.

### Agitation and proselytization

The discipline and rigorousness of the highly developed sectarian association makes it eminently suitable as an instrument for agitation. The contrast between sectarian associations that are "exclusive" and those that are "universalistic" in their aim has probably been overemphasized. Every developing sect seems to have an urge to find a larger following, even if that following is not initiated into its innermost life. As a matter of fact, sectarian exclusiveness and the quest for universal influence are complementary, rather than antagonistic, principles. The search for influence stems from the imbalance between the divine inspiration of the sectarian group and its rejection by others. The sectarian's total commitment, the conclusion that outsiders are misguided, and the separateness of the sect helps to make the doctrine an effective instrument of persuasion.

Again, it is in political and religious sects that one finds the most active and dedicated proselytizers. The ordinary person is not a *homo politicus*, and his dedication to ideals is only partial. The religious and political ideas that are, as the historians say, always "in the air," are brewed in the sectarian association; to say that ideas are being discussed everywhere is only to say that by one route or another they have entered men's minds. Thus, Trotsky raised the question: Who led the February revolution in Russia which so suddenly led to the abdication of the Czar? He argued against the theory of spontaneous conception: the revolution was not impersonal but merely nameless. . . .[7]

Conscious and experienced workers educated in the party of Lenin brought the unrest to fruition. But, Trotsky immediately adds, they, while able to guarantee the victory of the insurrection, were "not adequate to . . . transfer immediately into the hands of the proletarian vanguard the leadership of the revolution."[8] Clearly, for that, conscious preparation and planning by an active inner core were required. What gives the sectarian revolt or the unfocused collective crime the name of revolution is its ultimate victory. As the sectarian ideology becomes universally sanctioned, there results the kind of mass conversion that genuinely ushers in a new order.

## NOTES

1. John L. Gillin, "A Contribution to the Sociology of Sects," *American Journal of Sociology,* XVI (September, 1910), p. 241.
2. Albert K. Cohen, *Delinquent Boys: The Culture of the Gang* (Glencoe, Ill.: The Free Press, 1955). For another approach, see A. R. Crane, "Pre-Adolescent Gangs: a Socio-Psychological Interpretation," *Journal of Genetic Psychology,* LXXXVI (June, 1955), pp. 275-79.
3. Ernst Troeltsch, *The Social Teachings of the Christian Churches* (London: George Allen and Unwin, Ltd., 1931), p. 339.
4. Ellsworth Faris, "The Sect and the Sectarian," *American Journal of Sociology,* LX (May, 1955), pp. 75-89.
5. Liston Pope, *Millhands and Preachers: A Study of Gastonia* (New Haven: Yale University Press, 1942), p. 137.
6. Marie Hossenlopp, *Essaie psychologique sur les bandes de voleurs jeunes* (Clermont-Ferrand: Imprimerie generale, 1944).
7. Leon Trotsky, *History of the Russian Revolution* (New York: Simon and Schuster, Inc., 1937), p. 151.
8. *Ibid.,* p. 152.

# 5.

# SOCIAL CONTROL

## Neil J. Smelser

Although social control refers to the minimization of the effects of *any* of the stages of value-added, we shall discuss control in the following special sense. A value-oriented belief, once crystallized, has a potential for moving in many directions—it may come to naught; it may form into a cult, a sect, or eventually a denomination; it may become an underground conspiracy; it may secede from the parent body that spawned it; it may grow into a revolutionary attempt to overthrow constitutional authorities. Even at an advanced stage of the development of a value-oriented belief, then, considerable indeterminacy remains as to the direction in which the movement may turn. A major determinant of the course of the movement lies in the behavior of agencies of social control in response to the movement.

*A Model for Containing Value-oriented Movements.* A value-oriented belief arises when the conditions of conduciveness and strain combine in particular ways. What happens to these beliefs once they have arisen is still an open question. To analyze the fortunes of value-oriented movements further, we shall create a model statement of how such a movement can be peacefully contained within a system. This containment involves the selective closing of certain behavioral alternatives and the selective

Reprinted with permission of The Macmillan Co. from *Theory of Collective Behavior*, by Neil J. Smelser. Copyright 1963 by Neil J. Smelser.

opening of others. It involves four kinds of behavior on the part of authorities:

(1) Ruling out uninstitutionalized expression of hostility. . . .

(2) Ruling out direct challenges to legitimacy. This involves drawing a definite circle around those governmental activities which are constitutionally inviolable. Any change in the definition of legitimacy must be carefully restricted and governed by defined procedures—such as the procedures of constitutional amendment.

In the following discussion we shall refer to the successful ruling out of these two behavioral alternatives as "political effectiveness" on the part of the authorities.

(3) Opening channels for peaceful agitation for normative change, and permitting a patient and thorough hearing for the aggrieved groups. We shall refer to this practice as "flexibility" on the part of the authorities.

(4) Attempting to reduce the sources of strain that initiated the value-oriented movement. We shall refer to such behavior as "responsiveness" on the part of the authorities.

If authorities behave in these ways, we should expect the value-oriented movement either to disappear, to change into some other, less threatening kind of movement (e.g., a norm-oriented movement) or to assume a value-oriented form which is containable within the system (e.g., an institutionalized cult, sect, or denomination). This model of containment is not always followed by political authorities, however; correspondingly, a value-oriented movement may take other directions. We shall examine the effects of two frequent ideal-type deviations from the model: (*a*) the effects of permanent political effectiveness, unresponsiveness and inflexibility—or, stated more simply, the effects of permanent repression; (*b*) the effects of a period of repression followed by a weakening of effectiveness. The first tends to drive the movement underground and then into passivity; the second tends to drive the movement underground, or at least into an extreme value-oriented position, and then permits it to rise as a full-scale, and frequently bloody value-oriented revolutionary movement.

*The Effects of Permanent Repression.* Toward the last third of the nineteenth century the white encroachments on Indian lands had reached an apex, and a multiplicity of strains had been imposed on many Indian tribes. The major wars to resist this encroachment had been put down effectively in the mid-1870's. Furthermore, the United States government permitted the continued deterioration of Indian life and failed to respond to the entreaties, petitions, and delegations of the Indians.[1] The whites were pursuing policies, in short, which were effective, inflexible, and unresponsive from the Indians' standpoint.

From the late 1870's onward, Indian protest began to assume a new guise. Active warfare against the whites was by and large limited to guerrilla outbursts; even those were more or less completely repressed by the early 1880's. The Plains Indians, "finding naturalistic forms of readjustment inadequate, . . . turned increasingly to new religions."[2] Many of these were tribal and localized religions; others, notably the Grass Dance and the Hand Game, spread widely. In the 1880's the strongest value-oriented religion was the Ghost Dance, which by and large was millenarian. The ideology of the Ghost Dance limited itself to fantasy destruction of the whites on the whole; on occasion, however, it gave way to violent outbreaks.[3] Also in the late nineteenth century the Peyote religion appeared. This cult was based on a belief envisioning the return of native ways; its ritual centered on the consumption of a powerful drug made from the Peyote cactus.

After the critical turning point of the early 1890's, during which the whites not only effectively crushed the sporadic outbursts associated with the Ghost Dance, but actively discouraged it, the Peyote religion gradually came to represent the dominant Indian mode of adjustment. Slotkin accounts for this evolution as follows:

> The Ghost Dance was not only nativistic but also militant, providing a supernatural means for overthrowing the domination-subordination relation between Whites and Indians. Its central doctrine was the imminent renovation in the world (including the destruction of White society and culture) as a solution for the problems confronting the Indians. The Ghost Dance succumbed to three circumstances. First, the anticipated world renovation did not take place. And there was no reinterpretation of the doctrine to make it viable. . . . Second, the Ghost Dance was involved in the Sioux Disturbance of 1890-91; therefore the rite was prohibited by

White officials in order to maintain the domination-subordination relation between Whites and Indians. Third, after the Sioux Disturbance was ferociously suppressed by the U.S. Army, the Indians became resigned to subordination; consequently they required a program of accommodation rather than the Ghost Dance program of opposition.

The Peyote Religion was nativistic but not militant. Culturally, it permitted the Indians to achieve a cultural organization in which they took pride. Socially, it provided a supernatural means of accommodation to the existing domination-subordination relation.[4]

To sum up, a value-oriented movement under conditions of continuous repression tends to become moribund. It evolves progressively toward the most passive and least politically threatening form of organization, even though the destruction of the oppressors is secretly envisioned. In extreme cases the organization of the movement disappears altogether.[5]

*The Effects of Repression Followed by a Weakening of Effectiveness.* Technically defined, a value-oriented revolution is a combination of a value-oriented belief with a hostile outburst. Hence the social control of hostility is very important for the control of revolutionary movements. In ideal-typical sequence, the value-oriented revolutionary movement unfolds in the following way: The society experiences a period of strain and dissatisfaction which is met by a posture of effectiveness, inflexibility, and unresponsiveness on the part of the agencies of social control. Thus the sequence starts in a way identical to that considered under the heading of permanent repression. After a period, however, when a value-oriented belief has developed, the agencies of social control change their posture; they begin to display inconsistency, vacillation or weakness. At this time the movement begins to evolve toward a value-oriented revolutionary movement. In this model summary of the build-up of the value-oriented revolutionary movement, we are not attempting to account for all revolutionary outbursts. If authorities are ineffective *from the very beginning* of the development of the period of strain, grievances do not smoulder and build into a value-oriented belief. The aggrieved simply overthrow the authorities quickly, as in a *coup d'état* or a palace revolution.

The nationalist revolutions under colonial domination correspond roughly to this ideal-type sequence of repression followed by relaxation. The first phase of colonial domination is pacification, or closing off the possibility of hostile outbursts and challenges to the legitimacy of the colonial power. As strains build up in the colonial situation, value-oriented beliefs begin to crystallize; these remain passive, however, because of the effective repression on the part of the colonial power. The beliefs become revolutionary only when repression relaxes, i.e., when the colonial power changes its policies or weakens to the point of being unable to contain the movement. . . .

The response of the agencies of social control in the Russian Revolution of 1917 displays a similar pattern. During earlier periods of potential revolution—in the Decembrist period of the early nineteenth century, in the terrorist period of the late nineteenth century, and in the two decades leading up to the explosion of 1905—the military forces had remained loyal to the Tsars.[6] In 1917, however, the army and bureaucracy itself were disorganized and unable to contain the protest. The contrast between 1917 and 1905 is especially instructive, since many of the social forces in operation were similar. At both times Russia was experiencing the pains of the early stages of industrialization.[7] In both 1905 and 1917 Russia had been fighting in a foreign war for a substantial period, though the Japanese War was not nearly so exhausting as World War I. The same political parties were struggling for power in 1905 and 1917.[8] The difference between the two periods lay primarily in the degree to which the wielders of force permitted or joined in the revolutionary activity. As Gross notes,

> . . . the revolution of 1905 was to an extent a microcosm of 1917. The Japanese War and defeat was of much smaller dimensions. The workers and peasants revolted, but the army and bureaucracy was still intact. Here and there soldiers and sailors rebelled, it is true. But, in 1905 the whole bureaucratic system and the army apparatus were still intact. Here and there soldiers and sailors rebelled, it is true. But, in 1905 the whole bureaucratic system and the army apparatus were still in operation. *In 1917 the pillars of the tsarist system—the bureaucracy and the army—were disintegrating even before the workers and the people of St. Petersburg revolted.* When the February days came the workers struck, and there were no organized social forces strong enough to support the regime. The workers struck, the population rebelled, the army regiments disintegrated and joined the revolution.[9]

What the Tsarist regime lacked before the February revolution Kerensky also lacked between the February and October revolutions. Faced with mounting inflation and military defeat, unable to introduce reforms of any sort,[10] erratic in its use of force,[11] and unable to command the loyalty or discipline of the military forces,[12] the Kerensky government was snarled in the trap of unresponsiveness, inflexibility and ineffectiveness which made it a target for revolutionary overthrow.

The French Revolution, finally, poses difficult problems of interpretation. For, as Lefebvre has observed, it was not one but several revolutions under a single name.[13] If we restrict our attention to the days of 1789, however, it is possible to observe the interplay of unresponsiveness, inflexibility, and ineffectiveness in this case, too. It should be noted that upon the date of convening the Estates-General in the spring of 1789 no significant body of opinion felt that a political revolution was imminent, even though the utopian ideology of the Enlightenment—in the name of which the Revolution was ultimately perpetrated—was already highly developed.[14] Most of the delegates who convened hoped for certain reforms to be granted in return for financial support of the government. Many preconditions for revolution had, however, been long in the making. These included the definition of opposition to the regime in value-oriented terms; the decay of feudal patterns of authority, with consequent divisions among the traditional ruling classes; widespread strain which affected adversely the nobility, the middle class, the clergy, the peasants, and the workmen; and finally, the crystallization of a set of generalized beliefs of a value-oriented character. What was required for a revolution was a setting in which these conditions could be combined with a successful defiance of authority. The convocation of the Estates-General and the events of the next several months provided the occasion for a succession of such defiances. Actually, these defiances did not always involve a display of violence; sometimes the revolution was accomplished when the King failed to utilize his forces.

The first major governmental capitulation in the face of defiance appeared in connection with the Oath of the Tennis Court on June 20, 1789. Having declared themselves on June 15, in defiance of the King, to be the National Assembly of France, the Third Estate had been ordered suspended until a royal session of June 22. Refusing to suspend operations, the delegates nevertheless found themselves blocked from the usual meeting hall. Thereupon they retired to the tennis court, where they swore they would never separate until a constitution was formed. After a brief period of confusion, the King capitulated without any use of violence on either side and ordered the nobles to join the assembly for further deliberations. This was, in effect, a partial revolution, for there had been a successful defiance of authority and a partial transfer of power.

A second shift in power occurred in the series of riots beginning on July 12, 1789. Necker, the finance minister in whom the Third Estate placed many of its hopes for reforms, was dismissed by the King on July 12. On this day, and the several days following (including July 14, the day of the attack on the Bastille), mobs roamed the streets of Paris, generally unquelled by the King's troops, who were either unable or unwilling to put down the crowds. After these outbursts the King submitted further to the demands of the assembly. He promised to recall Necker; he paid a visit to Paris on July 17; he appointed Lafayette head of the new National Guard and went along with the election of Bailly as Mayor of Paris. Much of the violence in the riots of July 12 and the few days thereafter did not have as a *direct* objective the revolutionary overthrow of the monarchy; indeed the National Assembly wished not to be held responsible for the violence. But the display of violence, and, more important, the inability and unwillingness of the King's troops to put it down forthwith, led to a further capitulation of the King and to another partial revolution.[15]

A third phase of the revolution also involved a show of violence and an equivocal attitude on the part of the authorities. On October 5, a large gathering of starving women marched on Versailles; the next day they attacked the palace. Under the pressure of such events, and under the urging of Lafayette, the King agreed to move to Paris (where he would be under more direct threat and control of the people), and also agreed finally to accepting the Declaration of the Rights of Man.[16]

By such stages the revolution proceeded to run its course, changes of power gradually shifting as it became apparent that the forces of order were inadequate to control the displays of violence. Sometimes this violence arose for reasons such as hunger, price changes, etc. In each case, however, the disturbance revealed the fundamental weakness of the constituted authorities.

These examples from revolutions in underdeveloped areas and from the West illustrate the importance of agencies of social control in the later stages of value-oriented movements. Other examples could be given. To summarize: If a value-oriented movement is to assume a revolutionary cast, authorities *at some level*—perhaps at the top level, perhaps at some regional level, perhaps at the middle-officer level, perhaps at the level of the troops themselves—must appear to be unable or unwilling to enforce their authority. Since force is an ultimate sanction in political control, the *possibility* of its use always is present when a movement turns in a revolutionary direction. This is not to say that violence always appears in a value-oriented revolution. Perhaps the authority capitulates without a show of force if he considers himself sufficiently at a disadvantage. Perhaps adherents of the movement itself will not engage in a show of force if they appear unlikely to succeed. Sometimes the appearance of force will not involve a frontal attack on the authorities by a revolutionary group itself, but will be the occurrence of violence *somewhere else* in the system which the authority is unable to handle. The revolutionary opposition may capitalize on this incapacity, even though the revolutionary group did not perpetrate the violence. Thus, when a movement becomes revolutionary, violence is always a possibility; whether it becomes an actuality, and how it becomes an actuality are open questions.

## NOTES

1. Slotkin, *The Peyote Religion* (Glencoe, Ill., 1956), pp. 9-17.
2. *Ibid.*, p. 17.
3. The most notable occasion is the Ghost Dance outbreak of violence among the Sioux in 1890-91. Cf. Mooney, "The Ghost-Dance Religion and the Sioux Outbreak of 1890," *Fourteenth Annual Report of the Bureau of Ethnology*, Part 2 (Washington, 1896),

pp. 819-828; also pp. 706-724 for other instances of outbreaks. See also MacGregor, *Warriors Without Weapons* (Chicago, 1946), pp. 32-33, and Lesser, *The Pawnee Ghost Dance Hand Game* (New York, 1933), pp. 53-67.

4. *The Peyote Religion*, p. 21. See also B. Barber, "A Socio-Cultural Interpretation of the Peyote Cult," *American Anthropologist*, Vol. 43 (1941), pp. 673-674; Petrullo, *The Diabolic Root* (Philadelphia, 1934), pp. 26-27.

5. For an example of the organizational collapse of a native movement under the arrest of its leader, cf. Krader, "A Nativistic Movement in Western Siberia," *American Anthropologist*, Vol. 58 (1956), p. 288.

6. Gross, *The Seizure of Power in a Century of Revolutions* (New York, 1958), pp. 63-79, 125-130, 151-186.

7. Kohn, *Revolutions and Dictatorships* (Cambridge, Mass., 1939), pp. 91-92.

8. Gross, *The Seizure of Power in a Century of Revolutions*, p. 183; L. Gottschalk, "Causes of Revolution," *American Journal of Sociology*, Vol. 50 (July, 1944), p. 7.

9. *The Seizure of Power in a Century of Revolutions*, p. 194. One further difference between 1905 and 1917 was that in the former the Tsar made an "ersatz" capitulation to popular demands and created a parliamentary or advisory body which was soon to lose any effectiveness which was originally promised. Pp. 182-193. For further evidence on the disorder in the Tsarist regime, cf Florinsky, *The End of the Russian Empire* (New Haven, 1931), Chs. IV, IX; N.N. Golovine, *The Russian Army in the World War* (New Haven, 1931), Chs. X, XI; Trotsky, *History of the Russian Revolution* (Ann Arbor, 1957), Vol. 1, pp. 16-32, 76-79.

10. Trotsky, *History of the Russian Revolution*, Vol. I, pp. 183, 203-204, 224, 271, 376; Vol. II, pp. 140-331.

11. *Ibid.*, Vol, II, pp. 50, 223.

12. *Ibid.*, Vol. I, pp. 248-266, 373, 389; Vol. II, pp. 283, 346; Vol. III, pp. 69, 187, 288.

13. *The Coming of the French Revolution* (New York, 1959), p. 5.

14. *Ibid.*, p. 179; Tocqueville, *The Old Regime and the French Revolution* (New York, 1856), p. 15; Stephens, *History of the French Revolution* (New York, 1886), Vol. I, pp. 9-10.

15. The accounts of the last two paragraphs are taken from Stephens, *History of the French Revolution*, Vol. I, pp. 60-155.

16. *Ibid.*, pp. 221-228.

# 6.

# ARMIES AND THE ART OF REVOLUTION

## K. C. Chorley

The position of the armed forces in a modern state runs parallel to that of the civil service. The armed forces are responsible for the maintenance of law and order and for the defence of the realm. The civil service is responsible for the administration of communal life. Both are at the orders of the duly chosen government of the day and are constitutionally bound to carry out the policy of that government. This position is, however, rather a constitutional conception than a constitutional fact. So far as the armed forces are concerned the theory has been evolved with the evolution of standing armies in order to guard against the perils of irresponsible military force. But in practical political life it is found that the theory is apt to break down in application at times of crisis; it puts too great a strain on political human nature. Armies are not in fact set apart from politics. In smooth political periods, where there are no particular clashes of interest between governors and governed, or between various sections of a community, the army is to all appearance merely a part of the machinery of government and politically innocuous. But in communities where deep fissures of angry opinion develop to separate classes and political parties the soldiers appear in their true colours and take their political stand on whatever side their sentiments may lie.

Reprinted with permission of the author and Faber and Faber from *Armies and the Art of Revolution*, by K. C. Chorley. Copyright 1943 by K. C. Chorley.

Broadly speaking, an army reproduces in its own character the structure of society in which it has grown up. Where this is a class structure it means in practice that the main features of army character will square with those of the traditionally strongest classes in the community. The corps of officers will be chosen from those classes and the rank and file will be subjected to a system of discipline and influence designed to make them so much docile material in the hands of their officers. Experience proves that the process of politically sterilizing the rank and file can be carried through, given favorable conditions of service, to an astonishing degree of success. The importance attached by a politician like Pitt to keeping the army from civil contacts is significant. As a result, an enormous reservoir of power is in effect placed at the disposal of the officers and can be used by them without let or hindrance to further their own political aims. Experience also proves that the officers have seldom hesitated to use this power when their interests have been seriously threatened. Hence, when they are drawn mainly from one particular class of the community, or from the ranks of one particular political party, their power will effectually be at the beck and call of that class or party.

In a static society this condition of affairs offers no particular danger, but where a society is gradually but steadily changing in character it is a different story. In such a case it may easily happen that the army does not keep pace with the rest of society and that its structure still reflects the social forces of an earlier time. Here the danger from the army is obvious. It may at any time clash with the progressive drive of the community. The social and political structure of this country, for instance, evolved slowly but surely all through the nineteenth century away from the traditional balance between Whigs and Tories and in the direction of modern democracy, reaching perhaps its zenith of development under the great Radical Governments of 1906-14. But the social structure of the armed forces showed no parallel development. It lagged behind and was no longer a reflection of the structure of society at large. Thus, when the democratic Liberal Government required the sanction of armed force, not perhaps in a very just but certainly in a legal cause, it found that the army, as represented by its officers, was to all intents and purposes a private army of the Conservative party. Disliking the cause it was asked to support, it had no hesitation in jamming the machine of democratic government.

Where a social structure is crumbling and unstable the chances that the army will back partisan politics by force or the threat of force are even greater. The causes of the crumbling are of secondary importance. It may be that an incapable democracy finds itself unable to rule the differences of turbulent political parties or to ride an economic storm as in Italy and Germany before the triumph of Fascism and Nazism. It may be that, as in nineteenth-century Spain, the system of rule has become so effete and out of touch with the spirit of the times that it can no longer effectively control the machinery of government. The result in any event is the same; the army becomes by one means or other the arbiter of policy.

In modern times, these dangers are enormously increased owing to the complexity and power of modern weapons of war which put a regular army in an invincible position as against amateur levies. The exclusive or preponderating weight of guns, tanks, and airplanes, besides munitions, on one side of the balance is decisive. Hence the more modern and efficient the technical equipment of an army, the more it is to be feared by a government with whose policy it seriously disagrees. It follows then that the position of the army in almost any society is the pivot on which that society swings; and in practice this usually means the position of the corps of officers.

Owing to the immense technical superiority of trained and fully equipped troops, it can be laid down that no revolution will be won against a modern army when that army is putting out its full strength against the insurrection. Practical experience proves this to be the case. No revolution has in fact been won under those conditions. And apparent exceptions to this rule show on investigation special features which mean that the striking power of the army has been in effect seriously curtailed and weakened. In a revolutionary situation the attitude of the army is therefore of supreme importance. It is the decisive factor on which will depend success or failure. The army's attitude will be determined in part by the corps of officers and in part by the rank and file.

The evidence suggests that widespread disaffection among officers is generally sufficient in practice to paralyze the striking power of the army. We have the testimony of 1688 and of 1913-14 in this country, and in Spain the witness of 1936, where the disaffected officer corps not only paralyzed the army by depriving it of leadership but dragged it over almost intact to its own side. Since most armies, and this has been particularly true of the British, are officered by men drawn from the propertied classes of the community, it is scarcely reasonable to suppose that the officers will in any circumstances be drawn over to support a proletarian revolution. In modern times, disaffection in an officers' corps is likely to have other aims. It may be used to further a Fascist revolt against a democratic government as it has been in Spain; or it may be used to hamstring some particular policy of an advanced government bent on reform of the social system, and which has not had the foresight or perhaps the power to reform its army before attacking the system on whose character that army has been modeled.

Revolutionary leaders of the Left depend upon disaffection in the rank and file if they are to gain the support of the army or paralyze its opposition during a revolution. In practice, the rank and file whatever may be their apparent class interests and sympathies, are far more politically sluggish than their officers and far less easily moved to mutinous action on their own account. This is due to the care with which a ring fence is built round them in order to cut them off from civilian interests and provide an empty field in which they may be conditioned to accept unquestioningly their officers' influence. Again and again, as the evidence of the preceding pages has shown, the rank and file have accepted their officers' lead to the extent of breaking an insurrection on whose success their own class interests depended.

Practical grievances relating to conditions of service will have some effect in promoting mutinous agitation among the rank and file. But it is very doubtful how far the discontent they feel can be turned to political ends, unless it is very widespread and deep and is identified in the minds of the men with a particular system of government, and not merely with a particular set of governing officials. This is an important distinction. It is a valid difference between the disaffection in the Stuart Navy in 1692 and the disaffection in the Navy during the Spithead and Nore mutinies. In the Stuart case the king represented the system of society; in the other case the Admiralty represented only a particular ministry and a particular House of Commons. In any event, practical grievances have an inherent weakness which counteracts their strength as solvents fit to disintegrate the rank and file of an army. They can always be remedied by the government of the *status quo* and once the cause for discontent is removed the rank and file slip back to their old position. It has been shown how the Russian Government took care to remedy the soldiers' grievances in 1905-6 thereby checking their temptation to support the revolution. Practical grievances have a second inherent weakness. It is extraordinarily difficult to turn them to revolutionary account because the agitation they occasion is unlikely to be under the control of political leaders, and mutinies will break out regardless of any general revolutionary situation. It has been shown for instance how Wolfe Tone tried to gain direction of the discontent in the British fleet and yet how unready he was to make use of it when the actual explosion came. It will be a mere matter of luck whether such outbreaks can be related to a general revolutionary situation. In the pre-revolutionary period leaders will no doubt exploit them to the fullest possible extent but they will not rely upon them when gauging the attitude that the army will take up when the revolution breaks out.

History suggests that the only solvent likely to disintegrate the rank and file against the will of their officers in an unsuccessful large-scale war. The army will be ripe for disintegration either immediately after the war or towards its end when it is disillusioned by suffering and defeat. The way is cleared for disintegration by two fundamental changes in the character of the army brought about by wartime conditions. One change regards the rank and file. The enormous wastage of modern war added to the necessary expansion of the armed forces means that the ranks must be filled on a vast scale from the civilian population. And the civilians must be taught soldiering in the shortest possible space of time. Hence there is no opportunity to wean them from their civilian interests and cut them off from their civilian background. The rank and file approximates to the type of a citizen army and the soldiers of citizen armies, as has been shown in some detail with reference to the French National Guard and the English militia, are not politically emasculated. The terms of their service prevent this; they carry with them into their military life all the political and class affiliations and sympathies of their civilian life.

The second change regards the corps of officers. Here again the wastage and expansion are both enormous. Thus, as the war drags on, it will be found that the officers' corps is manned more and more by men who have little or nothing in common with those sections of the community from which the old officers' corps was drawn and do not share the old professional and social ideals. It will be manned by promotion from the ranks and by a wide recruitment from all classes of the civil population. In practice this means that the old influence of the officers' corps over the rank and file is completely undermined. It is undermined partly because the rank and file are now politically alive on their own account and partly because the officers' corps has lost every characteristic of a military caste. The army, both officers and men, is in fact the nation in arms. It is an army of individuals subject like other individual citizens to every storm of political passion which may sweep over the country.

From the foregoing summing up of the position of a modern army in the state, and its social and political characteristics and the circumstances in which it may be expected to take partisan political action, as regards both officers and men, two general conclusions may be drawn: the one regards revolutionary action, the other regards the defence of democracy.

Revolutionary action, whether social or nationalist, implies a clash with trained troops who have all the advantage of modern equipment, supplies, and administrative machinery behind them. Where these troops are exerting their full effort it is impossible to win a revolution against them. In certain circumstances an unsuccessful revolt may be worthwhile on the score of long-term revolutionary strategy. It may frighten and intimidate the government of the *status quo* into making concessions, or it may consolidate and inspire a revolutionary party, as for instance happened in Italy in 1848, in Ireland after the Easter Rebellion, or in Spain after the Asturias Insurrection. On the whole, however, an unsuccessful revolt does not justify itself and frequently does irremediable harm to the movement it seeks to further.

The object of a revolution is to win it. It follows therefore that the first business of revolutionary leaders will be to assess, before launch'ng the revolution, the probable strength and attitude of the armed forces which will be opposed to them. This assessment will be made, not only in regard to the objective strength and the subjective character of those forces, but also in regard to the special conditions in which the revolution will be fought out. It may happen that the theoretical strength of the opposing forces is in practice sufficiently weakened owing to the circumstances, sometimes geographical, sometimes political, and sometimes both, in which they have to operate. This is particularly true of the American Revolution, where the distance from the base in England and the extreme difficulty of the transport of men and supplies, coupled with the fact that the British Army was on the whole fighting to penetrate a hostile area, contributed in no small measure to the ultimate success of the Colonists. It is also to a large extent true of the Sinn Fein Revolution, where the opposition of a large section of public opinion in England and the fear of awkward repercussions abroad added to the advantages which the Irish derived from conducting guerrilla warfare against the background of a friendly population and in a rural territory, crippled the effective striking power of the British Army and police. These favorable conditions will be more likely to occur in nationalist than in social revolts. In social revolts it is unlikely that the revolutionaries will have the benefit of a homogeneous population behind them. Nor is it likely that they will have the benefit of any compact geographical region to use as an undisturbed base for training their levies and assembling their supplies.

The social revolt presents, therefore, on the whole a more difficult problem than the nationalist revolt. Under certain rather rare conditions, as in France in 1830 and 1848, and in Spain in 1931, social revolt has succeeded without active disintegration of the army. The explanation of this is simple. The government of the *status quo* feels weak and uncertain and prefers to abdicate without provoking a serious armed clash.

Charles X, Louis Philippe, and Alphonso XIII never tried out the issue between troops and people. Thus the question of army disintegration did not seriously arise. It was never put to the test whether the common soldier would follow his general or swing back to his natural social place among the revolting populace. But under a strong and courageous government, which is prepared and able to fight out the issue to the bitter end, the disintegration of the armed forces is essential for success. Where armies of the old non-democratic type are in question this disintegration will almost certainly only take place towards the end of or after an unsuccessful war, since it is probable that only unsuccessful war produces a set of conditions sufficiently strong to act as solvents of army unity. Hence, where severe opposition is to be expected, the chances for revolutionary action are most favourable at this period. The apparent exception to this rule, presented by the swing-over of the French Army to the Revolution in 1789, can be explained in terms of special conditions. Outstanding among them was the fact that the officers at first encouraged discontent by their attitude and at no period presented a united active front against the revolution except as èmigrés.

In planned insurrections the leaders are in a position to work before the outbreak to increase all conditions favouring disintegration of the army. Practical grievances of the soldiers can be exploited, political propaganda can be carried on, the insurrection can be timed for an advantageous date. Finally, at the moment of outbreak, fraternization can be attempted.

In spontaneous mass uprisings, which catch revolutionary leaders unawares, or before their plans are matured, less will be effected beforehand. It will then be their business to gain control as rapidly as possible of the instinctive revolutionary movement and direct it to the best advantage. Fraternization will be the only means open to them of influencing the morale of the troops.

In those armies which have the character described for citizen armies, the influence of the officers' corps over the rank and file is weak. Hence, at the impact of social revolution, the armed forces may be expected to split according to their class and political interests. This conclusion, however, is based on general reasoning from the behaviour of citizen armies. It has never been put to a large-scale practical test, since no serious social revolution has taken place in those countries which maintain exclusively armies of militia type.

The long-service army with a professional officers' corps is not amenable to influence from the Left in any serious degree, but it does appear markedly amenable to fascist influences coming through Right channels. The reasons for this lie in the character of the officers' corps which makes it in effect the custodian of conservatism and the privileges of property, in the tendency of the officers' corps to support party politics with the sanction of force when their political interests are gravely threatened or their political emotions aroused, and in the ascendancy which the officers' corps gains over the rank and file.

A progressive government which is driving its way along the road of social reconstruction by constitutional means may find itself hamstrung if it maintains an army of this type.

A democracy, struggling against some storm of political disillusion and economic depression which finds a fascist focus, may discover too late that its armed forces are no defense.

# PART V

# Consequences of Revolution

# 1.

# RADICALIZATION OF
# REVOLUTIONARY GOVERNMENT

## Crane Brinton

At this stage in revolution, then, the moderates in control of the formal machinery of government are confronted by the extremists, or if you prefer, merely by radical and determined opponents, in control of machinery devised for propaganda, pressure-group work, even insurrection, but now increasingly used as machinery of government. This stage ends with the triumph of the extremists and the merging of the dual sovereignty into a single one. We must now inquire into the reasons for the failure of the moderates in these revolutions to hold power.

There is first the paradox we have previously noted, that in the early stages of revolution the control of the machinery of government is in itself a source of weakness for those who hold such control. Little by little the moderates find themselves losing the credit they had gained as opponents of the old regime, and taking on more and more of the discredit innocently associated by the hopeful many with the status of heir to the old regime. Forced on the defensive, they make mistake after mistake, partly because they are so little used to being on the defensive. They are in a position from which only a superhuman wisdom could extricate them; and the moderates are among the most human of revolutionaries.

Faced with the opposition of more radical groups organized in the network we have called the illegal government, the moderates have broadly but three choices: they may try to suppress the illegal government; they may try to get control of it themselves; or they may let it alone. Actually their policy shifts around among these three policies, combining one with another; in these circumstances, the net effect is to produce a fourth policy, which amounts to a positive encouragement of their enemies in the illegal government.

In the revolutions we are studying the moderates are particularly handicapped in their efforts to suppress these enemy organizations. The revolutions were all made in the name of freedom, were all —even the Russian February Revolution—associated with what the Marxists call a bourgeois individualistic ideology. The moderates found themselves obliged to observe certain "rights" of their enemies—notably those of freedom of speech, of the press, of assembly. What is more, many if not most of the moderates sincerely believed in such rights, held that truth is great and will prevail. Had it not just prevailed against the tyranny of the old regime? Even when under pressure the moderate begins to try to suppress an extremist newspaper, forbid an extremist meeting, jail a few extremist leaders, his conscience troubles him. More important, any unsuppressed extremists raise a mighty howl. The moderates are betraying the revolution; they are using exactly the same methods the villainous tyrants of the old regime had used.

The Russian Revolution is here an excellent example. The Kadets and compromisists between February and October could not conveniently suppress Bolshevik propaganda, nor indeed any form of Bolshevik political activity. When they tried to do so after a premature Bolshevik rising, the street troubles in Petrograd known as the "July Days," they were met by protests from all sorts of people, including notably the Bolsheviks. This was despotism, this was Czarism of the worst sort. Had not the February Revolution brought political freedom, freedom of the press and association, to Russia forever? Kerensky mustn't make use of the kind of weapons the Czars had used. Stalin of course could later use methods worthy of Peter the Great or Ivan the

Terrible, but that is only to say that the moderate, the "liberal" phase of the Russian Revolution was unquestionably over by the time Stalin took power. In 1917, however, even had Kerensky been the sort of man who could successfully organize repressive measures—and he plainly was not that sort of man—what we are bound to call public opinion would not in those days have permitted the execution of such measures. Much the same situation is to be found in France, where the Jacobins were permitted free speech and free association, and firmly and publicly insisted on their rights as free men to get ready for a dictatorship by suppressing the "enemies of the fatherland"—that is, what was left of royalists, non-juring priests, active conservatives.

Nor are the moderates more successful in their attempts to get —or rather to retain—control of the machinery which they and the extremists had jointly built up as a means of overthrowing the old regime. For this there seems to be no single preponderant reason. The moderates are, of course, occupied with a good deal of the work of actual governing, and they have less time for army committees or Jacobin clubs or soviet meetings. They feel themselves perhaps a trifle superior to such activity. They are temperamentally unfitted for the rougher and dirtier work of the politics of direct action. They have moral scruples. They are not quite the noble souls historical legend makes out the Girondin moderates in the French Revolution to have been; indeed many of them, like Brisot and Kerensky, have a good many of the gifts of the political manipulator. But they are in power, and they seem to set about quite naturally cultivating the sober virtues that go with power. Such virtues, however, make them inadequate leaders of militant revolutionary societies.

Whatever the explanation, the fact of the uniformity is clear. This particular failure of the moderates is well shown in the French Revolution. The Jacobin network of societies of "Friends of the Constitution" was in its inception hardly to the Left of Lafayette and his friends. When, however, it began to move further to the Left the Fayettists made a few feeble efforts to retain control, and then went off and founded their own society, the Feuillants. The Feuillants, however, could not spread with much success beyond narrow upper-class and intellectual Parisian circles. Later groups founded here and there throughout the country as "Friends of the Monarchy," or "Friends of Peace," tried to compete with the Jacobins, but with very little luck. If they gave bread to the poor, the Jacobins cried out that they were attempting bribery. If they did nothing, the Jacobins complained that they lacked social conscience. Finally the Jacobins worked out a fairly systematic procedure. They would hire a few hoodlums—sometimes it was not necessary to hire them—to break up a meeting of the rival Friends of Peace, and would then send a deputation to the municipal authorities asking that the Friends of Peace be closed as a public nuisance. The authorities were either Jacobins themselves, or more afraid of the Jacobins than of the Friends of Peace, so that the matter received a suitable revolutionary solution.

Similarly the Presbyterians found themselves powerless to control the spread of Independency, not only in the army, but in local parishes. And in Russia the compromisists found the Bolsheviks formidable in all the important soviets. A detailed study of the Petrograd soviet from February to October will show how cleverly the party of Lenin took advantage of every mistake of its opponents, how successfully it burrowed from within, spreading its control from factory soviets on up until finally the city soviet was captured. Such a study will also show the compromisists gradually losing ground, in spite of the great oratorical gifts of leaders like Tseretelli, Chkheidze, and Kerensky.

There is, indeed, an almost organic weakness in the position of the moderates. They are placed between two groups, the disgruntled but not yet silenced conservatives and the confident, aggressive extremists. There are still freedom of speech and the other political rights, so that even conservatives have a voice. Now the moderates seem in all these revolutions to be following the slogan used so conspicuously for French politics of the *Cartel des Gauches* in 1924, a slogan that still gives difficulties to the noncommunist Left throughout the Western world today: "no enemies to the Left." They distrust the conservatives, against whom they have so recently risen; and they are reluctant to admit that the extremists, with whom they so recently stood united, can actually be their enemies. All the force of the ideas and sentiments with which the moderates entered the revolution give them a sort of twist toward the Left. Emotionally they cannot bear to think of themselves as falling behind in the revolutionary process. Moreover, many of them hope to outbid the extremists for popular support, to beat them at their own game. But only in normal times can you trust in the nice smooth clichés of politics like "beat them at their own game." The moderates fail by this policy of "no enemies to the Left" to reconcile these enemies to the Left; and they make it quite impossible to rally to their support any of the not yet quite negligible conservatives. Then, after the moderates get thoroughly frightened about the threatening attitude of the extremists, they turn for help to the conservatives, and find there just aren't any on hand and available. They have emigrated, or retired to the country, hopeless and martyred in spirit. Needless to say, a martyred conservative is no longer a conservative, but only another maladjusted soul. This last turn of theirs toward the conservatives, however, finishes the moderates. Alone, unsupported in control of a government as yet by no means in assured and habitual control of a personnel, civil or military, they succumb easily to insurrection. It is significant that Pride's Purge, the French crisis of June 2, 1793, and the Petrograd October Revolution were all hardly more than *coups d'état*.

In the English, French, and Russian revolutions it is possible to distinguish one critical measure around which all these currents converge, a measure which, espoused by the moderates, cuts them off from support on the Right and leaves the radicals in a position to use this very measure against its authors. Such are the Root-and-Branch Bill in the English Revolution, the Civil Constitution of the Clergy in the French, and Order Number One in the Russian.

The Root-and-Branch Bill originated in a petition with 15,000 signatures presented to the House of Commons late in 1640, asking for the abolition of Episcopacy "with all its roots and branches." Naturally the moderate Episcopalians, from Hyde and Falkland to Digby, were against a measure which destroyed their Church; and just as naturally the Presbyterians were inclined to favor it. It is possible that politically minded moderates like Pym might have left the bill alone, but the refusal of the bishops to give up their seats in the House of Lords seems to have determined Pym to support the bill. This espousal made almost every thorough Episcopalian some kind of Royalist, and when the Civil War broke out in 1642 the Presbyterians were stranded on the extreme Right of the party groupings within the region controlled by the Parliamentarians. They could find no possible allies except to the Left. The Independents—and Cromwell had first actually introduced the Root-and-Branch Bill in the House—could now argue that presbyters were no better than bishops, that the reasons which held for the abolition of one held incontrovertibly for the abolition of the other. Later, when the moderates proved incapable of carrying the war to a successful conclusion, measures like the Self-Denying Ordinance and the creation of the New Model Army had to be accepted by a Presbyterian majority which was not by any means a commanding majority, and which had left itself with no possibility of conservative support.

The Civil Constitution of the Clergy emerged after months of discussion in the National Assembly as a charter for renewed Christianity in France. The moderates who put it through seem mostly to have been sincere men, bad Catholics in some ways, perhaps, but rather because they had absorbed some of the practical wordly spirit of the age than because they were outright anticlericals or "freethinkers." Yet their measure alienated the good Catholics and merely encouraged the violent freethinkers to try to root out the "vile superstitions" of Christianity altogether. The Civil Constitution in all innocence provided for the election of parish priests by the same local electoral bodies that chose lay officials for the new government positions, and for the election of bishops by the same departmental body that elected representatives to the Legislative Assembly. It scrapped all the historic dioceses of old France, and substituted nice, nearly uniform dioceses identical with the new *départements* into which France was governmentally divided. It did consent to "notify" the Pope of such elections.

Since the property of the Church as a corporation had been taken over to serve as security for the new paper money of the revolution, the *assignats*, the State was to support the expenses of the clergy under the new constitution. The election of priests and bishops by bodies to which Protestants, Jews, and avowed atheists were theoretically eligible was so completely uncanonical that no Pope could for a moment have considered accepting it. Although there was the usual diplomatic delay, the break between the Pope and the revolutionary government was inevitable, and with it a powerful and conservative group of Catholics was forced irreconcilably into opposition. The new Constitutional Church was hardly more acceptable to the real radicals than the old Roman Catholic Church, and as the critical days of the Terror drew nearer the moderates found themselves saddled with the protection of a church which returned them no important support.

Order Number One emerged from no such long debate as did the Root-and-Branch Bill and the Civil Constitution of the Clergy. Indeed, it is not quite fair to list it as a definite measure sponsored by the moderates, though the soviet leader most prominent in the group which prepared it was the moderate N. D. Sokolov, and the compromisists energetically promulgated it. The Order emerged in the very last days of the February Revolution from the headquarters of the Petrograd soviet. It was addressed to the army, and in addition to the usual revolutionary measures toward a standing army of the old regime—abolition of salutes, social and political equality of privates with officers, and so on—it provided for elected company and battalion committees which were to have entire charge of arms, above all of those of officers; and it ordered that every military unit obey the soviets in political matters. The military committee of the duma might be obeyed in military matters, provided the soviet did not object in a specific case. The Order was devised primarily with the Petrograd garrison in mind, but its main provisions were rapidly taken up at the front. This order at once convinced the conservatives that there was nothing to be hoped for from the revolution, and put even the more liberal officers in a state of mind to welcome later attempts at a conservative *coup d'état*. It made the subsequent task of the moderates in bringing Russia back to military efficiency for the war on Germany more difficult than ever. And it by no means served to reconcile the soldiers themselves with the continuation of the war. Most of the popularity of Order Number One eventually redounded to the credit of the Bolsheviks; most of its unpopularity came back on the compromisists. This is the typical fate of the moderates in these revolutions.

Again, the moderates are in all our societies confronted sooner or later with the task of fighting a war; and they prove poor war leaders. In England the fighting broke out in 1642, and before the first Civil War was over Cromwell and the Independents had made themselves indispensable, and were on the threshold of power. Foreign war in France broke out in the spring of 1792, and a few months later the monarchy had fallen; the war went very badly in the spring of 1793, and in June the moderate Girondins, who had on the French side been the most eager for war, were turned out by the Montagnards. The Russian Revolution was born in the midst of a disastrous war, and the Russian moderates never had a chance at peaceful administration. The fact is clear. The moderates cannot seem to succeed in war. The reasons why are less clear. No doubt the commitment of the moderates to protect the liberties of the individual is a factor. You cannot organize an army if you take Liberty, Equality, and Fraternity at all seriously.

Modern wars seem to carry with them the necessity for organizing civil government along military lines, for the exercise of strong, centralized governmental authority in which the liberty of the individual is far from a matter of first concern, in which there is very little debate, very little of the government by discussion so prized by the moderates, very little compromise and moderation. War, said Madison, is the mother of executive aggrandizement, and even here in America our wars have borne him out. But in the midst of a revolution the executive that gets aggrandized is not the moderate executive. The Reigns of Terror in France and in Russia are in part explicable as the concentration of power in a government of national defense made necessary by the fact of war. This is by no means a complete explanation of the Reigns of Terror. But certainly the necessity for a strong centralized government to run the war is one of the reasons why the moderates failed. They simply could not provide the discipline, the enthusiasm, the unpondered loyalty necessary to fight a war, and they went out. . . .

### The Accession of the Extremists

The rule of the extremists we have called the crisis period. This period was not reached in the American Revolution, though in the treatment of Loyalists, in the pressure to support the army, in some of the phases of social life, you can discern in America many of the phenomena of the Terror as it is seen in our three other societies. We cannot here attempt to go into the complicated question as to why the American Revolution stopped short of a true crisis period, why the moderates were never ousted in this country, or at least ousted only in 1800. We must repeat that we are simply trying to establish certain uniformities of description, and are not attempting a complete sociology of revolutions.

The extremists are helped to power no doubt by the existence of a powerful pressure toward centralized strong government, something which in general the moderates are not capable of providing, while the extremists, with their discipline, their contempt for half measures, their willingness to make firm decisions, their freedom from libertarian qualms, are quite able and willing to centralize. Especially in France and Russia, where powerful foreign enemies threatened the very existence of the nation, the machinery of government during the crisis period was in part constructed to serve as a government of national defense. Yet though modern wars, as we know in this country, demand a centralization of authority, war alone does not seem to account for all that happened in the crisis period in those countries.

What does happen may be a bit oversimply summarized as follows: emergency centralization of power in an administration, usually a council or commission, and more or less dominated by a "strong man"—Cromwell, Robespierre, Lenin; government without any effective protection for the normal civil rights of the individual—or if this sounds unrealistic, especially for Russia, let us say the normal private life of the individual; setting up of extraordinary courts and a special revolutionary police to carry out the decrees of the government and to suppress all dissenting individuals or groups; all this machinery ultimately built up from a relatively small group—Independents, Jacobins, Bolsheviks—which has a monopoly on all governmental action. Finally, governmental action becomes a much greater part of all human action than in these societies in their normal condition: this apparatus of government is set to work indifferently on the mountains and molehills of human life—it is used to pry into and poke about corners normally reserved for priest or physician, or friend, and it is used to regulate, control, and plan the production and distribution of economic wealth on a national scale.

## Reigns of Terror and Virtue

This pervasiveness of the Reign of Terror in the crisis period is partly explicable in terms of the pressure of war necessities and of economic struggles as well as of other variables: but it must probably also be explained as in part the manifestation of an effort to achieve intensely moral and religious ends here on earth. The little band of violent revolutionists who form the nucleus of all action during the Terror behave as men have been observed to behave before when under the influence of active religious faith. Independents, Jacobins, Bolshcviks, all sought to make all human activity here on earth conform to an ideal pattern, which, like all such patterns, seems deeply rooted in their sentiments. A striking uniformity in all these patterns is their asceticism, or if you prefer, their condemnation of what we may call the minor as well as the major vices. Essentially, however, these patterns are a good deal alike, and all resemble closely what we may call conventional Christian ethics. Independents, Jacobins, and Bolsheviks, at least during the crisis period, really make an effort to enforce behavior in literal conformity with these codes or patterns. Such an effort means stern repression of much that many men have been used to regarding as normal; it means a kind of universal tension in which the ordinary individual can never feel protected by the humble routines to which he had been formed: it means that the intricate prerevolutionary network of customary interactions among individuals—a network which is still to the few men devoted to its intelligent study almost a complete mystery—this network is temporarily all torn apart. John Jones, the man in the street, the ordinary man, is left floundering.

We are almost at the point of being carried away into the belief that our conceptual scheme is something more than a mere conveneince, that it does somehow describe "reality." At the crisis, the collective patient does seem helpless, thrashing his way through a delirium. But we must try to avoid the emotional metaphorical appeal, and concentrate on making clear what seems to be the really important point here. Most of us are familiar with the favorite old Tory metaphor: the violent revolutionist tears down the noble edifice society lives in, or burns it down, and then fails to build up another, and poor human beings are left naked to the skies. That is not a good metaphor, save perhaps for purposes of Tory propaganda. Even at the height of a revolutionary crisis period, more of the old building is left standing than is destroyed. But the whole metaphor of the building is bad. We may take instead an analogy from the human nervous system, or think of an immensely complicated gridwork of electrical communications. Society then appears as a kind of network of interactions among individuals, interactions for the most part fixed by habit, hardened and perhaps adorned as ritual, dignified into meaning and beauty by the elaborately interwoven strands of interaction we know as law, theology, metaphysics, and similar noble beliefs. Now sometimes many of these interwoven strands of noble beliefs, some even of those of habit and tradition, can be cut out, and others inserted. During the crisis period of our revolutions some such process seems to have taken place; but the whole network itself seems so far never to have been altered suddenly and radically, and even the noble beliefs tend to fit into the network in the same places. If you kill off *all* the people who live within the network, you don't so much change the network of course as destroy it. This type of destruction is as yet rare in human history. Certainly in none of our revolutions was there even a very close approach to it.

What did happen, under the pressure of class struggle, war, religious idealism, and a lot more, was that the hidden and obscure courses which many of the interactions in the network follow were suddenly exposed, and passage along them made difficult in the unusual publicity and, so to speak, self-consciousness. The courses of other interactions were blocked, and the interactions went on with the greatest of difficulties by all sorts of detours. The courses of still other interactions were confused, short-circuited, paired off in strange ways. Finally, the pretensions of the fanatical leaders of the revolution involved the attempted creation of a vast number of new interactions. Now though for the most part these new interactions affected chiefly those

strands we have called the noble beliefs—law, theology, metaphysics, mythology, folklore, high-power abstractions in general—
still some of them did penetrate at an experimental level into
the obscurer and less dignified part of the network of interactions
among human beings and put a further strain on it. Surely it is
no wonder that under these conditions men and women in the
crisis period should behave as they would not normally behave,
that in the crisis period nothing should seem as it used to seem,
that, indeed, a famous passage from Thucydides, written two
thousand years before our revolutions, should seem like a
clinical report:

> When troubles had once begun in the cities, those who followed
> carried the revolutionary spirit further and further, and determined
> to outdo the report of all who had preceded them by the ingenuity
> of the enterprises and the atrocity of their revenges. The meaning
> of words had no longer the same relation to things, but was changed
> by them as they thought proper. Reckless daring was held to be
> loyal courage; prudent delay was the excuse of a coward; moderation
> was the disguise of unmanly weakness; to know everything was to
> do nothing. Frantic energy was the true quality of a man. A
> conspirator who wanted to be safe was a recreant in disguise. The
> lover of violence was always trusted, and his opponent suspected. He
> who succeeded in a plot was deemed knowing, but a still greater
> master in craft was he who detected one. On the other hand, he
> who plotted from the first to have nothing to do with plots was a
> breaker up of parties and a poltroon who was afraid of the enemy.
> In a word, he who could outstrip another in a bad action was
> applauded, and so was he who encouraged to evil one who had
> no idea of it. . . . The tie of party was stronger than the tie of blood,
> because a partisan was more ready to dare without asking why.

With this we may put a quotation from a much humbler
source, an obscure Siberian co-operative leader protesting against
Red and White Terror alike. Mr. Chamberlin quotes:

> And we ask and appeal to society, to the contending political
> groups and parties: When will our much-suffering Russia outlive
> the nightmare that is throttling it, when will deaths by violence
> cease? Doesn't horror seize you at the sight of the uninterrupted
> flow of human blood? Doesn't horror seize you at the consciousness
> that the deepest, most elementary bases of the existence of human
> society are perishing: the feeling of humanity, the consciousness of
> the value of life, of human personality, the feeling and consciousness
> of the necessity of legal order in the state? . . . Hear our cry and

despair: we return to prehistoric times of the existence of the human race; we are on the verge of the death of civilization and culture; we destroy the great cause of human progress, for which many generations of our worthier ancestors labored.

# 2.

# POLITICAL DISINTEGRATION AFTER THE CHINESE REVOLUTION OF 1911

## C. Martin Wilbur

In the decade centering on 1920, regional militarism was dominant in China. Throughout the country there existed independent military-political groupings, each of which controlled territory and exploited local resources. Each, as a system, was similar to all the others; they differed primarily in scale. Yet each system was flavored by the geographical and cultural characteristics of its particular region and by the personalities of its leaders.

### The Crucial Problem: Centralized vs. Decentralized Control

The Chinese military regimes in the 1920's were structured hierarchies usually organized for both civil administration and warfare. They seem to have been held together in varying degrees by strong leaders, organization and discipline, bonds of personal loyalty between leaders and followers, ideological commitment, local ties, and personal advantage. These military groupings were characterized by two conflicting tendencies: centralization vs. decentralization of control. Most armies were, in theory, parts of a national army under the central government in Peking, or were provincial armies. In fact, many were independent of any higher authority. But within any independent system the same

Reprinted with permission of the University of Chicago Press from *China's Heritage and the Communist Political System: Book One,* edited by Ping-Ti Ho and Tang Tsou. Copyright 1968 by the University of Chicago Press.

problem—centralized control against lower-unit autonomy—existed. Divisions and brigades might in theory be subordinate to the higher authority of the system of which they were parts, yet they separately garrisoned cities or districts and might attempt to secure and control their own finances. Usually the center was unable to procure adequate finances for the entire system and had to allow the subordinate units to secure their own revenues. The same conflict occurred in procurement of arms, the basic stuff of all military units. . . .

### Inter-Regime Politics

Practically every base was surrounded by bases controlled by other regimes. This called for a high degree of political skill on the part of a military leader to protect his own base and to manipulate the larger political situation for aggrandizement. Every military leader had to count on the possibility of his rivals combining against him, and he had to protect his rear if he launched a campaign to improve his position. He must be alert to every conference, troop movement, or arms shipment in a neighbor's regime. He also must keep a sharp eye on his own subordinates and their secret negotiations. Only the crafty and the well-connected could survive. This was an additional reason why militarists employed old bureaucrats skilled at factional intrigue and having wide personal connections.

Many of the stronger military leaders kept ambassadors in other Chinese centers of power to conduct negotiations and to report on conditions and plans in the rival camp. The situation was not unlike international relations, with alliance systems and balances of power. But the system was unstable because military bases were not well-defined and institutionalized nation-states. Few of the important regimes were actually secure in their "own" bases; they might be toppled from within by defection of subordinates. Few bases had clearly demarcated boundaries. The two outstanding exceptions were those of Yen Hsi-shan in Shansi and Chang Tso-lin in Manchuria.

Another great difference between a nation-state and the province-wide bases in China was the absence of institutionalized nationalism. In spite of strong provincialism, the provinces were not nations but parts of the greater China. Provincial regimes could not be buttressed by national loyalty. Defection and treachery were not inhibited by patriotism. Preceding every military campaign there was likely to be extensive secret negotiation to form alliances, neutralize potential rivals, and secure the defection of subunits in the camp of the regime against which the war was to be fought.

The party which was persuaded to turn over required assurance that he and his troops would either be incorporated as an independent unit into the other system or be left in control of his sub-base or given a better one. He must also be promised money and arms.

## Some Impressions

The documents and the press of the period leave several strong impressions. One is of political instability—of alarms, threats, and counterthreats, of alliances, defections, and realignments, of campaign after campaign in various parts of China. The second impression is of the brevity of civil wars, if actually fought, and their indecisive nature. Few regimes were permanently knocked out or their troop units destroyed. Defeated brigades or regiments were either incorporated into stronger systems or driven into poorer bases. The line between "banditry" and "legitimacy" was arbitrary.

These impressions evoke an image of constant turmoil, with only one clear line of development—that toward an ever-increasing number of military units and men under arms, and a growing burden of taxes. Estimates of the number of men under arms rise from about 500,000 in 1913 to 1.2 million in 1920. At the end of 1925 the figure may have reached 1.8 or 1.9 million. By July, 1928, at the end of the Northern Expedition, KMT forces were thought to number about 1.6 million and those of the whole country more than 2.2 million.[1]

Rural China provided an unlimited supply of young males eager to enlist for the promise of regular pay. Demobilization was difficult not only because commanders usually refused to reduce their capital—that is, their reputed troop strength—but also because demobilized troops might simply turn to banditry.

In a sense, armies were a form of relief for the unemployable. But they were a drain on the nation's scanty resources and contributed very little to the economy.

Another impression is that the turmoil caused by civil wars from 1911 onward, and the increasing but unpredictable taxation, so exhausted the Chinese people that they were prepared to accept any government that seemed likely to end such disorder. During the 1920's, every important commander proclaimed his intention to restore peace and denounced his rivals for fomenting wars. . . .

## Factors Giving Rise to Twentieth-Century Separatism and Militarism

No *single* explanation for the emergence of militarism in China will get us far in understanding how the phenomenon arose or why it has arisen many times during China's long history.

### Latent Factors

Several factors inherent in China's geography and history might conduce to the rise of autonomous military-political regimes if the general political situation made such a development possible. Differences in topography and climate throughout the great land mass we now call China resulted in varying cultural adaptations that are evident from the dawn of Chinese history. The gradual expansion of the Chinese realm brought into one nation peoples of diverse cultures, while the frequent invasions of China by peoples from outside its frontiers brought in other groups with non-Chinese attributes. These historic processes left residues of ethnic and linguistic differences between the populations in various parts of the empire, as well as separate traditions, which presented obstacles to political unity. Merely to call to mind the differences in speech and customs between the peoples of Shantung and Kwangtung or of Szechwan and Chekiang will make this evident. Even such adjoining provinces as Kwangtung and Hunan had markedly different dialects and historical traditions. Thus centrifugal tendencies were always powerful, and the area we think of as China was divided for periods nearly as long as those in which it was united. Yet the historical trend from Mongol times onward was toward national unity; periods of disunity were brief.

China's size and poor communications created great obstacles to centralized control over the diverse regions, provinces, and local districts. Statesmen tried to solve this problem through the device of the imperial institution acting through civil and military bureaucracies recruited and controlled by the imperial government and infused with a common ideology. This ideology, "Confucianism," was also purposely inculcated in the vast population in order to internalize a spirit of social harmony and obedience to the imperial will.

The ethic of loyalty to closely related individuals—parents, kin, teachers, sponsors—and to small collectivities such as family, clan, village, and common-interest associations, was stronger in China than loyalty to abstract ideals such as impartial justice or the nation; it was probably stronger even than loyalty to the emperor. This ethic often expressed itself in the tendency toward cliques and factions in bureaucracies and other large collectivities. Such factions were organized along lines of personal attachment or common provincial origin for mutual protection and advancement of the members. In a society characterized by intense struggle for advancement and security, and lacking a system of impartial law or strongly developed institutions outside the state which could protect the individual, the control of military power—from local militia or bandit gangs up to provincial forces or regional armies—was extremely important for ambitious men and cliques.

Thus the geographic expanse and diversity of China, the cultural and linguistic differences and separate historic traditions among its people, and the ethic of particularistic loyalty conduced in times of stress to regional separatism and military autonomy. Such tendencies might prevail against the counter-tendency of political unity and centralized control if the one over-arching institution—the imperial government—was weak. When the central government was weak, power gravitated to men with the sword—a phenomenon not peculiar to China. Such was the case during the closing decades of the Ch'ing dynasty.

## Recent Historical Developments
China's military regimes as they existed in the 1920's were the outgrowth of a long development in which we may distinguish

several important strands.[2] One was the creation of provincial or regional armies under such leaders as Tseng Kuo-fan, Tso Tsung-t'ang, and Li Hung-chang in the 1850's and 1860's to combat the Taiping and other rebel forces attempting either to overthrow the Manchu dynasty or to detach border areas from imperial control. These provincial armies were internally unified by ties of personal loyalty within their officer corps. The commanders who organized these forces and who then were appointed as provincial governors and viceroys gained considerable control of local finances, and organized their own staffs of experts and infiltrated them into the imperial bureaucracy. The armies gradually declined in military effectiveness and were replaced by more modern forces trained along Western lines and equipped with modern arms. They had left, however, an important legacy —erosion of centralized control over military power. The imperial government no longer firmly controlled the armed forces or disposed the finances of the separate provinces.

The modernization of China's armies during the last three decades of the Manchu dynasty was carried out by Chinese viceroys such as Li Hung-chang, Chang Chih-tung, and Liu K'un-i. These men operated in their various domains with some coordination between their efforts and yet with much factional rivalry. They created separate military academies to train officers, built arsenals, hired Western instructors and technicians, and purchased arms abroad using such provinicial finances as they controlled or, with permission of the Court, percentages of specified customs revenues. The form of army building strengthened the trend toward regional autonomy. This autonomy was evident during the Sino-Japanese War of 1894-95, and was clearly shown during the Boxer disturbance of 1900.

After the military disasters of 1900, Yüan Shih-k'ai began to rebuild the Peiyang Army in the north. It became China's strongest force. Yüan used senior officers loyal to himself and trained junior officers in his military academies. The Peiyang Army played a crucial role in the elimination of the Manchu dynasty and the imperial institution and made possible Yüan's ascendancy as China's first president from 1912 to 1916.

Parallel to the development of the Peiyang Army, other modern armies had been formed in Hunan and Hupei by Chang

Chih-tung, in the Nanking viceroyalty by Liu K'un-i, and in Fukien, Kwangtung, Szechwan, and the southwestern provinces. After the Revolution of 1911-12, these southern units, outside the Peiyang system, tried to maintain their independence from Yüan's control. Many of them opposed Yüan's effort to make himself emperor in 1915-16.

After Yüan's death, his generals became the principal holders of military power throughout most of China. Then the Peiyang Army itself broke apart into several contending factions. There were many other armies in China with long histories and independent territorial bases of power, and new ones were quickly formed. Thousands of Chinese had been trained as military officers in the provincial military schools, the Paoting Academy, or Japan. China had many arsenals operating in separate provinces and foreign-made arms had been imported in large amounts. Thus a once unified political system became fragmented.

This account of the development of military separatism does not imply an autonomous process. Other important historic processes closely interacted with it and with each other in the nineteenth and early part of the twentieth century. We may mention the gradual breakdown of the Chinese social fabric in the nineteenth century under the pressure of a rapidly growing population and increasing economic inequality between social classes; the decay of the imperial institution and decline in the efficiency of the Ch'ing bureaucracy; and foreign competition for paramountcy over parts of China's territory and wealth. Western imperialism challenged the old order while Western nations and Japan provided new models for government and social organization. Confucianism as the national ethical system withered under the competition of many alien ideologies such as Christianity, republicanism, social Darwinism, socialism, Marxism-Leninism, and, above all, nationalism. Nor should we forget the influences exerted by individuals upon events and popular attitudes, individuals such as the Empress Dowager Tz'u-hsi, and Kuang-hsü Emperor, K'ang Yu-wei, Yen Fu, Liang Ch'i-ch'ao, Sun Yat-sen, Ch'en Tu-hsiu, and Hu Shih, to mention only a few. Likewise the rulers of military satrapies were Chinese human beings. They were the products of their environment, thought as Chinese, had aspirations for their country as well as for themselves. To use the term "warlord" to embrace such a diversity of human personalities as Wu P'ei-fu, Chang Tso-lin, Yen Hsi-shan, Ch'en Chiung-ming, Feng Yü-hsiang, Li Tsung-jen, or Chiang Kai-shek and a great many other leaders of military-political regimes may conceal more than it reveals. They all operated within a system which none of them had created.

## NOTES

1. *China Year Book, 1919-20,* (Peking and Tientsin Press) pp. 318-30; *ibid., 1921-22,* pp. 518-19; *ibid., 1926-27,* p. 1065; Kao Yin-chu, *Chung-hua-min-kuo ta-shih-chi* [A Record of Important Events during the Chinese Republic] (Taipei, 1927), p. 300, "July 2, 1928." For a more detailed estimation as of the end of 1928, see the report of Ho Ying-ch'in *Ke-ming wen-hsien* [Documents of the revolution] vol. 24 Taipei: 1953 onward), pp. 4856-63.
2. The following is based on W.L. Bales, *Tso Tsüng-t'ang: Soldier and Statesman of Old China* (Shanghai: Kelly and Walsh, 1937); Stanley Spector, *Li Hung-chang and the Huai Army: A Study in Nineteenth Century Chinese Regionalism* (Seattle: University of Washington Press, 1964) Ralph L. Powell, *The Rise of Chinese Military Power, 1895-1912* (Princeton University Press, 1955).

# 3.

# CONFINING CONDITIONS AND REVOLUTIONARY BREAKTHROUGHS

## Otto Kirchheimer

I want to try to connect the course of several regimes with what, for want of a better name, I shall call "confining conditions"—the particular social and intellectual conditions present at the births of these regimes. Do I prejudice the case by calling the sum total of the prerevolutionary situation confining conditions rather than calling them more neutrally, as Val Lorwin suggested to me, simply antecedent conditions? Yet every situation which a new regime finds at its inception is an antecedent one. I am concerned specifically—and only—with the conditions that have to be overcome if the new regime is to continue. How the new regime may accomplish this, or may fail to, is the subject of this paper. Therefore I consider the nature of the confining conditions, chiefly those of social structure; the nature of the new regime; and the nature of the methods available to it, as well as those it adopts to overcome the confining conditions.

In discussing political action, we often ask the question: did the man or the group have to act the way he, or they, did? What other options were open, *e.g.*, to Stalin in the late 1920s? Not being satisfied with the answer that, given the character of Stalin, the eventual course of action was really to be expected all along,

Reprinted with permission of the author and publisher from the *American Political Science Review*, Vol. 59 No. 4, 1965. Copyright 1965 by Otto Kirchheimer.

we might profitably shift the question to a different level. To what extent do the circumstances attendant upon the rise of a new regime determine its subsequent actions? The late Franz Neumann raised such questions in regard to the course of the National Socialist regime. His *Behemoth* was an impressive attempt to show how the confining conditions under which the regime worked—especially the fact that it came to power with the help of leaders of German heavy industry—not only switched the track for the National Socialists, but explained many of their patterns of actions long after their regime was firmly established.

Yet Neumann's account of the German state organization and its supersession by the movement-type party already foreshadows the problems which increasingly preoccupied his thoughts (although only in fragmentary publications) in his later years. To what extent can a revolutionary power structure move away from the specific constellation of forces which presided over its origin, and move off in a different direction of its own?

# I

Neumann had little difficulty with the negative test. Whoever fails to put his hands on the switch—either because of a lack of the social prerequisites (France in 1848) or because of a lack of will power (Germany in 1918)—cannot deflect the current into new circuits. Neither the leaders of the incipient French labor and Socialist movement of 1848, nor the leaders of the numerically strong but unimaginative organizations of the German Socialists in 1918, ever tried to put their hands on the switches. Crowded from the center of power, they soon could not even hold to the position of initiating incremental changes. Even the modest role of setting into motion long-range changes, with all due anticipatory consideration of other power-holders' reactions, escapes the group which fails to make a political breakthrough. Such a group becomes an object, rather than a subject, of the political process.

The capacity to compress thoroughgoing or revolutionary change—as distinct from incremdntal change—into a minimum of time, according to the new power-holders' own timetable, is the test of revolutionary victory. What are the possible dimensions, and what are the limits, of such capacity for change? In his later publications, and on the basis of Soviet experience, Neumann held that political power could make itself supreme and thereby make itself the font of economic power.[1]

## II

But what does this supremacy amount to? . . . Let us turn to the case of the Soviet Union. In order to obtain a measure of initial acceptance, the leaders of the Petrograd Revolution had to put their stamp of approval on the seizure of the gentry's land by the peasantry. However, this policy aggravated the age-old difficulties which had beset the Russian polity and which Stolypin's dissolution of the *Obshina* had only started to tackle: the need of accelerating transformation to an industrial society by simultaneously shifting population to the cities and modernizing agricultural methods. Stalin's forced collectivization was an answer to the difficulties caused by the lower rate of industrial growth and reagrarianization of the country in the 1920s, which coincided with the considerable rural exodus to the cities.[2] Having at his disposal a strong enough administrative apparatus to reverse the process of Kulakization under the NEP and to collectivize agriculture, Stalin had a range of choices in regard to the methods of collectivization. If he wanted to industrialize rapidly, however, he probably had little choice about the principle of collectivization. Left alone, the peasants would have dictated both the pace and the direction of industrialization by consuming more and delivering less food to the rest of the country.

What matters in this context is the interrelation between socioeconomic conditioning and the discretionary element left to the decision of the regime. The setting up of larger agricultural units and the shifting of agricultural surplus population to industrial life were bound to take place under almost any regime. The revolutionary approval of land seizure by the peasantry, plus the conditions of the NEP period, had aggravated the regime's difficulties by creating an important new proprietary interest at a time when the regime was unable to offer enough industrial goods to entice the peasants to part voluntarily with their produce. Yet, at the same time, a coercive apparatus was at hand to collectivize the land, and collect food surpluses. The general problem of the relations between the agricultural sector and the industrial sectors of a modernizing society was given, irrespective of whether the country was to be governed by an autocracy, a bourgeois democracy, or the Communist Party. What the supremacy of a revolutionary group entailed was a much wider choice of means and strategies to carry out the transformation. The "whole-hog Stalin"[3] was not necessary, and Stalin's methods were counterproductive, if measured by the yard-stick of what more gradual, part-cooperative collectivization could have obtained in both good will and direct production results. Yet given the need for accelerating the transformation as a condition for survival of the revolutionary group, the internal leadership struggle resulted in the decision that the gain in time would outweigh the costs of forced collectivization. Zigzagging in the course of the great industrialization debate, Stalin used changes in his own position to eliminate actual and potential rivals, and then used his ensuing supremacy over the dominant political group to enforce the most ruthless of the available options. But the need for industrialization created fundamental claims on any regime, as it had even on the Tsarist regime.

The social and economic frame of the particular society, then, lays down a conditioning perimeter within which the original choice has to be made and solutions have to be sought. . . .

The leaders of the USSR have achieved such a breakthrough, transforming Russia into a major industrial system. While they still experience difficulties with agrarian organization, and these in turn delay the fulfillment of urgent consumer expectations, such problems can scarcely endanger the subsistence level. Most of the confining conditions have been removed, at whatever cost to those who lived through—or died during—the long decades it took to accomplish that feat. . . .

The argument that the major outcome—conversion into an industrial society—would have taken place in any event does not upset our conclusion. The fact is that a "premature" industrial revolution, compressing various stages of social development into an extremely limited time span determined by its political elite— moreover, with primitive accumulation by the state and not private owners, and with national sovereignty exalted in the process—did take place. This is highly relevant to our original question: here a revolutionary regime did move beyond the confining conditions under which it arose.

## III

To illuminate another facet of the problem, I want to discuss the conditions of collaboration of various political forces under a revolutionary regime. Where lies the well-spring of common action? To what extent does the variation in composition and orientation of such forces determine the confines of their actions from the very outset?

I have in mind here the well known episode of the relations between Robespierre and the Committee of Public Safety toward the Paris *sans-culottes* from autumn 1793 to early summer 1794. One might describe the situation after the autumn days of 1793 as an uneasy coalition between the committee and the Paris *sans-culottes*, ideologically represented and sometimes led by Hébert and Chaumette.[4] Neither group could have acted effectively without the other. Their presence served as a means for Robespierre to keep his hold over the Convention, as much as the Committee served as a means for the *sand-culottes* to push their political and economic demands. The common ground which provided both their dynamics and their larger justification was the unconditional pursuit of the revolutionary war. There was at best a partial meeting of minds and never a complete convergence on social and economic goals. In order to carry on the war and to avoid spiralling inflation, price and wage controls were indicated. Yet—apart from military procurement—farmers and merchants were frequently able to circumvent price controls. The Paris city administration, on the other hand, was lukewarm in enforcing wage controls. Such contradictions were partly solved by the trial and guillotining of Hébert and Chaumette. Although their execution was followed in *jeu de bascule* fashion within two weeks by the execution of Danton and Desmoulins, the victory of Fleurus in June 1794 lifted, to some extent, the radical mortgage on Robespierre and allowed the dismantling of price controls. The result was to do away with the often uncontrollable district clubs, and to restrict the more egalitarian policies, in an attempt at securing a steady flow of bread at the official price to the urban population. The payoff came on the

9th of Thermidor when the National Guard did not come out for Robespierre, but went home; and when the district assemblies meeting that evening were split wide open between loyalty to the Convention or to the more radical politics of the *sans-culottes*.

But is this the only, or a sufficient, reason for the turn of events? First, a seemingly more accidental fact: on the decisive afternoon, when the National Guard was assembled on the Place de Grève with all its equipment, there was no leader resolute enough to make them march against the Convention. What about the less obvious links in the chain of causation? There was the matter of sheer physical fatigue of the Paris *militants*, who had been in the thick of the political struggle for the previous five years; and the fact that many of the younger ones had departed for the war fronts. There was the phenomenon which we now call the circulation of elites: the most vigorous and the most intelligent of them had meanwhile taken government jobs in the central administration and war machine, and had formed new and different bonds of allegiance. This brings us nearer to another, more Protean constellation: *sans-culottes* are a political, not a social, category. Their major ties were common political sympathies: hatred of the aristocracy and support of the new regime and the military program. This motley crew of unemployed, journeymen, artisans, shopkeepers, lawyers, teachers, government employees, and even a sprinkling of merchants, could scarcely have a unified *social* outlook. Some of them being independent producers and middlemen, and others being wage earners, they would scarcely see eye-to-eye on economic issues. They remained parcels of various occupational groups. They could join the revolutionary battle all the more easily because their social and occupational distinctions had not always jelled into class-consciousness. They remained accessible to a variety of sometimes contradictory appeals, guiding their behavior in speech and action.

Suppose that Robespierre had saved his neck on the 9th of Thermidor due to a fresh intervention of the National Guard. Could this coalition of the national revolutionary government and its advanced urban clientele have lasted? While trying to find its way through a bedlam of conflicting interests, the Committee of Public Safety was ideologically committed to uphold the sanctity of private property—with exceptions necessitated by the conduct of the war. Moreover, its policy toward the disposal of the agricultural properties of the *émigré* nobles and the church bears little evidence of a sustained interest in the cause of the small peasant and the landless farmhand. How would it have related itself in the long run to the interests not only of the merchants but of the upper echelons of the peasants? Even if we disregard the discordant interests among the *sand-culottes*—bound to come out more sharply after the most urgent war pressures had receded—could the Robespierre-*sans-culotte* combination have long outlasted the immediate danger period of the war?

Seventeen hundred ninety-three marks the definitive entry of the urban masses upon the French political scene. But, given the forces present at that particular historical juncture, the 1793-94 episode is a great precursor of problems yet to come. Whenever they were in a position to make their own political contribution in the decades ahead, the peasants would make short shrift of "prematurely" radical political ideas.

If we except exceedingly short periods in 1848 and 1871, and abortive movements remaining below the most provisional governmental level, the people at large did not move into the center of political decision. It is for this reason that the coalition of the Committee of Public Safety and the *sans-culottes* of 1793-94 still retains such a paradigmatic interest. For here we must raise the question, to what extent the possibility existed—which became so important in the Chinese and Russian revolutions of the 20th century—of jumping stages of societal development and compressing two revolutions into one? To what extent could the 1793-94 combination have possessed the organizational cohesion, the unity of purpose, and the technical means to overcome its confining conditions—*i.e.,* its being surrounded by a sea of peasantry and torn by the discordances between two constituent elements, the bourgeois-governmental wing and the popular Paris-street wing? The attitude of the governmental wing toward economic and social policy issues shows how alien the conscious reshaping of society by governmental fiat remained to them. They tried to keep the backdoor through which such measures entered—war-time necessity and the pressure of their Paris allies—as well guarded as they could under the circumstances of the day. The breakup of the combination and Robespierre's subsequent defeat without serious intervention by his erstwhile radical associates highlight the lack of cohesive social consciousness needed to take the revolution beyond its pristine bourgeois phase.

The heterogeneous nature of the short-lived coalition of the 1793-94 period of the Revolution was in itself the chief confining condition of that Revolution. The Paris *avant-garde,* with all its revolutionary fervor, was anything but unified and anything but uniformly proletarian (however we define "proletarian" in pre-industrial Paris). The National government, temporary coalition partner of the revolutionary Paris Commune, was riven by personal quarrels and conflicts among the various organs of government. Beyond that, and even more fundamental, the revolutionary government was unwilling to injure the interests of merchants and agricultural property owners beyond what the conduct of the war in its most desperate phase seemed to make necessary. Organizational centralization, the "maximum" for food prices, and the unfulfilled promise of the famous "Ventôse decrees": these were adopted to win the war, not to establish a social millennium or create the cadres to maintain the revolutionary regime. . . .

With the First World War as a watershed, we are able to see the decisive differences between 19th and 20th century revolutions. Masses had been brought together in the 19th century by political organizations on a semi-permanent basis; their minds had been exercised by expectations of economic benefit, social innovation, or patriotic or religious exaltation. But only the First World War showed how the public authorities, first with the joyous and later on the increasingly reluctant cooperation of the population, could mobilize huge masses of men and technical forces of hitherto unknown destructiveness and link them in huge organizations for official national goals.

While the official apparatus was everywhere quickly dismantled after the war, the experience was not lost on a new crop of political organizers. If such great results could be reached for the traditional goal of acting on the power structure of other societies, why not use similar methods on the domestic structure? The official state apparatus with its limited vistas, its simultaneous mixture of tradition-bound procedure and immersion in the particular interests of one group or another, with its hesitant and uneasy role of arbitration, was neither intellectually nor technically equipped for such a task. It is the merger of political movement and official state organization, the simultaneous unfolding of the mechanisms of change and the purveying of new loyalties, which mark the differences between the revolutionary dynamics of the 20th and the largely uncontrolled social and economic revolution of the 19th century. The 19th-century government concentrated the energies of its much more slender and haphazard apparatus on emergency periods.

The revolution of the 20th Century obliterates the distinction between emergency and normalcy. Movement plus state can organize the masses because: (a) the technical and intellectual equipment is now at hand to direct them toward major societal programs rather than simply liberating their energies from the bonds of tradition; (b) they have the means at hand to control people's livelihood by means of job assignments and graduated rewards unavailable under the largely agricultural and artisanal structure of the 1790s and still unavailable to the small enterprise and commission-merchant-type economy of the 1850s and 1860s; (c) they have fallen heir to endlessly and technically refined propaganda devices substituting for the uncertain leader-mass relations of the previous periods; and (d) they faced state organizations shaken up by war dislocation and economic crisis. Under these conditions Soviet Russia could carry through simultaneously the job of an economic and a political, a bourgeois and a post-bourgeois revolution in spite of the exceedingly narrow basis of its political elite. On the other hand, the premature revolutionary combination of 1793-94 not only dissolved quickly, but left its most advanced sector, the *sans-culottes*, with only the melancholy choice between desperate rioting—Germinal 1795— or falling back into a pre-organized stage of utter helplessness and agony.

# NOTES

1. See esp. ch. 1, "Approaches to the study of political power," and ch. 10, "Economics and Politics in the 20th century," in Franz Neumann, *The Democratic and the Authoritarian State* (Glencoe, 1957).

2. Alexander Gerschenkron, *Economic Backwardness in Historical Perspective* (Harvard University Press, 1962), pp. 119-151.

3. Alex Nove, *Economic Rationality in Soviet Politics* (New York, 1964), p. 32. *Cf.* M. Erlich, *The Soviet Industrialisation Debate 1924-1928* (Harvard University Press, 1960): "A policy of moderate tempos would strengthen the position of the upper strata of the villages and would make the adroit balancing between them and the unruly radicals of the cities a necessity which could be adopted only as a temporary expedient. Had such a course been pursued over a long period of time the regime would have stood to lose not only from its possible failures but also from its successes. The alternative to such retreats and maneuvers leading to the gradual erosion of the dictatorial system was clearly a massive counterattack which would have broken once and for all the peasants' power over the basic decisions of economic policy. A high speed industrialisation with a strong emphasis on the capital goods sector which Stalin now favored provided the logical line for such a counterattack." (p. 174)
   "The overhang of agricultural excess population permitted the manning of equipment which was physically usable with the surplus peasants of yesterday, which could be removed from the countryside without a notable detriment to agricultural output and be employed at a real wage barely exceeding their wretchedly lower consumption levels of the earlier status." (p. 184)

4. For literature on the episode see the general discussion in Georges Lefebvre, *La Révolution francaise,* 3d ed. (Paris, 1963), pp. 354-430, and most interesting in this context his remarks on pp. 407-409; two more specialized works by Daniel Guérin, *La Lutte de Classes sous la Première République, Bourgeois et "bras nus" (1793-1797),* 2 vols. (Paris, 1946), and Albert Soboul, *Les Sans-culottes Parisiens en l'an II, Mouvement Populaire et Gouvernement Révolutionnaire, 2 Juin, 1793—9 Thermidor an II* (Paris, 1958), esp. pp. 427-433, 503-504, 1025-1035. Guérin draws explicit conclusions as to the class content of the struggle between Robespierre and the *sans-culottes.* Soboul analyzes a wealth of hitherto unknown documents, among them papers of district assemblies and district clubs. His conclusions from the assembled material, though more shaded, are in line with those of Guérin as to the *sans-culottes*-Revolutionary Government relation. For the social composition of the *sans-culottes* see also G. Rudé, *The Crowd in the French Revolution* (London, 1959), pp. 178-84.

# 4.

# THE ROUTINIZATION OF CHARISMA

## Max Weber

In its pure form charismatic authority has a character specifically foreign to everyday routine structures. The social relationships directly involved are strictly personal, based on the validity and practice of charismatic personal qualities. If this is not to remain a purely transitory phenomenon, but to take on the character of a permanent relationship forming a stable community of disciples or a band of followers or a party organization or any sort of political or hierocratic organization, it is necessary for the character of charismatic authority to become radically changed. Indeed, in its pure form charismatic authority may be said to exist only in the process of originating. It cannot remain stable, but becomes either traditionalized or rationalized, or a combination of both.

The following are the principal motives underlying this transformation: (a) The ideal and also the material interests of the followers in the continuation and the continual reactivation of the community, (b) the still stronger ideal and also stronger material interests of the members of the administrative staff, the disciples or other followers of the charismatic leader in continuing their relationship. Not only this, but they have an interest in

Reprinted with permission of The Macmillan Co. from *The Theory of Social and Economic Organization*, by Max Weber, translated by Talcott Parsons and A. M. Henderson. Copyright 1947 by Talcott Parsons.

continuing it in such a way that both from an ideal and a material point of view, their own status is put on a stable everyday basis. This means, above all, making it possible to participate in normal family relationships or at least to enjoy a secure social position in place of the kind of discipleship which is cut off from ordinary worldly connexions, notably in the family and in economic relationships.

These interests generally become conspicuously evident with the disappearance of the personal charismatic leader and with the problem of succession, which inevitably arises. The way in which this problem is met—if it is met at all and the charismatic group continues to exist—is of crucial importance for the character of the subsequent social relationships. The following are the principal possible types of solution: —

(a) The search for a new charismatic leader on the basis of criteria of the qualities which will fit him for the position of authority. This is to be found in a relatively pure type in the process of choice of a new Dalai Lama. It consists in the search for a child with characteristics which are interpreted to mean that he is a reincarnation of the Buddha. This is very similar to the choice of the new Bull of Apis.

In this case the legitimacy of the new charismatic leader is bound to certain distinguishing characteristics; thus, to rules with respect to which a tradition arises. The result is a process of traditionalization in favour of which the purely personal character of leadership is eliminated.

(b) By revelation manifested in oracles, lots, divine judgments, or other techniques of selection. In this case the legitimacy of the new leader is dependent on the legitimacy of the technique of his selection. This involves a form of legalization. It is said that at times the *Schofetim* of Israel had this character. Saul is said to have been chosen by the old war oracle.

(c) By the designation on the part of the original charismatic leader of his own successor and his recognition on the part of the followers. This is a very common form. Originally, the Roman magistracies were filled entirely in this way. The system survived most clearly into later times in the appointment of 'dictators' and in the institution of the 'interrex.' In this case legitimacy is acquired through the act of designation.

(d) Designation of a successor by the charismatically qualified administrative staff and his recognition by the community. In its typical form this process should quite definitely not be interpreted as 'election' or 'nomination' or anything of the sort. It is not a matter of free selection, but of one which is strictly bound to objective duty. It is not to be determined merely by majority vote, but is a question of arriving at the correct designation, the designation of the right person who is truly endowed with charisma. It is quite possible that the minority and not the majority should be right in such a case. Unanimity is often required. It is obligatory to acknowledge a mistake and persistence in error is a serious offence. Making a wrong choice is a genuine wrong requiring expiation. Originally it was a magical offence.

Nevertheless, in such a case it is easy for legitimacy to take on the character of an acquired right which is justified by standards of the correctness of the process by which the position was acquired, for the most part, by its having been acquired in accordance with certain formalities, such as coronation. This was the original meaning of the coronation of bishops and kings in the Western World by the clergy or the nobility with the 'consent' of the community. There are numerous analogous phenomena all over the world. The fact that this is the origin of the modern conception of 'election' raises problems which will have to be gone into later.

(e) By the conception that charisma is a quality transmitted by heredity; thus that it is participated in by the kinsmen of its bearer, particularly by his closest relatives. This is the case of hereditary charisma. The order of hereditary succession in such a case need not be the same as that which is in force for appropriated rights, but may differ from it. It is also sometimes necessary to select the proper heir within the kinship group by some of the methods just spoken of; thus in certain Negro states brothers have had to fight for the succession. In China, succession had to take place in such a way that the relation of the living group to the ancestral spirits was not disturbed. The rule either of seniority or of designation by the followers has been very common in the Orient. Hence, in the house of Osman, it has been obligatory to eliminate all other possible candidates.

Only in Medieval Europe and in Japan universally, elsewhere

only sporadically, has the principle of primogeniture, as governing the inheritance of authority, become clearly established. This has greatly facilitated the consolidation of political groups in that it has eliminated struggle between a plurality of candidates from the same charismatic family.

In the case of hereditary charisma, recognition is no longer paid to the charismatic qualities of the individual, but to the legitimacy of the position he has acquired by hereditary succession. This may lead in the direction either of traditionalization or of legalization. The concept of 'divine right' is fundamentally altered and now comes to mean authority by virtue of a personal right which is not dependent on the recognition of those subject to authority. Personal charisma may be totally absent. Hereditary monarchy is a conspicuous illustration. In Asia there have been very numerous hereditary priesthoods; also, frequently, the hereditary charisma of kinship groups has been treated as a criterion of social rank and of eligibility for fiefs and benefices.

(f) The concept that charisma may be transmitted by ritual means from one bearer to another or may be created in a new person. The concept was originally magical. It involves a dissociation of charisma from a particular individual, making it an objective, transferrable entity. In particular, it may become the charisma of office. In this case the belief in legitimacy is no longer directed to the individual, but to the acquired qualities and to the effectiveness of the ritual acts. The most important example is the transmission of priestly charisma by anointing, consecration, or the laying on of hands; and of royal authority, by anointing and by coronation. The *caracter indelibilis* thus acquired means that the charismatic qualities and powers of the office are emancipated from the personal qualities of the priest. For precisely this reason, this has, from the Donatist and the Montanist heresies down to the Puritan revolution, been the subject of continual conflicts. The 'hireling' of the Quakers is the preacher endowed with the charisma of office.

Comcomitant with the routinization of charisma with a view to insuring adequate succession, go the interests in its routinization on the part of the administrative staff. It is only in the initial stages and so long as the charismatic leader acts in a way which is completely outside everyday social organization, that it is possible for his followers to live communistically in a community of faith and enthusiasm, on gifts, 'booty,' or sporadic acquisition. Only the members of the small group of enthusiastic disciples and followers are prepared to devote their lives purely idealistically to their call. The great majority of disciples and followers will in the long run 'make their living' out of their 'calling' in a material sense as well. Indeed, this must be the case if the movement is not to disintegrate.

Hence, the routinization of charisma also takes the form of the appropriation of powers of control and of economic advantages by the followers or disciples, and of regulation of the recruitment of these groups. This process of tradionalization or of legalization, according to whether rational legislation is involved or not, may take any one of a number of typical forms.

1. The original basis of recruitment is personal charisma. With routinization, the followers or disciples may set up norms for recruitment, in particular involving training or tests of eligibility. Charisma can only be 'awakened' and 'tested'; it cannot be 'learned' or 'taught.' All types of magical asceticism, as practiced by magicians and heroes, and all novitiates, belong in this category. These are means of closing the group which constitutes the administrative staff.

Only the proved novice is allowed to exercise authority. A genuine charismatic leader is in a position to oppose this type of prerequisite for membership. His successor is not, at least if he is chosen by the administrative staff. This type is illustrated by the magical and warrior asceticism of the 'men's house' with initiation ceremonies and age groups. An individual who has not successfully gone through the initiation, remains a 'woman'; that is, is excluded from the charismatic group.

2. It is easy for charismatic norms to be transformed into those defining a 'traditional social status on a hereditary charismatic basis. If the leader is chosen on a hereditary basis, it is very easy for hereditary charisma to govern the selection of the administrative staff and even, perhaps, those followers without any position of authority. The term 'familistic state' will be applied when a political body is organized strictly and completely in terms of this principle of hereditary charisma. In such a case, all appropriation

of governing powers, of fiefs, benefices, and all sorts of economic advantages follow the same pattern. The result is that all powers and advantages of all sorts become traditionalized. The heads of families, who are traditional gerontocrats or patriarchs without personal charismatic legitimacy, regulate the exercise of these powers which cannot be taken away from their family. It is not the type of position he occupies which determines the rank of a man or of his family, but rather the hereditary charismatic rank of his family determines the position he will occupy. Japan, before the development of bureaucracy, was organized in this way. The same was undoubtedly true of China as well where, before the rationalization which took place in the territorial states, authority was in the hands of the 'old families.' Other types of examples are furnished by the caste system in India, and by Russia before the *Mjestnitschestvo* was introduced. Indeed, all hereditary social classes with established privileges belong in the same category.

3. The administrative staff may seek and achieve the creation and appropriation of individual positions and the corresponding economic advantages for its members. In that case, according to whether the tendency is to traditionalization or legalization, there will develop (a) benefices, (b) offices, or (c) fiefs. In the first case a praebendal organization will result; in the second, patrimonialism or bureaucracy; in the third, feudalism. These become appropriated in the place of the type of provision from gifts or booty without settled relation to the everyday economic structure.

Case (a), benefices, may consist in rights to the proceeds of begging, to payments in kind, or to the proceeds of money taxes, or finally, to the proceeds of fees. Any one of these may result from the regulation of provision by free gifts or by 'booty' in terms of a rational organization of finance. Regularized begging is found in Buddhism; benefices in kind, in the Chinese and Japnese 'rice rents'; support by money taxation has been the rule in all the rationalized conquering states. The last case is common everywhere, especially on the part of priests and judges and, in India, even the military authorities.

Case (b), the transformation of the charismatic mission into an office, may have more of a patrimonial or more of a bureaucratic character. The former is much the more common; the latter is found principally in Mediterranean Antiquity and in the modern Western World. Elsewhere it is exceptional.

In case (c), only land may be appropriated as a fief, whereas the position as such retains its originally charismatic character. On the other hand, powers and authority may be fully appropriated as fiefs. It is difficult to distinguish the two cases. It is, however, rare that orientation to the charismatic character of the position disappears entirely; it did not do so in the Middle Ages.

For charisma to be transformed into a permanent routine structure, it is necessary that its anti-economic character should be altered. It must be adapted to some form of fiscal organization to provide for the needs of the group and hence to the economic conditions necessary for raising taxes and contributions. When a charismatic movement develops in the direction of praebendal provision, the 'laity' become differentiated from the 'clergy'; that is, the participating members of the charismatic administrative staff which has now become routinized. These are the priests of the developing 'church.' Correspondingly, in a developing political body the vassals, the holders of benefices, or officials are differentiated from the 'tax payers.' The former, instead of being the 'followers' of the leader, become state officials or appointed party officials. This process is very conspicuous in Buddhism and in the Hindu sects. The same is true in all the states resulting from conquest which have become rationalized to form permanent structures; also of parties and other movements which have originally had a purely charismatic character. With the process of routinization the charismatic group tends to develop into one of the forms of everyday authority, particularly the patrimonial form in its decentralized variant or the bureaucratic. Its original peculiarities are apt to be retained in the charismatic standards of honour attendant on the social status acquired by heredity or the holding of office. . . .

The more highly developed the interdependence of different economic units in a monetary economy, the greater the pressure of the everyday needs of the followers of the charismatic movement becomes. The effect of this is to strengthen the tendency to routinization, which is everywhere operative, and as a rule has rapidly won out. Charisma is a phenomenon typical of prophetic religious movements or of expansive political movements in their early stages. But as soon as the position of authority is well established, and above all as soon as control over large masses of people exists, it gives way to the forces of everyday routine.

One of the decisive motives underlying all cases of the routinization of charisma is naturally the striving for security. This means legitimization, on the one hand, of positions of authority and social prestige, on the other hand, of the economic advantages enjoyed by the followers and sympathizers of the leader. Another important motive, however, lies in the objective necessity of adaptation of the patterns of order and of the organization of the administrative staff to the normal, everyday needs and conditions of carrying on administration. In this connexion, in particular, there are always points at which traditions of administrative practice and of judicial decision can take hold; since these are needed both by the normal administrative staff and by those subject to its authority. It is further necessary that there should be some definite order introduced into the organization of the administrative staff itself. Finally, as will be discussed in detail below, it is necessary for the administrative staff and all its administrative practices to be adapted to everyday economic conditions. It is not possible for the costs of permanent, routine administration to be met by 'booty,' contributions, gifts, and hospitality, as is typical of the pure type of military and prophetic charisma.

The process of routinization is thus not by any means confined to the problem of succession and does not stop when this has been solved. On the contrary, the most fundamental problem is that of making a transition from a charismatic administrative staff, and the corresponding principles of administration, to one which is adapted to everyday conditions. The problem of succession, however, is crucial because through it occurs the routinization of the charismatic focus of the structure. In it, the character of the leader himself and of his claim to legitimacy is altered. This process involves peculiar and characteristic conceptions which are understandable only in this context and do not apply to the problem of transition to traditional or legal patterns of order and types of administrative organization. The most important of the modes of meeting the problem of succession are the charismatic designation of a successor and hereditary charisma.

# PART VI

# Psychological Factors in Revolution

# 1.
# PSYCHOLOGICAL FACTORS IN CIVIL VIOLENCE

## Ted R. Gurr

The primary object of this article is to demonstrate that many of the variables and relationships identified in social psychological research on the frustration-aggression relationship appear to underlie the phenomenology of civil violence.[1] Juxtaposition of these two diverse types of material provides a basis for an inter-related set of propositions that is intended to constitute the framework of a general theory of the conditions that determine the likelihood and magnitude of civil violence. These propositions are of two types, whose proposed relationships are diagrammed in Figure 1: (1) propositions about the operation of *instigating variables*, which determine the magnitude of anger, and (2) propositions about *mediating variables*, which determine the likelihood and magnitude of overt violence as a response to anger.[2]

This approach does not deny the relevance of aspects of the social structure, which many conflict theorists have held to be crucial. The supposition is that theory about civil violence is most fruitfully based on systematic knowledge about those properties of men that determine how they react to certain characteristics of their societies.

Reprinted with permission of the author and publisher from *World Politics*, Vol. 20 No. 2, 1968. Copyright 1968 by the Princeton University Press.

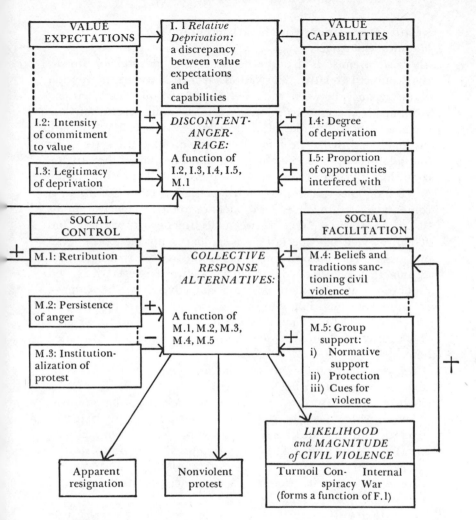

a. The direction(s) of proposed effects on magnitude of civil violence are indicated by $+$ and $-$.

**Figure 1. Variables Determining the Likelihood and Magnitude of Civil Violence**

## Relative Deprivation: Variables Determining the Magnitude of Anger

My basic premise is that the necessary precondition for violent civil conflict is relative deprivation, defined as actors' perception of discrepancy between their *value expectations* and their environment's apparent *value capabilities*.[3] Value expectations are the goods and conditions of life to which people believe they are justifiably entitled. The referents of value capabilities are to be found largely in the social and physical environment: they are the conditions that determine people's perceived chances of getting or keeping the values they legitimately expect to attain. In a comparable treatment, Aberle defines relative deprivation as "a negative discrepancy between legitimate expectation and actuality," viewing expectations as standards, not mere prophecies or hopes.[4] For purposes of general theoretical specification I assume that perceived discrepancies between expectations and capabilities with respect to any collectively sought value—economic, psychosocial, political—constitute relative deprivation. The extent to which some values may be more salient than others is a subject of theoretical and empirical inquiry not evaluated here.

Relative deprivation can be related to the concept of frustration by extending Yates's distinction between the frustrating situation and the frustrated organism.[5] A frustrating situation is one in which an actor is, by objective standards, thwarted by some social or physical barrier in attempts to attain or continue enjoyment of a value. The actor can be said to be frustrated, however, only when he is aware of interference or thwarting. The awareness of interference is equivalent to the concept of relative deprivation as defined above.

A further distinction is necessary between two general classes of deprivation: those that are personal and those that are group or category experiences.[6] For given groups, and for some classes of societies, it is possible to identify events and patterns of conditions that are likely to be widely seen as unjust deprivation. Such events may occur abruptly—for example, the suppression of a political party or a drastic inflation—or slowly, like the decline of a group's status relative to other social classes. Such conditions can be called collective frustrations[7] to distinguish them from such unexpected personal frustrations as failure to obtain an expected promotion or the infidelity of a spouse, which may be relatively common but randomly incident in most populations.

Whether empirical research ought to focus on conditions defined as collectively frustrating or directly on perceived deprivation is an operational question whose answer depends on the researcher's interest and resources, not upon the following theoretical formulation. Survey techniques permit more or less direct assessment of the extent and severity of relative deprivation.[8] To the extent that the researcher is prepared to make assumptions about measurable conditions that are collectively frustrating in diverse nations, cross-national aggregate data can be used in correlational studies.[9]

The basic relationship can be summarized in a proposition analogous to and assuming the same basic mechanism as the fundamental theorem of frustration-aggression theory:[10]

> *Proposition I.1:* The occurrence of civil violence presupposes the likelihood of relative deprivation among substantial numbers of individuals in a society; concomitantly, the more severe is relative deprivation, the greater are the likelihood and intensity of civil violence.

This proposition may be truistic, although theories were noted above which attempt to account for civil strife without reference to discontent. Moreover, relative deprivation in some degree can be found in any society. The usefulness of the basic proposition is best determined by reference to the set of propositions that qualify it. These propositions specify the conditions that determine the severity and in some cases the occurrence of deprivation, whether or not it is likely to lead to civil violence, and the magnitude of violence when it does occur. The fundamental question, which is susceptible to a variety of empirical tests, is whether the proposed precise relationship between severity of deprivation, as determined by variables I.2 through I.5, and magnitude of violence does hold when the effects of the mediating variables M.1 through M.5 are taken into account.

*Definitions and qualifications*
Civil violence and relative deprivation are defined above. If

relative deprivation is the perception of frustrating circumstances, the emotional response to it tends to be anger. Obviously there are degrees of anger, which can usefully be regarded as a continuum varying from mild dissatisfaction to blind rage. The severity of relative deprivation is assumed to vary directly with the modal strength of anger in the affected population; the determinants of strength of anger are specified in propositions I.2 to I.5, below.

The concept of magnitude requires elaboration. Various measures of quantity or magnitude of aggression are used in psychological research on the frustration-aggression relationship —for example, the intensity of electric shocks administered by frustrated subjects to a supposed frustrater, numbers of aggressive responses in test situations, or the length of time frustrated children play destructively with inanimate objects. A consideration of theory, however, suggests that no single measure of magnitude of aggression is *prima facie* sufficient. Assuming the validity of the basic frustration-aggression postulate that the greater the strength of anger, the greater the quantity of aggression, it seems likely that strong anger can be satisfied either by inflicting severe immediate damage on the source of frustration or by prolonged but less severe aggression, and that either of these tactics is probably more or less substitutable for the other. Which alternative is taken may very well be a function of opportunity, and while opportunities can be controlled in experimental situations, in civil violence they are situationally determined. Hence neither severity nor duration alone is likely to reflect the modal strength of collective anger or, consequently, to constitute an adequate measure of magnitude of civil violence.

Moreover, there are evidently individual differences—presumably normally distributed—in the strength of anger needed to precipitate overt aggression. Hence the proportion of a population that participates in collective violence ought to vary with the modal strength of anger: discontent will motivate few to violence, anger will push more across the threshold, rage is likely to galvanize large segments of a collectivity into action. This line of argument suggests that magnitude of civil violence has three component variables: the degree of participation within the affected population, the destructiveness of the aggressive actions, and the length of time violence persists.

Frustration-aggression theory stipulates a set of variables that determine the strength of anger or discontent in response to a given frustration. Dollard and others initially proposed that the strength of instigation to aggression (anger) varies with "(1) the strength of instigation to the frustrated response, (2) the degree of interference with the frustrated response, and (3) the number of frustrated response-sequences."[11] The first of these variables, modified in the light of empirical evidence, provides the basis for propositions about characteristics of value expectations that affect the intensity of anger. The second and third variables, similarly modified, suggest several propositions about value capabilities.

Before the propositions are presented, two qualifications of the classic behaviorist conceptualization of frustration as interference with specific, goal-directed responses must be noted. First, it appears from examination of specific outbreaks of civil violence that abrupt awareness of the likelihood of frustration can be as potent a source of anger as actual inferference. The Vendée counterrevolution in eighteenth-century France was triggered by the announcement of military conscription, for example.[12] A survey of twentieth-century South African history shows that waves of East Indian and Bantu rioting historically have coincided with the parliamentary discussion of restrictive legislation more than with its actual imposition. The Indian food riots in the spring of 1966 were certainly not instigated by the onset of starvation but by its anticipation.

Second, it seems evident that the sense of deprivation can arise either from interference with goal-seeking behavior or from interference with continued enjoyment of an attained condition. As an example from psychological experimentation, frustration is often operationalized by insults; it seems more likely that the insults are a threat to the subjects' perceived level of status attainment or personal esteem than they are an interference with behavior directed toward some as-yet-unattained goal. Several examples from the history of civil violence are relevant. A student of the coup d'état that overthrew the Perón regime in Argentina states that the crucial events that precipitated the anti-Perónists into action were Perón's public insults to the Catholic hierarchy and isolated physical depredations by his supporters against Church properties—events symbolizing an attack on the moral foundations of upper-middle-class Argentine society.[13] In Soviet Central Asia, according to Massell, the most massive and violent resistance to Sovietization followed systematic attempts to break Muslim women loose from their slavish subordination to Muslim men.[14] The two kinds of interference may have differential effects on the intensity and consequences of anger; the point to be made here is that both can instigate violence.

Consequently, analysis of the sources of relative deprivation should take account of both actual and anticipated interference with human goals, as well as of interference with value positions both sought and achieved. Formulations of frustration in terms of the "want: get ratio," which refers only to a discrepancy between sought values and actual attainment, are too simplistic. Man lives mentally in the near future as much as in the present.[15] Actual or anticipated interference with what he has, and with the act of striving itself, are all volatile sources of discontent.

*Value expectations*

The propositions developed here concern the effects on perceived deprivation of the salience of an expectation for a group, rather than the absolute level of the expectation.[16] The first suggestion derived from psychological theory is that the more intensely people are motivated toward a goal, or committed to an attained level of values, the more sharply is interference resented and the greater is the consequent instigation to aggression. One can, for example, account for some of the efficacy of ideologies in generating civil violence by reference to this variable. The articulation of nationalistic ideologies in colonial territories evidently strengthened preexisting desires for political independence among the colonial bourgeoisie at the same time that it inspired a wholly new set of political demands among other groups. Similarly, it has been argued that the desire of the nineteenth-century European factory worker for a better economic lot was intensified as well as rationalized by Marxist teachings.

Experimental evidence has suggested qualifications of the basic proposition which are equally relevant. One is that the closer men approach a goal, the more intensely motivated toward it they appear to be.[17] This finding has counterparts in observations about civil violence. Hoffer is representative of many theorists in noting that "discontent is likely to be highest when misery is bearable [and] when conditions have so improved that an ideal state seems almost within reach. . . . The intensity of discontent seems to be in inverse proportion to the distance from the object fervently desired."[18] The intensity of motivation varies with the perceived rather than the actual closeness of the goal, of course. The event that inflicts the sense of deprivation may be the realization that a goal thought to be at hand is still remote. The mechanism is clearly relevant to the genesis of post-independence violence in tropical Africa. Failure to realize the promises of independence in the Congo had extraordinarily virulent results, as is evident in a comparison of the intensive and extensive violence of the uprisings of the "Second Independence" of 1964-1965 with the more sporadic settling of accounts that followed the "First Independence" of 1960.[19]

The proposition relates as well to the severity of discontent in societies in the full swing of socioeconomic change. The rising bourgeoisie of eighteenth-century France, for example, individually and collectively had a major commitment to their improving conditions of life, and great effort invested in them. Many felt their aspirations for political influence and high social status to be close to realization but threatened by the declining responsiveness of the state and by economic deprivations inherent in stumbling state efforts to control trade and raise taxes.[20]

Although much additional evidence could be advanced, the relationships cited above are sufficient to suggest the following proposition and its corollaries:

*Proposition I.2:* The strength of anger tends to vary directly with the intensity of commitment to the goal or condition with regard to which deprivation is suffered or anticipated.

*I.2a:* The strength of anger tends to vary directly with the degree of effort previously invested in the attainment or maintenance of the goal or condition.

*I.2b:* The intensity of commitment to a goal or condition tends to vary inversely with its perceived closeness.

It also has been found that, under some circumstances, anticipation or experience of frustration tends to reduce motivation toward a goal. This is particularly the case if frustration is thought to be justified and likely.[21] Pastore, for example, reports that when subjects saw frustration as reasonable or justifiable, they gave fewer aggressive responses than when they perceived it to be arbitrary. Kregarman and Worchel, however, found that the reasonableness of a frustration did not significantly reduce aggression and that anticipation of frustration tended not to reduce anger but rather to inhibit external aggressive responses.[22]

The low levels of motivation and the moderate nature of interference that characterize these studies make generalization to "real," collective situations doubtful. If applied to a hypothetical example relevant to civil strife—say, the effects of increased taxation on a population under conditions of varying legitimacy attributed to the action—the experimental findings suggest three alternatives: (1) that anger varies inversely with the legitimacy attributed to interference; (2) that anger is constant, but inhibition of its expression varies directly with legitimacy; or (3) that no systematic relationship holds between the two. If the sources of legitimacy are treated in Merelman's learning-theory terms, the first of these alternatives appears most likely: if legitimacy is high, acceptance of deprivation (compliance) provides symbolic substitute rewards.[23] It may also be that the first alternative holds in circumstances in which legitimacy is high, the second in circumstances in which it is moderate. The first relationship can be formulated in propositional form, with the qualification that evidence for it is less than definitive:

*Proposition I.3:* The strength of anger tends to vary inversely with the extent to which deprivation is held to be legitimate.

## Value capabilities

The environment in which people strive toward goals has two general characteristics that, frustration-aggression theory suggests, affect the intensity of anger: the degree of interference with goal attainment and the number of opportunities provided for attainment.

Almost all the literature on civil strife assumes a causal connection between the existence of interference (or "frustration," "cramp," or "disequilibrium") and strife. "Discontent" and its synonyms are sometimes used to symbolize the condition of interference without reference to interference *per se*. A direct relationship between degree of interference and intensity of strife is usually implicit but not always demonstrated. Rostow has shown graphically that poor economic conditions—high wheat prices, high unemployment—corresponded with the severity of overt mass protest in England from 1790 to 1850.[24] Variations in bread prices and in mob violence went hand in hand in revolutionary France.[25] There is correlational evidence that the frequency of lynchings in the American South, 1882-1930, tended to vary inversely with indices of economic well-being.[26] From cross-national studies there is suggestive evidence also— for example, Kornhauser's correlation of—.93 between per capita income and the Communist share of the vote in sixteen Western democracies in 1949.[27] The Feierabends devised "frustration" measures, based on value capability characteristics of sixty-two nations, and correlated them with a general measure of degree of political stability, obtaining a correlation coefficient of .50.[28]

As far as the precise form of the relationship between extent of interference and intensity of aggression is concerned, the experimental results of Hamblin and others are persuasive. Three hypotheses were tested: the classic formulation that instigation to aggression varies directly with the degree of interference, and the psychophysical hypotheses that aggression ought to be a log or a power function of interference. The data strongly support the last hypothesis, that aggression is a power function of degree of interference—i.e., if magnitude of aggression is plotted against degree of interference, the result is a sharply rising "J-curve." Moreover, the power exponent—the sharpness with which the J-curve rises—appears to increase with the strength of motivation toward the goal with which interference was experienced.[29] It is at least plausible that the J-curve relationship should hold for civil strife. Compatible with this inference, though not bearing directly on it, is the logarithmic distribution curve that characterizes such cross-polity measures of intensity of civil violence as deaths per 100,000 population.[30] It also may account for the impressionistic observation that moderate levels of discontent typically lead to easily quelled turmoil but that higher levels of discontent seem associated with incommensurately intense and persistent civil violence. In propositional form:

> *Proposition I.4:* The strength of anger tends to vary as a power function of the perceived distance between the value position sought or enjoyed and the attainable or residual value position.[31]

Experimental evidence regarding the hypothesis of Dollard and others that the greater the number of frustrations, the greater the instigation to aggression is somewhat ambiguous. Most people appear to have hierarchies of response to repeated frustration, a typical sequence being intensified effort, including search for alternative methods or substitute goals, followed by increasingly overt aggression as other responses are extinguished, and ultimately by resignation or apparent acceptance of frustration. Berkowitz suggests that most such evidence, however, is congruent with the interpretation that "the probability of emotional reactions is a function of the degree to which all possible nonaggressive responses are blocked, more than to the interference with any one response sequence."[32]

The societal equivalents of "all possible nonaggressive responses" can be regarded as all normative courses of action available to members of a collectivity for value attainment, plus all attainable substitute value positions. Relevant conditions are evident in the portraits of "transitional man" painted by Lerner and others. Those who are committed to improving their socioeconomic status are more likely to become bitterly discontented if they have few rather than many prospective employers, if they can get no work rather than some kind of work that provides a sense of progress, if they have few opportunities to acquire requisite literacy and technical skills, if associational means for influencing patterns of political and economic value distributions are not available, or if community life is so disrupted that hearth and kin offer no surcease from frustration for the unsuccessful worker.[33] All such conditions can be subsumed by the rubric of "opportunities for value attainment," with the qualification that perception of opportunities tends to be more crucial than actual opportunities.

Much evidence from studies of civil strife suggests that the greater are value opportunities, the less intense is civil violence. The argument appears in varying guises. Brogan attributes the comparative quiescence of mid-nineteenth-century English workers vis-à-vis their French counterparts in part to the proliferation in England of new cooperatives, friendly and building societies, and trade unions, which provided positive alternatives to violent protest.[34] The first of the American Negro urban rebellions in the 1960's occurred in a community, Watts, in which by contemporary accounts associational activity and job-training programs had been less effective than those of almost any other large Negro community. Cohn explains the high participation of unskilled workers and landless peasants in the violent millenarian frenzies of medieval Europe by reference to the lack of "their kinship groups had disintegrated and they were not effectively organised in village communities or in guilds; for them there existed no regular, institutionalised methods of voicing their grievances or pressing their claims."[35] Kling attributes the chronic Latin American pattern of coup d'état to the lack of adequate alternatives facing elite aspirants with economic ambitions; political office, seized illicitly if necessary, provides opportunity for satisfying those ambitions.[36]

More general observations also are relevant. Economists suggest that government can relieve the discontents that accompany the strains of rapid economic growth by providing compensatory welfare measures—i.e., alternative means of value satisfaction.[37] Numerous scholars have shown that migration is a common response to deprivation and that high emigration rates often precede outbreaks of civil violence. In a cross-national study of correlates of civil violence for 1961-1963, I have found a rather consistent association between extensive educational opportunities, proportionally large trade union movements, and stable political party systems on the one hand and low levels of strife on the other, relationships that tend to hold among nations whatever their absolute level of economic development. Education presumably increases the apparent range of opportunity for socioeconomic advance, unionization can provide a secondary means for economic goal attainment, and parties serve as primary mechanisms for attainment of participatory political values.[38] Hence:

> *Proposition I.5:* The strength of anger tends to vary directly with the proportion of all available opportunities for value attainment with which interference is experienced or anticipated.

## The Mediation of Anger: The Effects of Social Control and Social Facilitation

For the purpose of the theoretical model I assume that the average strength of anger in a population is a precise multiple function of the instigating variables. Whether or not civil violence actually occurs as a response to anger, and its magnitude when it does occur, are influenced by a number of mediating variables. Evidence for these variables and their effects is found both in the psychological literature and in studies of civil violence *per se*. It is useful to distinguish them according to whether they inhibit or facilitate the violent manifestation of anger.

### Social Control: The Effects of Retribution

The classic formulation is that aggression may be inhibited through fear of "such responses on the part of the social environment as physical injury, insults, ostracism, and deprivation of goods or freedom."[39] Good experimental evidence indicates that anticipation of retribution is under some circumstances an effective regulator of aggression.[40] Comparably, a linear relationship between, on the one hand, the capacity and willingness of government to enforce its monopoly of control of the organized instrumentalities of force and, on the other, the likelihood of civil violence is widely assumed in the literature on civil strife. Strong apparent force capability on the part of the regime ought to be sufficient to deter violence, and if violence should occur, the effectiveness with which it is suppressed is closely related to the likelihood and intensity of subsequent violence. Smelser states that a major determinant of the occurrence of civil strife is declining capacity or loyalty of the police and military control apparatus. Johnson says that "the success or failure of armed insurrection and . . . commonly even the decision to attempt revolution rest . . . upon the attitude (or the revolutionaries' estimate of that attitude) that the armed forces will adopt toward the revolution."[41] In Janos' view, the weakening of law-enforcement agencies "creates general disorder, inordinate concrete demands by various groups, and the rise of utopian aspirations."[42] Military defeat is often empirically associated with the occurrence of revolution. Race riots in the United States and elsewhere have often been associated with tacit approval of violence by authorities.[43] Paret and Shy remark that "terror was effective in Cyprus against a British government without sufficient political strength or will; it failed in Malaya against a British government determined and able to resist and to wait."[44]

It also has been proposed, and demonstrated in a number of experimental settings, that if aggression is prevented by fear of retribution or by retribution itself, this interference is frustrating and increases anger. Maier, for example, found in animal studies that under conditions of severe frustration, punishment increased the intensity of aggression.[45] Walton inferred from such evidence that a curvilinear relationship ought to obtain between the degree of coerciveness of a nation and its degree of political instability, on the argument that low coerciveness is not frustrating and moderate coerciveness is more likely to frustrate than deter, while only the highest levels of coerciveness are sufficient to inhibit men from civil violence. A permissiveness-coerciveness scale for eighty-four nations, based on scope of political liberties, has been compared against the Feierabends' political stability scale, and the results strongly support the curvilinearity hypothesis.[46] Bwy, using a markedly different measure of coerciveness—one based on defense expenditures—found the same curvilinear relationship between coerciveness and "anomic violence" in Latin America.[47] Some theoretical speculation about civil strife implies the same relationship—for example, Lasswell and Kaplan's stipulation that the stability of an elite's position varies not with the actual use of violence but only with ability to use it,[48] and Parsons' more detailed "power deflation" argument that the repression of demands by force may inspire groups to resort to increasingly intransigent and aggressive modes of making those demands.[49]

One uncertainty about the curvilinear relationship between retribution and aggression is whether or not it holds whatever the extent of initial deprivation-induced anger. It is nonetheless evident that the threat or employment of force to suppress civil violence is by no means uniform in its effects, and that it tends to have a feedback effect that increases the instigation to violence. Such a relationship is diagrammed in Figure 1 and is explicit in the following proposition and its corollary:

> Proposition M.1: The likelihood and magnitude of civil violence tend to vary curvilinearly with the amount of physical or social retribution anticipated as a consequence of participation in it, with likelihood and magnitude greatest at medium levels of retribution.

> M.1a: Any decrease in the perceived likelihood of retribution tends to increase the likelihood and magnitude of civil violence.

These propositions and corollaries, and all subsequent propositions, hold only, of course, if deprivation-induced anger exists. If the modal level of collective discontent is negligible, a condition that holds for at least some small, although few large, collectivities, the mediating variables have no inhibiting or facilitating effects by definition.

The propositions above do not exhaust frustration-aggression evidence about effects of retribution. Experimental evidence further indicates that a delay in the expression of the aggressive response increases its intensity when it does occur.[50] Observations about civil violence also suggest that the effects of feared retribution, especially external retribution, must take account of the time variable. The abrupt relaxation of authoritarian controls is repeatedly associated with intense outbursts of civil violence, despite the likelihood that such relaxation reduces relative deprivation. Examples from recent years include the East German and Hungarian uprisings after the post-Stalin thaw, the Congo after independence, and the Dominican Republic after Trujillo's assassination.

A parsimonious way to incorporate the time dimension into frustration-aggression theory is to argue that in the short run the delay of an aggressive response increases the intensity of anger and consequently the likelihood and magnitude of aggression, but that in the long run the level and intensity of expectations decline to coincide with the impositions of reality, and anger decreases concomitantly. Cognitive dissonance theory would suggest such an outcome: men tend to reduce persistent imbalances between cognitions and actuality by changing reality, or, if it proves intransigent, by changing their cognitive structures.[51] The proposed relationship is sketched in Figure 2.

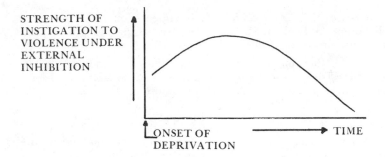

STRENGTH OF INSTIGATION TO VIOLENCE UNDER EXTERNAL INHIBITION

ONSET OF DEPRIVATION

TIME

Figure 2. Displacement of Instigation to Violence over Time

One example of experimental evidence to this point is the finding of Cohen and others that once subjects became accustomed to certain kinds of frustration—withdrawal of social reinforcement in the experimental situation used—they were less likely to continue to seek the desired value or condition.[52] One can, moreover, speculate that the time-scale is largely a function of the intensity of commitment to the frustrated response or condition. The effects of South Africa's apartheid policies and the means of their enforcement offer an example. These policies, which impose substantial and diverse value-deprivations on non-whites, especially those in urban areas, were put into effect principally in the 1950's. Violent protests over their implementation were repressed with increasing severity, culminating in the Sharpeville massacre of 1960 and a series of strikes and riots. By the mid-1960's, when deprivation was objectively more severe than at any time previously in the twentieth century, levels of civil strife were very low, inferentially the result of very high levels of deterrence (feared retribution). Since deprivation remains severe and has affected a wide range of values, avoidance of violence in this case probably would require the maintenance of very high and consistent deterrence levels beyond the active life-span of most of those who have personally experienced the initial value-deprivation. Any short-run decline in the perceived likelihood or severity of retribution, however, is highly likely to be followed by intense violence. In propositional form:

> *Proposition M.2:* Inhibition of civil violence by fear of external retribution tends in the short run to increase the strength of anger but in the long run to reduce it.

> *M.2a:* The duration of increased anger under conditions of inhibition tends to vary with the intensity of commitment to the value with respect to which deprivation is suffered.

### *Social Control: The Effects of Institutionalized Displacement*

On the evidence, the effects of repression in managing discontent are complex and potentially self-defeating in the short run. Displacement theory suggests means that are considerably more effective. Several aspects of displacement theory are relevant for civil violence. Among Miller's basic propositions about object and response generalization is the formulation that the stronger the fear of retribution relative to the strength of anger, the more dissimilar will the target of aggression be from the source of interference and the more indirect will be the form of aggression.[53] With reference to object generalization, Berkowitz has proposed and demonstrated that hostility tends to generalize from a frustrater to previously disliked individuals or groups.[54] A counterpart of this thesis is that displaced aggressive responses tend to be expressed in previously used forms.

Examples of object generalization in civil violence are legion. Several studies have shown positive relationships between poor economic conditions and lynchings of Negroes in the American South. An initial reaction of urban white colonialists to

African rural uprisings in Madagascar in 1947 and Angola in 1961 was vigilante-style execution of urban Africans who had no connections with the rebellions. English handweavers, when their livelihood was threatened by the introduction of new weaving machines, destroyed thousands of machines in the Luddite riots of 1811-1816, but almost never directly attacked the employers who installed the machines and discharged superfluous workers.[55]

Object generalization is a crucial variable in determining who will be attacked by the initiators of particular acts of civil violence, but is only peripheral to the primary concern of the theory, the determination of likelihood and magnitude of violence as such. Most important in this regard is the psychological evidence regarding response generalization. Experimental evidence suggests that only a narrow range of objects provides satisfying targets for men's aggressive responses, but that almost any form of aggression can be satisfying so long as the angry person believes that he has in some way injured his supposed frustrater.[56]

By extension to the collectivity, insofar as adequate response displacement options are available, much anger may be diverted into activity short of civil violence. The evidence is diverse and extensive that participation in political activity, labor unions, and millenarian religious movements can be a response to relative deprivation which permits more or less nonviolent expression of aggression. Studies of voting in the United States show that politicians in farm states are rather consistently voted out of office after periods of low rainfall and that the occurrence of natural disasters may lead to hostility against officials.[57] Extremist voting—which may be regarded as nonviolent aggression—in nine European countries during the Depression has been shown to correlate $+.85$ with the percentage of the labor force unemployed.[58] Studies of labor movements repeatedly document the transformation of labor protest from violent to nonviolent forms as unionization increases. Comparative and case studies similarly document the development of aggressive millenarian religious movements as a response to natural disaster or political repression, in places and eras as diverse as medieval Europe, colonial Africa, and among the indigenous peoples of the Americas and the South Pacific.[59]

This is not to imply that displacement is a sole or exclusive function of such institutions. Their instrumental functions for participants (Proposition I.5) can be crucial: peaceful political and union activism are alternative means to goals whose attainment by other means is often impaired; religious chiliasm provides hope and belief for those whose social universe has been destroyed. But insofar as men become accustomed to express discontents through such institutional mechanisms, the likelihood that anger will lead to civil violence is diminished. In propositional form:

> *Proposition M.3:* The likelihood and magnitude of civil violence tend to vary inversely with the availability of institutional mechanisms that permit the expression of nonviolent hostility.

## Social Facilitation: Cognitive Factors

Experimental, developmental, and field studies of the effects of rewarding individual aggression demonstrate that habitual aggression may be developed and maintained through intermittent rewards and may also be generalized to situations other than those in which the habits were acquired. A number of experiments indicate that the presence of cues or stimuli associated with anger instigators is necessary for most aggressive responses to occur. A summary proposition is that "a target with appropriate stimulus qualities 'pulls' (evokes) aggressive responses from a person who is ready to engage in such actions either because he is angry or because particular stimuli have acquired cue values for aggressive responses from him."[60]

For members of a collectivity a variety of common experiences can contribute to the acquisition of aggressive habits and the recognition of aggression-evoking cues. Among them are socialization patterns that give normative sanction to some kinds of aggressive behavior; traditions of violent conflict; and exposure to new generalized beliefs that justify violence. The literature on civil violence suggests at least four specific modes by which such experiences facilitate violent responses to deprivation. They can (1) stimulate mutual awareness among the deprived, (2) provide explanations for deprivation of ambiguous origin, (3) specify accessible targets and appropriate forms of violence, and (4) state long-range objectives to be attained through violence.

Subcultural traditions of violent protest are well documented in European history. The frequency with which Parisian workers and shopkeepers took to the streets in the years and decades following the great *journées* of 1789 is one example. At least 275 food riots, most of them similar in form and sequence, took place in rural England between 1725 and 1800 in close correlation with harvest failures and high food prices.[61] Hobsbawm points out that in Southern Italy "every political change in the nineteenth century, irrespective from what quarter it came, automatically produced its ceremonial marches of peasants with drums and banners to occupy the land," while in Andalusia "millenarian revolutionary waves occurred at roughly ten-year intervals for some sixty or seventy years."[62] Lynching as a Southern white response to Negro transgressions and the mobbing of white policemen by Negroes are comparable expressions of subcultural traditions that facilitate civil violence.

The theoretical point is that the initial occurrences of civil violence among some homogeneous group of the deprived— those events that set the pattern—tend to be nonrational responses to extreme deprivation. If violence provides a satisfactory outlet for tensions or if it motivates authorities to remedy the sources of deprivation, civil violence tends to become a sanctioned group activity. The fact that normative support for violence thus develops does not mean that violence subsequently occurs without instigation. Deprivation remains a necessary precondition for violence; the strength of anger at which it is likely to occur is lowered.

A related source of attitudinal support for collective violence is the articulation of ideology or, more generally, what Smelser calls generalized belief among the deprived. Such beliefs, ranging from rumors to fully articulated ideologies, are said to develop in situations characterized by social strain that is unmanageable within the existing framework for social action. It is evident that in many social settings relative deprivation is manifest but its sources obscure. In psychological terms, no cues associated with the anger instigator are present. The agency responsible for an unwanted tax increase is apparent to the most ignorant villager; the causes of economic depression or of the disintegration of traditional mores are often unclear even to economists and sociologists. A new ideology, folk-belief, or rumor can serve to define and explain the nature of the situation, to identify those responsible for it, and to specify appropriate courses of action.

Moreover, there usually are a number of competing generalized beliefs circulating among the deprived. Those most likely to gain acceptance tend to be those with substantial aggressive components, i.e., those that rationalize and focus the innate drive to aggression. Cohn's comparative study of the waves of chiliastic excitement that swept medieval Europe in times of plague and famine, for example, documents the fact that the heresies that most effectively mobilized the deprived were those that suited or could be molded to their states of mind: "when . . . eschatological doctrines penetrated to the uprooted and desperate masses in town and country they were re-edited and reinterpreted until in the end they were capable of inspiring revolutionary movements of a peculiarly anarchic kind."[63]

Some of these observations can be summarized in this proposition and its corollary:

*Proposition M.4:* The likelihood and magnitude of civil violence tend to vary directly with the availability of common experiences and beliefs that sanction violent responses to anger.

*M.4a:* Given the availability of alternative experiences and beliefs, the likelihood that the more aggressive of them will prevail tends to vary with the strength of anger.

*Social Facilitation: Sources of Group Support for Violence*

A classic subject of social psychological theory is the extent to which some social settings facilitate overt aggression. It is incontrovertible that individuals tend to behave in crowds differently from the way they act alone. The crowd psychologies of scholars such as Le Bon and Sorokin have emphasized the "unconscious" nature of crowd behavior and its "de-individuating" effects.[64] It appears more fruitful to examine experimentally identified variables that contribute to the "crowd behavior" phenomenon. From this point of departure one can distinguish at least three modes by which groups affect individuals' disposition to violence: (1) by providing normative support, (2) by providing apparent protection from retribution, and (3) by providing cues for violent behavior.

1. *Normative support.* There is good experimental evidence that individuals alone or in poorly cohesive groups are less likely to express hostility than those in highly cohesive groups. Members of highly cohesive friendship groups respond to external frustrations with greater hostility than randomly formed groups. Similarly, if individuals believe that their peers generally agree with them about a frustrater, their public display of antagonism more closely resembles their privately expressed antagonism than if they do not perceive peer agreement.[65]

Theoretical and empirical studies of civil violence repeatedly refer to the causal efficacy of comparable conditions. Social theorists describe the perception of anonymity and of universality of deprivation characteristic of riotous crowds. Hopper's classic picture of group interaction under conditions of relative deprivation in the early stages of the revolutionary process is relevant: by participating in mass or shared behavior, discontented people become aware of one another; "their negative reactions to the basic factors in their situations are shared and begin to spread. . . . Discontent . . . tends to become focalized and collective."[66] Comparative studies of labor unrest show that the most strike-prone industries are those whose workers are relatively homogeneous and isolated from the general community.[67] Some of the efficacy of revolutionary brotherhoods and tightly knit bands of rebels in prosecuting civil violence can be interpreted in terms of the reinforcement of mutual perception of deprivation and the justification of violence as a response to it.

2. *Protection from retribution.* Groups appear capable of reducing fears of external retribution for violence in at least three ways. Crowd situations in particular provide members with a shield of anonymity. In an experimental study by Meier and others, two-thirds of subjects who were prepared to join a lynching mob said, *inter alia*, that they would do so because in the crowd they could not be punished. The same relationship is apparent in the handful of studies made of riot participants: crowd members usually feel insulated from retribution.[68]

Organized groups can provide apparent protection from retribution by acquiring sufficient force capability to prevent the agents of retribution—i.e., military and internal security forces—from effectively reaching them. Increases in the relative force capability of a deprived group may also reinforce rationalization for violence by raising hopes of success or may merely facilitate the expression of rage by providing desperate men with the means to strike at tormentors who had previously been unassailable.

A third aspect of group protectiveness is the perceived effect of hierarchical organization and the presence of highly visible leaders. Leaders of revolutionary organizations, in addition to their other manifest functions, not only foment but assume responsibility for illicit violence. Their followers tend to see such leaders as the likely objects of retaliatory efforts and hence feel less personal risk.

3. *Cues for violence.* The transition from anger to aggression is not automatic or even abrupt. Laboratory studies of imitative behavior repeatedly document the significance of aggression-releasing cues provided by social models. The act of punishing aggression itself can serve as a model for imitation by the person punished. Aggression-releasing cues need not necessarily originate with high-status persons. Polansky and others found that when frustrations were imposed on groups of children, "impulsive" but low-status children were both initiators and ready followers of aggressive behavioral contagion. On the other hand, not any aggressive model evokes aggression from angered subjects; the models that evoke greatest aggression are those associated with the subjects' present situation or with settings in which they were previously aggressive.[69]

Angry crowds of men also appear to require some congruent image or model of violent action before they will seize cobblestones or rope or rifles to do violence to fellow citizens. Such models may be symbolic: invocation of a subcultural tradition of violence by a leader, or articulation of a new generalized belief that is explicit in its prescription of violence. In general, however, a "call to arms" or an appeal to a tradition of violence appears less effective by itself than when accompanied by the sight or news of violence. The calculated use of terrorism by rebels can have such an effect, and so can a soldier's random shot into a crowd of demonstrators. Many specific cases of civil violence have been set off by comparable acts of violence elsewhere. "Revolutionary contagion" is evident in the 1830 and 1848 waves of European revolutionary upheavals and in the post-Stalin uprisings in Eastern Europe and Siberia. The same phenomenon is apparent in the initiation of innumerable cases of small-scale, unstructured violence. Series of riots in rural France and England have graphically been shown to spread outward from one or a few centers, riots occurring in the furthest villages days or weeks after the initial incident. Such patterning is evident, to mention a few cases, in the French Corn Riots of 1775, the "Plug-Plot" riots around Manchester in 1842, and the incidence of farmers' protest meetings and riots in Brittany in the summer of 1961.[70] The demonstration effect apparent in such series of events appears to have affected their form and timing more than the likelihood of the occurrence of strife. The people who responded to the events were already angered; they probably would have erupted into violence in some form sometime in the proximate future.

These three modes of group facilitation of civil violence can be summarized in propositional form:

> *Proposition M.5:* The likelihood and magnitude of civil violence tend to vary directly with the extent to which the deprived occupy organizational and/or ecological settings that provide (1) normative support through high levels of interaction, (2) apparent protection from retribution, and (3) congruent models for violent behavior.

**The Forms of Civil Violence**
The theoretical framework comprising the ten propositions is formally restricted to physically violent collective behavior. It is likely that it is as applicable to a still larger class of events, including those characterized by the threat of violence or by high levels of verbal aggression—for example, bloodless coups, demonstrations, and political strikes. Violent events tend to be more salient for the political system, however, and for most operational purposes constitute a more workable and clearly defined universe.

I have not discussed the propositions with reference to

specific forms of civil violence on grounds that all of the variables specified are relevant to each form specified in current typologies.[71] It is nonetheless likely that the propositions are of differential weight for different forms, and it is useful to demonstrate how variations in form may be generally accounted for in the context of the theoretical model. The first question to be asked is how detailed a listing of forms one should attempt to account for. A series of factor analytic studies provide a systematic, empirical answer to that question. In each of eleven studies, data on the incidence and characteristics of various types of strife were collected and tabulated, by country, and the "country scores" (number of riots, assassinations, deaths from civil violence, coups, mutinies, guerrilla wars, and so on, in a given time period) were factor analyzed. Whatever the typology employed, the period of reference, or the set of countries, essentially the same results were obtained. A strong *turmoil* dimension emerges, characterized by largely spontaneous strife such as riots, demonstrations, and non-political clashes, quite distinct from what we may call a *revolutionary* dimension, characterized by more organized and intense strife. This revolutionary dimension has two components, appearing in some analyses as separate dimensions: *internal war*, typically including civil war, guerrilla war, and some coups; and *conspiracy*, typically including plots, purges, mutinies, and most coups.[72] Events within each of the three types tend to occur together; events within any two or all three categories are less likely to do so. The implication is that they are substantively distinct forms of strife for each of which separate explanation is required.

Two complementary approaches to accounting for these three basic types of civil violence can be proposed within the context of the theoretical model. The first is that the two major dimensions, turmoil and revolution, reflect the varying class incidence of deprivation among societies. The defining characteristic of "turmoil" events is mass participation, usually rather spontaneous, disorganized, and with low intensity of violence; the forms of "revolution" reflect organized, often instrumental and intense, application of violence. The ability to rationalize, plan, and put to instrumental use their own and others' discontent is likely to be most common among the more skilled, highly educated members of a society—its elite aspirants. Thus if the incidence of mass deprivation is high but elite deprivation low, the most likely form of civil violence is turmoil. But if severe discontent is common to a substantial, alienated group of elite aspirants, then organized, intensive strife is likely.

The forms of revolution differ principally in their scale and tactics: internal wars are large-scale, and their tactics are typically to neutralize the regime's military forces; conspirators, usually few in number, attempt to subvert the regime by striking at its key members.

The differences between internal war and conspiracy can be accounted for by several characteristics. If severe deprivation is restricted largely to elite aspirants, the consequence is likely to be "conspiracy" phenomena such as plots, coups d'état, and barracks revolts. If discontent is widespread among substantial numbers of both mass and elite aspirants, the more likely consequence is large-scale, organized violence—civil and guerrilla war. The strategic position of the discontented elite aspirants may be relevant as well. If they are subordinate members of the existing elite hierarchy, they are likely to attack the regime from within, hence coups, mutinies, and plots. If they are instead excluded from formal membership in the elite though they possess elite qualities—acquired, for example, through foreign education—they must organize violent resistance from without. These are essentially Seton-Watson's explanation for the relative frequency of conspiracy in underdeveloped societies compared with the frequency of massive revolutionary movements in more developed states. In summary, "it is the combination of backward masses, extremist intellectuals and despotic bureaucrats which creates the most conspiratorial movements."[73]

These observations are of course only the beginning of an accounting of the forms of civil strife. They are intended to demonstrate, however, that such a theoretical explanation not only is compatible with but can be formulated within the framework of the theoretical model by showing the loci of deprivation in a society. They can be stated thus in propositional form:

> *Proposition F.1:* The characteristic form of civil violence tends to vary with the differential incidence of relative deprivation among elite aspirants and masses: (1) mass deprivation alone tends to be manifested in large-scale civil violence with minimal organization and low intensity; (2) elite-aspirant deprivation tends to be manifested in highly organized civil violence of high intensity.
>
> *F.1a:* Whether organized and intense civil violence is large-scale or small-scale is a joint function of the extent of mass deprivation and the strategic access of deprived elite aspirants to the incumbent political elite.

## Conclusion

I have advanced eleven general propositions about the variables operative in generating and structuring violent political unrest. They are based on the assumption that the frustration-aggression mechanism, however culturally modified, is the source of most men's disposition to illicit collective violence. The propositions do not constitute a theory of the revolutionary process or of the outcomes of strife, but of the conditions that determine the *likelihood* and *magnitude* of strife. On the other hand, the variables stipulated by the propositions are not irrelevant to revolutionary processes. Process models can be formulated wholly or partly in terms of changing patterns of weights on the component variables.

It is likely that most "causes" and "correlates" of the occurrence and intensity of civil strife can be subsumed by these variables, with one exception: foreign intervention. This exception is no oversight but simply recognition that decisions to intervene are external to domestic participants in civil strife. The effects of foreign intervention can be readily interpreted by reference to the model, however: intervention on behalf of the deprived is likely to strengthen group support (M.5) and may, as well, heighten and intensify value expectations (I.2). Foreign assistance to a threatened regime is most likely to raise retribution levels (M.1), but may also alter aspects of value capabilities (I.4, I.5) and strengthen justification for violence among the deprived, insofar as they identify foreigners with invaders (M.4).

The framework has not been elaborated merely to provide a satisfying theoretical reconstruction of the general causes of civil violence. It is intended primarily as a guide for empirical research using the techniques of both case and comparative studies. The framework stipulates the variables for which information should be sought in any thorough case study of the origins of an act of civil strife.[74] For purposes of comparative analysis it stipulates relationships that should hold among cultures and across time. Its most important objectives are to encourage empirical validation of its component propositions in a variety of contexts by a variety of operational means, and specification of their separate weights and interacting effects in those contexts.[75]

## NOTES

1. The universe of concern, civil violence, is formally defined as *all collective, nongovernmental attacks on persons or property, resulting in intentional damage to them, that occur within the boundaries of an autonomous or colonial political unit.* The terms "civil strife," "violent civil conflict," and "civil violence" are used synonymously in this article. The universe subsumes more narrowly defined sets of events such as "internal war," which Harry Eckstein defines as "any resort to violence within a political order to change its constitution, rulers, or policies" (in "On the Etiology of Internal Wars," 133), and "revolution," typically defined in terms of violently accomplished fundamental change in social institutions.
2. The term "instigating" is adapted from the behavioristic terminology of Dollard and others. Instigating variables determine the strength of instigation, i.e., stimulus or motivation, to a particular kind of behavior. Mediating variables refer to intervening conditions, internal or external to the actors, which modify the expression of that behavior.
3. The phrase "relative deprivation" was first used systematically in Samuel A. Stouffer and others, *The American Soldier: Adjust-*

*ment During Army Life*, Vol. I (Princeton 1949), to denote the violation of expectations. J. Stacy Adams reviews the concept's history and some relevant evidence and suggests that feelings of injustice intervene between the condition of relative deprivation and responses to it, in "Inequity in Social Exchange," in Berkowitz, ed., *Advances in Experimental Psychology*, 267-300. The "injustice" aspect is implicit in my definition and use of relative deprivation as *perceived* discrepancy between what people think they will get and what they believe they are entitled to. The Stouffer concept has been related to levels of social satisfaction and to anomie, but has not, so far as I know, been associated with the discontent-anger-rage continuum in the frustration-aggression relationship.

4. David F. Aberle, "A Note on Relative Deprivation Theory," in Sylvia L. Thrupp, ed., *Millennial Dreams in Action: Essays in Comparative Study* (The Hague 1962), 209-14. Bert Hoselitz and Ann Willner similarly distinguish between expectations, regarded by the individual as "what is rightfully owed to him," and aspirations, which represent "that which he would like to have but has not necessarily had or considered his due," in "Economic Development, Political Strategies, and American Aid," in Morton A. Kaplan, ed., *The Revolution in World Politics* (New York 1962), 363.

5. Aubrey Y. Yates, *Frustration and Conflict* (New York 1962), pp. 175-78.

6. Aberle, 210.

7. The Feierabends use the comparable term "systemic frustration" to describe the balance between "social want satisfaction" and "social want formation."

8. Hadley Cantril's work offers examples, especially *The Pattern of Human Concerns* (New Brunswick 1965).

9. This approach is exemplified by the Feierabends' work and by Bruce M. Russett, "Inequality and Instability: The Relation of Land Tenure to Politics," *World Politics*. XVI (April 1964), 442-54.

10. The basic postulate of Dollard and others is that "the occurrence of aggressive behavior always presupposes the existence of frustration and, contrariwise, that the existence of frustration always leads to some form of aggression" (p. 1). It is evident from context and from subsequent articles that this statement was intended in more qualified fashion.

11. *Ibid.*, 28.

12. Charles Tilly, *The Vendée* (Cambridge, Mass., 1964).

13. Reuben de Hoyos, personal communication.

14. Gregory Massell, "The Strategy of Social Change and the Role of Women in Soviet Central Asia: A Case Study in Modernization and Control," Ph.D. diss., Harvard University, 1966.

15. For this kind of approach, see Daniel Lerner, "Toward a Communication Theory of Modernization: A Set of Considerations," in Lucian W. Pye, ed., *Communications and Political Development* (Princeton 1963), 330-35.

16. This general statement of theory is concerned with specification of variables and their effects, not with their content in specific cases; hence the conditions that determine the *levels* of expectation and changes in those levels are not treated here, nor are the conditions that affect perceptions about value capabilities. For some attempts to generalize about such conditions see Ted Gurr, "The Genesis of Violence: A Multivariate Theory of Civil Strife," Ph.D. diss., New York University, 1965, esp. chaps. 6-8. For empirical evaluation or application of the theory, it is of course necessary to evaluate in some way levels of expectation in the population(s) studied. Some approaches to evaluation are illustrated in Ted Gurr with Charles Ruttenberg, *The Conditions of Civil Violence: First Tests of a Causal Model*, Center of International Studies, Princeton University, Research Monograph No. 28 (Princeton 1967), and Ted Gurr, "Explanatory Models for Civil Strife Using Aggregate Data," a paper read at the Annual Meeting of the American Political Science Association, 1967.

17. See Berkowitz, *Aggression*, 53-54.

18. Eric Hoffer, *The True Believer* (New York 1951), 27-28.

19. Compare Crawford Young, *Politics in the Congo* (Princeton 1965), chap. 13, with commentaries on the Kwilu and Stanleyville rebellions, such as Renée C. Fox and others, " 'The Second Independence': A Case Study of the Kwilu Rebellion in the Congo," *Comparative Studies in Society and History*, VIII (October 1965), 78-109; and Herbert Weiss, *Political Protest in the Congo* (Princeton 1967).

20. See, among many other works, Georges Lefebvre, *The Coming of the French Revolution* (Princeton 1947), Part II.

21. Value expectations are defined above in terms of the value positions to which men believe they are justifiably entitled; the discussion here assumes that men may also regard as justifiable some types of interference with those value positions.

22. Nicholas Pastore, "The Role of Arbitrariness in the Frustration-Aggression Hypothesis," *Journal of Abnormal and Social Psychology*, XLVII (July 1952), 728-31; John J. Kregarman and Philip Worchel, "Arbitrariness of Frustration and Aggression," *Journal of Abnormal and Social Psychology*, LXIII (July 1961), 183-87.

23. The argument is that people comply "to gain both the symbolic rewards of governmental action and the actual rewards with which government originally associated itself" and rationalize compliance with "the feeling that the regime is a morally appropriate agent of control . . ." (Richard M. Merelman, "Learning and Legitimacy,"

*American Political Science Review*, LX [September 1966], 551). The argument applies equally well to compliance, including acceptance of deprivation, with the demands of other social institutions.

24. Walt W. Rostow, *British Economy of the Nineteenth Century* (Oxford 1948), chap. 5.

25. George Rudé, "Prices, Wages, and Popular Movements in Paris During the French Revolution," *Economic History Review*, VI (1954), 246-67, and *The Crowd in History, 1730-1848* (New York 1964), chap. 7.

26. Carl Hovland and Robert Sears, "Minor Studies in Aggression, VI: Correlation of Lynchings with Economic Indices," *Journal of Psychology*, IX (1940), 301-10.

27. William Kornhauser, *The Politics of Mass Society* (New York 1959), 160.

28. "Aggressive Behaviors Within Polities."

29. Robert L. Hamblin and others, "The Interference-Aggression Law?" *Sociometry*, XXVI (1963), 190-216.

30. Bruce M. Russett and others, *World Handbook of Political and Social Indicators* (New Haven 1963), 97-100.

31. There is a threshold effect with reference to physical well-being. If life itself is the value threatened and the threat is imminent, the emotional response tends to be fear or panic; once the immediate threat is past, anger against the source of threat tends to manifest itself again. See n. 7 above, and Berkowitz, *Aggression,* 42-46.

32. Leonard Berkowitz, "Repeated Frustrations and Expectations in Hostility Arousal," *Journal of Abnormal and Social Psychology*, LX (May 1960), 422-29.

33. See, for example, Daniel Lerner, *The Passing of Traditional Society* (Glencoe 1958).

34. Denis W. Brogan, *The Price of Revolution* (London 1951), 34.

35. Norman R. C. Cohn, *The Pursuit of the Millennium*, 2d ed. rev. (New York 1961).

36. Merle Kling, "Toward a Theory of Power and Political Instability in Latin America," *Western Political Quarterly*, IX (March 1956), 21-35.

37. Ridker, 15; Mancur Olson, Jr., "Growth as a Destabilizing Force," *Journal of Economic History*, XXIII (December 1963), 550-51.

38. Gurr with Ruttenberg.

39. Dollard and others, 34.

40. For summaries of findings, see Richard H. Walters, "Implications of Laboratory Studies of Aggression for the Control and Regulation of Violence," *Annals of the American Academy of Political and*

*Social Science*, CCCLXIV (March 1966), 60-72; and Elton D. McNeil, "Psychology and Aggression," *Journal of Conflict Resolution*, III (September 1959), 225-31.

41. Chalmers Johnson, *Revolution and the Social System* (Stanford 1964), 16-17.

42. Andrew Janos, *The Seizure of Power: A Study of Force and Popular Consent*, Center of International Studies, Princeton University, Research Monograph No. 16 (Princeton 1964), 5.

43. See, for example, H. O. Dahlke, "Race and Minority Riots: A Study in the Typology of Violence," *Social Forces*, XXX (May 1952), 419-25.

44. Peter Paret and John W. Shy, *Guerrillas in the 1960's*, rev. ed. (New York 1964) 34-35.

45. *Frustration, passim*.

46. Jennifer G. Walton, "Correlates of Coerciveness and Permissiveness of National Political Systems: A Cross-National Study," M.A. thesis, San Diego State College, 1965.

47. Douglas Bwy, "Governmental Instability in Latin America: The Preliminary Test of a Causal Model of the Impulse to 'Extra-Legal' Change," paper read at the Annual Meeting of the American Psychological Association, 1966.

48. Harold Lasswell and Abraham Kaplan, *Power and Society: A Framework for Political Inquiry* (New Haven 1950), 265-66.

49. "Some Reflections on the Place of Force."

50. J. W. Thibaut and J. Coules, "The Role of Communication in the Reduction of Interpersonal Hostility," *Journal of Abnormal and Social Psychology*, XLVII (October 1952), 770-77.

51. See Leon Festinger, *A Theory of Cognitive Dissonance* (Evanston 1957).

52. Arthur R. Cohen and others, "Commitment to Social Deprivation and Verbal Conditioning," *Journal of Abnormal and Social Psychology*, LXVII (November 1963), 410-21.

53. Neal E. Miller, "Theory and Experiment Relating Psychoanalytic Displacement to Stimulus-Response Generalization," *Journal of Abnormal and Social Psychology*, XLIII (April 1948), 155-78.

54. *Aggression*, chap. 6.

55. Rudé, *The Crowd in History*, chap. 5. The high levels of verbal aggression directed against the employers suggest that displacement was involved, not a perception of the machines rather than employers as sources of deprivation. In the Luddite riots, fear of retribution for direct attacks on the owners, contrasted with the frequent lack of sanctions against attacks on the machines, was the probable cause of object generalization. In the Madagascar and Angola cases structural and conceptual factors were respon-

sible: the African rebels were not accessible to attack but local Africans were seen as like them and hence as potential or clandestine rebels.

56. Some such evidence is summarized in Berkowitz, "The Concept of Aggressive Drive," 325-27.

57. A critical and qualifying review of evidence to this effect is F. Glenn Abney and Larry B. Hill, "Natural Disasters as a Political Variable: The Effect of a Hurricane on an Urban Election," *American Political Science Review*, LX (December 1966), 974-81.

58. Kornhauser, 161. For interview evidence on the motives of protest voting, see Hadley Cantril, *The Politics of Despair* (New York 1958).

59. Representative studies are Cohn; James W. Fernandez, "African Religious Movements: Types and Dynamics," *Journal of Modern African Studies*, II, No. 4 (1964), 531-49: and Vittorio Lanternari, *The Religions of the Oppressed* (New York 1963).

60. Leonard Berkowitz, "Aggressive Cues in Aggressive Behavior and Hostility Catharsis," *Psychological Review*, LXXI (March 1964), 104-22, quotation from 106.

61. Rudé, *The Crowd in History*, 19-45.

62. E. J. Hobsbawm, *Social Bandits and Primitive Rebels*, 2nd ed. (Glencoe 1959), 63-64.

63. P. 31.

64. Gustave Le Bon, *The Psychology of Revolution* (London 1913); Pitirim Sorokin, *The Sociology of Revolutions* (Philadelphia 1925).

65. Representative studies include J. R. P. French, Jr., "The Disruption and Cohesion of Groups," *Journal of Abnormal and Social Psychology*, XXXVI (July 1941), 361-77; A. Pepitone and G. Reichling, "Group Cohesiveness and the Expression of Hostility," *Human Relations*, VIII, No. 3 (1955), 327-37; and Ezra Stotland, "Peer Groups and Reactions to Power Figures," in Dorwin Cartwright, ed., *Studies in Social Power* (Ann Arbor 1959), 53-68.

66. Pp. 272-75, quotation from 273.

67. Clark Kerr and Abraham Siegel, "The Isolated Mass and the Integrated Individual: An International Analysis of the Inter-Industry Propensity to Strike," in Arthur Kornhauser and others, eds., *Industrial Conflict* (New York 1954), 189-212.

68. Norman C. Meier and others, "An Experimental Approach to the Study of Mob Behavior," *Journal of Abnormal and Social Psychology*, XXXVI (October 1941), 506-24. Also see George Wada and James C. Davies, "Riots and Rioters," *Western Political Quarterly*, X (December 1957), 864-74.

69. See Walters; Norman Polansky and others, "An Investigation of Behavioral Contagion in Groups," *Human Relations*, III, No. 3 (1950), 319-48; and Leonard Berkowitz and Russell G. Geen, "Film Violence and the Cue Properties of Available Targets,"

*Journal of Personality and Social Psychology,* III (June 1966), 525-30.

70. Rudé, *The Crowd in History*; Henri Mendras and Yves Tavernier, "Les Manifestations de juin 1961," *Revue française des sciences politiques,* XII (September 1962), 647-71.

71. Representative typologies are proposed by Johnson, *Revolution and the Social System,* 26-68; Rudolph J. Rummel, "Dimensions of Conflict Behavior Within and Between Nations," *Yearbook of the Society for General Systems Research,* VIII (1963), 25-26; and Harry Eckstein, "Internal Wars: A Taxonomy," unpubl. (1960).

72. Two summary articles on these factor analyses are Rudolph J. Rummel, "A Field Theory of Social Action With Application to Conflict Within Nations," *Yearbook of the Society for General Systems Research,* X (1965), 183-204; and Tanter. What I call internal war is referred to in these sources as subversion; I label conspiracy what these sources call revolution. My terminology is, I believe, less ambiguous and more in keeping with general scholarly usage.

73. Hugh Seton-Watson, "Twentieth Century Revolutions," *Political Quarterly,* XXII (July 1951), 258.

74. For example, it has been used by Bryant Wedge to analyze and compare interview materials gathered in the study of two Latin American revolutions, in "Student Participation in Revolutionary Violence: Brazil, 1964, and Dominican Republic, 1965," a paper read at the Annual Meeting of the American Political Science Association, 1967.

75. Studies based on this theoretical model and using cross-national aggregate data include Ted Gurr, *New Error-Compensated Measures for Comparing Nations: Some Correlates of Civil Strife,* Center of International Studies, Princeton University, Research Monograph No. 25 (Princeton 1966); Gurr with Ruttenberg; Gurr, "Explanatory Models for Civil Strife"; and Gurr, "Why Urban Disorders? Perspectives From the Comparative Study of Civil Strife," *American Behavioral Scientist* (forthcoming).

# 2.

# SOCIAL AND PSYCHOLOGICAL DIMENSIONS OF COLLECTIVE BEHAVIOR

Neil J. Smelser

As indicated in the last section, many features of protest movements are explicable by reference to the social situations in
which they arise. To increase the power of our explanation of
them, however, reference must be made to their psychodynamic
significance. I shall conclude this essay by suggesting a number
of these deeper psychological meanings. In any given situation,
of course, participants may either "bring" these meanings to
a protest movement or have them "evoked" by the circumstances of the movement; most situations would show a continuous interplay between internal psychic determination and
external stimulation.

Let me begin by reviewing the psychic ingredients of two
common childhood situations—the Oedipal situation of the
child, in which he enters into competition with the parent of
the same sex for the love of the parent of the opposite sex;
and situations in which the child competes with his siblings
for the attention and affection of his parents. Needless to say,
these situations resemble one another in many respects and
may be fused in various ways in the child's psychological development; but they are distinguishable conceptually.

The Oedipal situation is marked by several types of ambi-

---

valence. Toward the father the boy experiences feelings of love, affection, and direct identification;[1] yet at the same time he is filled with feelings of competition and rage toward the father because he stands in the way of the boy's sexual desires for his mother. Simultaneously the boy is afflicted with the related feelings of castration anxiety and homosexual anxiety. Toward the mother the ambivalence is between positive sexual attraction on the one hand, and his frustration and anger because she refuses to be seduced away from the father on the other.

Typically the Oedipal conflict is resolved mainly by a process of repression and identification—repression of the anxiety-provoking elements, and identification with the opposite-sex parent.[2] Most conspicuously, the repressed elements are the hostile and erotic impulses toward both the father and the mother. What remains is the internalized superego, which becomes the seat of moral anxiety, and feelings of de-eroticized affection for the mother.

With respect to the relations among siblings, similar ambivalences, both toward the sibling and toward the parents whose affection is desired, are in evidence. In addition, the mechanisms of resolving the ambivalences are similar, though not quite so dramatic or phase-specific as in the Oedipal situation. The "preferred" solution is to repress the hostile and erotic elements of the ambivalences toward the siblings; to retain the gentler feelings of brotherhood, affection, and loyalty; and to identify with them. As Freud indicated, however, the identification in this case does not involve regarding them as superordinate, but rather regarding them as equally subordinate, loved—or whatever—by the parents.

Viewing these common psychodynamic processes with reference to the common features of protest movements, it seems to me that the protest movement is typically an occasion which permits the repressed elements of these crises to emerge and be gratified, though certain other defenses continue to operate.

This formulation applies most dramatically to the ambivalent attitudes toward authority figures manifested in protest movements. On the one hand there is the unqualified love, worship, and submission to the leader of the movement, who articulates and symbolizes "the cause." On the other hand there is the unqualified suspicion, denigration, and desire to destroy the agent felt responsible for the moral decay of social life and standing in the way of reform, whether he be a vested interest or a political authority. There is one important difference, however. In the Oedipal crisis the ambivalence is directed toward a single individual, the father; in the protest movement the ambivalence is split between two types of object. This splitting appears to serve a number of defensive purposes. It permits the gratification of the feelings of love and passivity as well as of the feelings of hostility toward the authority figure; but by a combination of projection and denial it also avoids the anxiety that is created when these ambivalent feelings are focused on the same object. In addition, these defenses— when combined with rationalization—permit certain kinds of behavior that might otherwise be reprehensible to the individual participants: passive dependency, now justified because of the sheer power and wonder of the leader; and destructive or even violent behavior, now justified because of the fundamental evil of the enemy. The same mechanisms of splitting, projection, denial, and rationalization also seem to operate when the hated object is not so much an authority figure as a sibling figure—such as a minority group that is perceived as gaining too many social advantages or "forgetting its proper place."

An ambivalence characterizes the relations of adherents to the movement to potential sources of outside support, but it is a different sort of ambivalence. This traces more to the child's Oedipal wish to seducing the opposite-sex parent into joining in the destruction of the same-sex parent;[3] or, in the sibling situation, his wish to seduce the parent into joining in the destruction of the sibling. It seems to me that one of the common meanings of a movement's desire for solidarity and support is often a manifestation of this kind of wish. This would account for the extraordinarily solidary, eroticized ties among "converts" who have become "committed" to the cause. At the same time these feelings are tinged with ambivalence. At the positive extreme is the joy of gratification if the seduction is accepted; at the negative extreme is the pain of bitter frustration if it is refused. Adherents to a movement must always be prepared to be disappointed with supporters who are less than totally committed. Perhaps this ambivalence lies behind the cynical disdain with which core members of a movement sometimes regard their less committed followers. Perhaps it also lies behind the attitude frequently expressed by adherents that "those who are not with us are against us," an attitude which suggests that the ambivalence toward outsiders is also subject to splitting and the associated defenses.

This kind of logic also throws some light on the future state of social bliss, peace, and harmony that is frequently envisioned by adherents to a cause. These visions tap very vivid Oedipal and sibling-destruction fantasies of what the world would be like if only the hated objects were obliterated and the child could have the loved object to himself. This fantasy, usually subjected to severe repression, comes closer to the surface, albeit in disguised form, in the ideologies of social protest.

Finally, the tendency for adherents of protest movements to create conditions that might reactivate the movement is also highlighted by these psychological considerations. The striking feature of the protest movement is what Freud observed: it permits the expression of impulses that are normally repressed. But the participant continues to defend against the impulses involved—especially the hostile and erotic ones—by mechanisms such as projection, denial, rationalization, and splitting. The efforts—sometimes conscious and sometimes unconscious—of leaders and adherents of a movement to create issues, to provoke authorities, and even to be martyred by these authorities, would seem to be in part efforts to "arrange" reality so as to "justify" the expression of normally forbidden impulses in a setting which makes them appear less reprehensible to the participants.

## NOTES

1. Sigmund Freud, "Group Psychology and the Analysis of the Ego," *Standard Edition* (London: The Hogarth Press and the Institute of Psycho-Analysis), XVIII, p. 105.

2. Sigmund Freud, "The Ego and the Id," *Standard Edition*, p. 32. Freud notes, however, that a number of different patterns of identification are possible.
3. This formulation extends the common meaning of the term "seduction" beyond the invitation to erotic stimulation to include an invitation to engage in a common attack on a hated object.

# 3.

# COLLECTIVE BEHAVIOR

## Ralph. H. Turner

Treatments of the dynamics of collective behavior reflect three different kinds of theory which have been presented with varying degrees of explicitness. *Contagion* theories explain collective behavior on the basis of some process whereby moods, attitudes, and behavior are communicated rapidly and accepted uncritically. *Convergence* theories explain collective behavior on the basis of the simultaneous presence of people who share the same predispositions and preoccupations. *Emergent norm* theories see collective behavior as regulated by a social norm which arises in a special situation.

### Contagion Theory
Some form of contagion, whereby unanimous, intense feeling and behavior at variance with usual predispositions are induced among the members of a collectivity, has been the focal point for most sociological study of collective behavior. From the early work of Bagehot (1869), LeBon (1896), and Tarde (1901), through the American tradition of Ross (1921), Park and Burgess (1921), Young (1945), Blumer (1946), and the Langs (1961), this approach has played a major part. The foremost problem which this type of theory sets for the investigator is to explain

how people in collectivities come to behave (a) uniformly, (b) intensely, and (c) at variance with their usual patterns. In differing degrees theorists of this bent accept LeBon's "law of the mental unity of crowds." "Under certain given circumstances, and only under those circumstances, an agglomeration of men presents new characteristics very different from those of the individuals composing it. The sentiments and ideas of all the persons in the gathering take one and the same direction, and their conscious personality vanishes".[1] The solutions to this problem focus upon psychological mechanisms such as imitation, suggestion, and emotional contagion, through which dissemination takes place, and anonymity and restricted attention, which neutralize ordinary behavior anchorages.

In summarizing a common view of the process leading to this condition of unanimity and intensity, Blumer[2] contrasted the *circular reaction* of the crowd with the *interpretative interaction* of normal groups. The former "refers to a type of interstimulation wherein the response of one individual reproduces the stimulation that has come from another individual and in being reflected back to this individual reinforces the stimulation".[3] Responses in the latter form of interaction follow upon interpretation, rather than directly upon the stimulus behavior, and are therefore likely to be different from the stimulus behavior. Since social structure ordinarily makes its impact through the interpretation phase, crowd behavior is thought to exhibit characteristics of herd behavior in animals.[4] It is similarly argued that the stripping away of "structured expectations of the participants" means that "psychological categories to supplement the categories of social structure" are required to explain collective behavior.[5]

Suggestion is the psychological mechanism upon which reliance has most often been placed. When writers such as Trotter (1919) asserted that suggestion is fundamental to all social behavior or Tarde (1901) that imitation is the basic process, suggestion in the crowd must be distinguished on the basis of the unusual limitation in the sources of suggestion. Tarde, accordingly, made the physical contiguity of crowd members a crucial criterion for the existence of the crowd. Trotter concluded that the degree to which the suggestion appears to emanate from the herd and embody the herd view determines its acceptance. Writers who distinguish the crowd according to the preponderance of suggestion and suggestibility are then led to search for the conditions which determine degrees of suggestibility. McDougall (1927) attributed suggestibility especially to the crowd's sense of power and to emotional excitement. Prestige, either of an individual or of the group, is the source characteristic most consistently viewed as conducive to acceptance of suggestion. Psychological research, beginning with Binet (1900), has accumulated a great deal of evidence on the conditions of suggestibility under laboratory conditions, whose extrapolation to crowd situations need not be of concern here.

Investigators have often asserted an inherent contagiousness of emotionally expressive behavior as the key mechanism in crowd behavior. McDougall enunciated a principle of primitive sympathy, that "each instinct . . . is capable of being excited in one individual by the expressions of the same emotion in another."[6] The fact that a situation is one that evokes emotional expression and that the emotion is a simple rather than complex one determines that contagion will take place. Control of a crowd by playing the national anthem, during which people must inhibit all emotional expression, is an effort to interrupt contagiousness of this sort.

The place of leaders in giving direction to crowds has generally been stressed, usually following the tradition of LeBon who asserted that the crowd seeks leaders and that "the leader has most often started as one of the led."[7] The opposite viewpoint, that there must be a leader before a crowd comes into being, was asserted by Gabriel Tarde (1901). Freud (1921) made a similar assumption the basis for a serious attempt to locate a more satisfactory mechanism than suggestion to account for the subservience of members to the group. Freud drew upon the similarity between crowd behavior and neurotic behavior and proposed that the explanation for suggestibility in groups be found in the harnessing of libidinal (or love) energy. An organized group is held together by two kinds of ties: to the leader and among the members. The suppression of the normal ambivalence among members of a group indicates that some new kind of libidinal tie must be at work since no other force would be strong enough to nullify negative reactions. The mechanism which accounts for the readiness of members to accept suggestions uncritically from others in the group is identification. Identification is the earliest form of emotional tie, but one which gives way to object-choice as the individual matures. When object-choice is blocked, however, there is a regression to identification. In groups the members form intense attachments to a common leader. Object-choice is blocked because the leader cannot reciprocate with an exclusive attachment to any of the group members. Consequently the members' attachments are transformed into identifications with the leader and with their fellows. Identification with their fellows is a protective device against special privilege: If I cannot possess the leader, neither must you, and complete uniformity and equality must be the rule among us. It is this two-way identification which makes for the rapid dissemination and uncritical acceptance of suggestion in the crowd.

Social contagion, imitation, suggestion, emotional contagiousness, and identification are the processes variously assumed to come into operation as vehicles for social contagion. In addition there are mechanisms which are believed to neutralize the normal inhibitions and social pressures against types of behavior which occur in the crowd. Normal social control is effective largely because the individual is known and identified and held responsible for his actions. In a large crowd people lose sight of individuals and mix with strangers before whom they can act without shame. Restriction of attention is another device which enables the present crowd to take the place of the normal range of reference groups in legitimating a course of action. If ability to carry out a course of action successfully is often a consideration in judging it legitimate, the apparent power of the crowd adds to its displacement of the usual behavioral anchorages.

While writers from the contagion point of view have in common their conception of crowd behavior as "not volitional but impulsive,"[8] they differ in the manner in which they distinguish it from organized group behavior. Freud nowhere made any sharp distinction, while Tarde (1901) and Trotter

(1919) differentiated in degree rather than kind. LeBon (1896), on the other hand, made the sharpest distinction on the basis of his law of mental unity. The preponderance of interpretative interaction (Blumer, 1939) and the control of interaction by shared expectations (Lang & Lang, 1961) have also been noted as characteristics of organized groups which distinguish them from crowds. While not denying that there are differences, Park and Burgess cautioned that none of the writers had "succeeded in distinguishing clearly between the organized or 'psychological' crowd, as LeBon calls it, and other similar types of social groups."[9]

There are certain common difficulties in the use of contagion theory as an approach to collective behavior. First, characterizations seem to rely excessively on the extreme and rare instances of behavior which the sociologist has no opportunity to observe for himself. The revivals, riots, demonstrations, and other events that sociologists visit appear to lack the contagiousness that purportedly whips disinterested bystanders into an emotional fury. Since the reports which support the contagion theories best are historical accounts by untrained and horrified observers, it is even conceivable that theorists have merely reconstructed the nightmare experienced by an observer in the face of something threatening and incomprehensible to him. But even if the reports are correct but apply only to rare events, it would be unwise to adopt the exceptional aberration as the model for collective behavior as a whole.

Second, the idea that crowds require a level of psychological explanation which organized groups do not require perpetuates a somewhat dubious conception of the human being as an animal with a removable veneer of socialization. Writers who employ the same level of explanation for crowd and organized groups escape this inconsistency, though they may do so as Freud (1922) did by extending the classical crowd model to include organized groups.

Third, the mechanisms cited to explain contagion appear to resist empirical verification. Least substantiated is the notion that the crowd develops out of love of a leader. There appear to be abundant instances in which shifting leadership is the rule and in which the leader only emerges after considerable crowd development has taken place. There may well be some contagiousness about a state of excitement, but it is doubtful that specific emotions are transmitted apart from some awareness of a situation to which they are appropriate responses. Suggestion is probably the best verified mechanism, but psychological research has led to narrower and narrower circumscription of the conditions under which suggestion takes place.

Fourth, contagion theory affords little basis for predicting the kinds of shifts which occur in crowd behavior. Contagiousness is perhaps the explanation for the existence of the shifting currents which have often been ascribed to crowds. But it affords no clues to the selective response that leads to a shift on one occasion and resistance on another.

Finally, contagion theory has nothing to offer in a study of the organization of collective behavior. Unless the simplistic model of the crowd as an undifferentiated mass of persons accepting suggestions uniformly is correct, a different sort of theory is essential to provide clues to differentiation of function within the crowd.

## Convergence Theory

While the most popular interpretations of collective behavior (i.e., contagion) have stressed the temporary transformation of individuals under group influence, there has always been an undercurrent of suspicion that participants were merely revealing their "true selves" and that the crowd served merely as the excuse. When this suspicion is exalted into the key assumption about which the analysis of crowds is focused, the writer is guided by a theory which accounts for crowd behavior on the basis of the *convergence* of a number of persons who share the same predispositions. The predispositions are activated by the event or object toward which their common attention is directed. The course of action of the crowd would have been predictable had the observers known sufficiently the composition of the group and the latent predispositions of its members.

For investigators employing this kind of theory, the problem of identifying a mechanism and specifying conditions under which contagion will create a homogeneous crowd out of a heterogeneous aggregate evaporates, as the product of a faulty assumption. The problems instead become those of identifying relevant latent tendencies in masses of people, the circumstances that will bring people with similar latencies together, and the kinds of events which will trigger these tendencies. There are three major ways in which the assumption of convergence has been used, not all of which merit the designation "theory." These are the identification of a special class or category of persons as crowd-prone, equation of the crowd with psychopathy, and the application of attitude and learning theory.

Popular accounts of crowd behavior lean heavily on the "outsider" theme. The medieval dancing manias were attributed to groups of dancers who entered the villages from outside, the Russian pogroms were attributed to a "barefoot brigade" traveling from place to place, and outside "agitators" are currently blamed for industrial and racial strife. Newspaper reports of race riots in the United States have often stressed the role of uniformed military personnel who come from outside of the local community and who take advantage of the stereotype of the military person on a pass. Such popular accounts vary in the degree to which they acknowledge a supplementary role for contagion.

Serious studies have put less emphasis on outsiders, but have been concerned with categories of people within the community who are not fully committed to the dominant mores. Distinguishing between the active mob participants and others, Cantril (1941) cited the findings of private investigation to show that, in the Leeville, Texas, lynching of 1930, the active members were chiefly from the lowest economic bracket, and several had previous police records. The poorest whites were the class most likely to compete for employment with Negroes and were most likely to find their own status threatened by the presence of Negroes more successful than themselves. The lack of commitment to lawful procedure among criminal elements and the aggravated state of relations between poor whites and Negroes created a reservoir of people who were ready for a lynching upon a minimum of provocation.

The view that man has an evil nature which can show itself upon occasion is an old one which has been given an intellectually respectable imprint by introduction of the psychoanalytic concept of the unconscious. Jung, while invoking a contagion principle by speaking of "a sort of collective possession . . . which rapidly develops into a psychic epidemic," attributed a key role in such manifestations to latent psychotics. They are the dangerous "sources of infection" because, "their chimerical ideas, upborne by fanatical resentment, appeal to the collective irrationality and find fruitful soil there, for they express all those motives and resentments which lurk in more normal people under the cloak of reason and insight."[10]

Extensive elaborations of the latent pathology explanation for crowd behavior were made by Martin (1920) and Meerloo (1950). Martin said that "a crowd is a device for indulging ourselves in a kind of temporary insanity by all going crazy together."[11] Released in the crowd are the primitive impulses of hate and egotism which in normal circumstances are repressed. For a crowd to develop, it is merely necessary that a sufficient number of persons with the same unconscious wishes assemble and that one person strike the blow that all the others unconsciously want to deliver.

An effort to retain elements of the pathology approach while eliminating some of the extremities of Martin's (1920) and Meerloo's (1950) analyses is found in the frustration-aggression approach. Dollard, Doob, Miller, Mowrer, and Sears (1939) applied the general proposition that frustration universally creates instigations to aggression in proportion to the extent of frustration and that, where aggression against a perceived source of frustration is blocked, aggression will be redirected toward available and safe objects. In a review of lynchings of Negroes in the United States, Dollard et al. showed a connection between the amount of frustration that poor southern whites have experienced, as indicated by economic indices, and the incidence of lynchings directed against Negroes. The high incidence of race riots in the United States during the period of readjustment after World War I and the frequency of wild-cat labor strife and race riots during the second and third years of World War II have likewise been attributed to accumulating frustrations. In such explanations the object of crowd behavior need have nothing directly to do with the source of frustration.

The most careful development of a convergence type of

theory is to be found among psychologists working in the learning theory tradition. The classic statement of this view was made by Allport (1924) and has been translated into the language of modern learning theory by Miller and Dollard (1941). Attacking LeBon's (1896) references to crowds in the French Revolution, Allport asserted,

> It was the *individual citizen* who did this—the man who "in a state of isolation" had for many years felt the same hatred and cherished the same spark of vengeance or lust for freedom that was now bursting into flame in the crowd. Nothing new or different was added by the crowd situation except an intensification of the feeling already present, and the possibility of concerted action. The individual in the crowd behaves just as he would behave alone, *only more so.*[12]

Allport suggested that the term social facilitation is more appropriate than contagion. "By the similarity of human nature the individuals of the crowd are all set to react to their common object in the same manner, quite apart from any social influence. Stimulations from one another release and augment these responses; but they do not originate them."[13]

Convergence theorists perform a valuable task in deflating the exaggerated claims of some contagion formulations. A compromise which stresses the importance of pre-existing attitudes while acknowledging that contagion may absorb persons without appropriate predispositions, in extreme circumstances, is logically tenable. The crucial empirical question of the power of contagion remains unanswered, however.

Apart from the unresolved empirical question there are some limitations to convergence theory. First, shifts in crowd behavior are difficult to explain under this approach. If the behavior in the crowd reflects the common predispositions of its members, then the development of the crowd should bring a clearer and more consistent, rather than a shifting, pattern to the fore. The one line of explanation available to convergence theory is that more intense impulses which are also more thoroughly repressed take longer to gain expression than surface impulses. Consequently, a crowd begins by expressing a fairly superficial but thinly repressed tendency, which then gives way to the deeper impulse whose repression is overcome by crowd facilitation. The test of this explanation would require examination of a large number of detailed accounts of actual crowds in which shifts occurred.

Second, like contagion theory, convergence theory offers no framework from which to approach organization in the crowd, unless it be the perpetuation of pre-existing relations within the crowd or the boosting of persons whose repressions are least intense to the positions of leaders.

A third limitation is more serious. It was a discovery of some importance that people have latent tendencies which they do not ordinarily express or recognize in themselves. That behavior in the crowd is an expression of these latencies is an observation that allows a more parsimonious explanation for phenomena that had mystified and terrified observers. But as the understanding of these latencies has progressed, it has also become clear that people have not one but often several latent tendencies which are relevant to a given situation. So long as there was thought to be only a single applicable latency, prediction of crowd behavior on the basis of convergence in connection with an appropriate stimulus situation seemed easy. But with the recognition of multiple latencies the original problem re-emerges in new form: Which of the latencies will make its appearance? The door is reopened for contagion or some other process to select from among several potential courses of action.

Finally, part of the simplification achieved by convergence theory arises from ruling out of analysis a portion of the phenomenon which is crucial in other theories. The Miller-Dollard (1941) formulation, in keeping with other statements from this point of view, concerns itself solely with the intensity of response, taking for granted the kind or direction of response in the crowd. The direction is taken for granted because it is assumed to be an automatic response to the nature of the situation. It is necessary, then, to assume that the situation is self-evident and that it is defined individually. But the "collective" definition of the situation may be the crucial part of crowd development, during which a situation which is ambiguous to individual perceptions is defined as dangerous, as reprehensible, as defenseless, or whatever other characterization serves to indicate the appropriate behavior. If the crowd determines how the situation is defined, the fact that people respond to the situation according to their predispositions may be true but of slight predictive utility.

## Emergent Norm Theory

Although convergence theories discount the sometimes exaggerated reports of contagion, they do not ordinarily dispute the unanimity, uniformity, and spontaneity attributed to the crowd by contagionists. A third type of theory makes its departure by challenging the empirical image of the crowd which both of these theories seek to explain. Turner and Killian (1957) suggested that the tendency for an observer to be overwhelmed by any dramatic happening and to see in wholes rather than in details leads to faulty observation and reporting of crowd behavior. The conspicuous actions of a few individuals are attributed to the entire group, and sentiments appropriate to the behavior and the situation are imputed to all of the members.

Observers trained to correct for these tendencies often report that many individuals in a crowd are merely amused or interested bystanders, some are even talking about other matters, and some may be quietly unfriendly to the dominant orientation of the crowd (Lee & Humphrey, 1943). The whole aggregation is characterized by *differential expression*, the behavior of a part of the crowd being taken by observers and crowd members as the sentiment of the crowd, and variant views and sentiments being sufficiently unrecognized to avoid destroying the illusion of unanimity. These observations raise an empirical question, but they also suggest a continuity between simpler and more commonplace phenomena and the dramatic episodes usually stressed. Observations of the former can be used as a basis for generalizations about the latter.

Emergent norm theory defines the key problem not as explaining why an unnatural unanimity develops, but as explaining the imposition of a pattern of differential expression which is perceived as unanimity by crowd members and observers. Taking the cue from the work of Sherif (1935) and Asch (1951), one can explain differential expression as the consequence of a social norm. The shared conviction of right, which constitutes a norm, sanctions behavior consistent with the norm, inhibits behavior contrary to it, justifies proselyting, and requires restraining action against those who dissent. Because the behavior in the crowd is different either in degree or kind from that in noncrowd situations, the norm must be specific to the situation to some degree—hence *emergent* norm. Specific further problems that take pre-eminence when these assumptions are made include accounting for the neutralization or inapplicability of existing norms, specifying the process by which a collectivity comes to acknowledge a norm as the rule of that body, and accounting for the character of the norm.

There are several important differences between emergent norm theory and contagion theory in their characterizations of the crowd. The first concerns the view that complete uniformity is a collective illusion. The image of Nazi crowds attacking Jewish merchants often distorted the true situation in which a few storm-troopers acted while a crowd of persons afraid to voice dissent stood silently by. A "crowd of looters" taking advantage of an overturned ice cream truck in southern California turned out upon careful observation to include many groups of two or three persons who disapproved of the looting, but who by their overt passivity gave some collective support to the activities of the minority.

The second difference is between the spontaneous induction of emotion under contagion and the imposition of conformity under the impact of a norm. Under contagion people find themselves spontaneously infected with the emotions of others so that they want to behave as others do; under a norm people first experience the social pressure against nonconformity and do not necessarily share the emotion themselves, as Asch's (1951) experiments have shown. The crowd suppresses incongruous moods, and a prevalent fear of the crowd expressed both by observers and members of even recreational crowds facilitates the imposition of the norm. Far from being "infected" by the crowd mood, the newcomer observes it, suppresses any inappropriate mood, and then seeks actively to determine the nature of the situation which gives rise to it.

A third difference between normative and contagion theory

is that the former is equally applicable to quiet and excited states, while the latter generally views contagion as a direct function of arousal. Moods of dread or of reverence may be as genuinely crowd phenomena as moods of violence and revelry. The observer who ran excitedly into the crowd at the site of a plane crash asking, "What happened?" was promptly silenced by disapproving gestures; students, present at a bonfire which exploded with injury to several persons, even though too far away to have observed the events directly, found it difficult to develop the proper mood for the subsequent home-coming dance.

Fourth, a conspicuous part of the symbolic exchange involved in the development of a crowd is the act of seeking and supplying justifications for the course of action of the crowd, or the recasting of conventional norms in a humorous or outgroup context so as to nullify their impact. Lynchings and riots never occur without extensive preparation, which consists of the development of collective assurance that the intended victims are outside of the ordinary moral order. Students cutting classes for a victory celebration were heard by observers to seek assurance that enough students would join to prevent professors from attempting to hold classes. Much of the content of the discussion and rumor which occurs in the crowd serves to define with group support the "facts" which are specifically necessary to determine the applicability of a particular norm. An empirical test of the two theories could be made by a content analysis of the exchanges that take place in observed crowds. The prime emphasis under contagion theory would be on communications which are expressive of the dominant emotion of the crowd and suggestions for action in accordance with the mood. While the latter would also be anticipated under norm theory, the former would be replaced by communications which have a normative character and which serve to indicate the applicability of a norm.

Fifth, limits to the development of crowd emotion and behavior are more readily explained as a function of a norm than as a product of contagion. The principle of contagion envisages a spiral of mutual reinforcement and neutralization of inhibitions typically leading the crowd to more extreme actions than were envisaged at its beginning. The evidence that southern lynchings were often followed by generalized devastation of Negro neighborhoods or that crowds soon get out of the hands of their original leaders appears to lend support to the spiral nature of contagion. Contradictory examples are available, however, and pose problems for contagion theory. In conventionalized crowds, the person whose expression of religious fervor (in a revival) or of abandonment of conventional mores (in an expressive jazz session) goes too far for the crowd serves to dampen the crowd mood rather than to facilitate its further development. Under contagion theory it might be argued that the crowd is not yet ready for the suggestion in question, but the fact that such crowds regularly reach limits beyond which they do not go calls this explanation into question. The further observation, drawn from careful historical research, that even so classical a crowd action as the storming of the Bastille during the French Revolution failed to follow up its action by attacks on the highly available director of the prison (Rudé, 1959), suggests that popular imagery of crowds has given insufficient attention to limits on crowd development. If an emergent norm defines behavior which is not usually acceptable as the rule in the crowd, it will usually also define the upper limits of acceptable behavior. Normative theory further gives rise to the hypothesis that many forms of crowd behavior are rendered possible as much by the conviction that behavior will not exceed certain upper limits as by the interstimulation of like-minded participants.

A final difference concerns the stress on anonymity which plays a part in many treatments of the crowd from a contagion viewpoint. Since social identity, by which the individual thinks of himself in certain stable social contexts and is recognizable to others, is a prime link in the chain of social control, its relevance is crucially different. If the crowd is a phenomenon of released impulse, then anonymity—the neutralization of identity—is important in eliminating the controls which ordinarily keep impulses in check. If the crowd represents behavior under an emergent norm, it is important that the individual in the crowd have an identity so that the control of the crowd can be effective over him. The latter assumption gives rise to the hypothesis that the control of the crowd is greatest among persons who are known to one another, rather than among anonymous persons.

Whereas convergence theory stresses the continuity between normal *individual* behavior and crowd behavior, emergent norm theory stresses the continuity between normal *group* behavior and crowd behavior. Just as behavior in normal groups gives rise to, and is governed by, norms, so the crowd generates and is governed by normative control. There is likewise a continuity between crowd norms and the norms which are usually in effect, the crowd supplying an atypical resolution of a longstanding normative conflict, defining a situation in which "emergency" norms can be invoked, or providing collective sanction for the conviction that the usual normative order has ceased to operate.

# REFERENCES

Asch, S.E. "Effects of Group Pressure Upon the Modification and Distortion of Judgment." In H. Gutzekow (ed.), *Groups, Leadership and Men*. Pittsburgh: Carnegie Press, 1951, Pp. 177-190.

Bagehot, W. *Physics and Politics: Thoughts on the Application of the Principles of "Natural Selection" and "Inheritance" to Political Society*. New York: Knopf, 1948 (first published 1869).

Binet, A. *La Suggestibilité*. Paris: Schleicher, 1900.

Cantril, H. *The Psychology of Social Movements*. New York: Wiley, 1941.

Dollard, J., Doob, L.W., Miller, N.E., Mowrer, O.H., and Sears, R.R. *Frustration and Aggression*. New Haven, Conn.: Yale University Press, 1939.

Freud, S. *Group Psychology and the Analysis of the Ego*. J. Strachey (Trans.). London: Hogarth, 1922.

Lee, A.M., and Humphrey, N.D. *Race Riot*. New York: Dryden, 1943.

Meerloo, J.A.M. *Patterns of Panic*. New York: International Universities Press, 1950.

Miller, N.E., and Dollard, J. *Social Learning and Imitation*. New Haven, Conn.: Yale University Press, 1941.

Ross, E.A. *Social Psychology*. New York: Macmillan, 1921.

Rudé, G. *The Crowd in the French Revolution*. Oxford: Oxford University Press, 1959.

Sherif, M. "A Study of Some Social Factors in Perception." *Arch. Psychol.,* No. 187, 1935.

Tarde, G. *L'opinion et la foule.* Paris: Librairie Félix Alcan, 1901.

Turner, R.H., and Killian, L.M. *Collective Behavior.* Englewood Cliffs, N.J.: Prentice-Hall, Inc., 1957.

Young, Kimball. *Social Psychology.* (2nd ed.) New York: Appleton-Century-Crofts, Inc., 1945.

## NOTES

1. G. LeBon, *The Crowd: A Study of the Popular Mind* (London: Ernest Benn Ltd., 1896), pp. 23-24.
2. H. Blumer, "Collective Behavior," in A.M. Lee (ed.) *New Outline of the Principles of Sociology* (New York: Barnes & Noble, Inc., 1946), pp. 165-220.
3. *Ibid.*
4. *Ibid;* W. Trotter, *Instincts of the Herd in Peace and War: 1916-1919* (London: Oxford University Press, 1919).
5. K. Lang & Gladys E. Lang, *Collective Dynamics* (New York: Crowell. 1961), p. 12.
6. W. McDougall, *The Group Mind: A Sketch of the Principles of Collective Psychology With Some Attempt to Apply Them to the Interpretation of National Life and Character* (Cambridge: Cambridge University Press, 1927), p. 25.
7. LeBon, p. 118.
8. McDougall, *op. cit.*
9. R.E. Park and E.W. Burgess, *Introduction to the Science of Sociology* (Chicago: University of Chicago Press, 1921), p. 876.
10. C.G. Jung, *The Undiscovered Self* (New York: Mentor, 1959), p. 14.
11. E.D. Martin, *The Behavior of Crowds* (New York: Harper, 1920), p. 37.
12. F.H. Allport, *Social Psychology* (Boston: Houghton, 1924), p. 295.
13. *Ibid.*

1 2 3 4 5 6 7 ← P Y → 9 8 7 6 5 4 3